Programming Languages: The Complete Guide

Programming Languages: The Complete Guide

Bruce Goodwin

MURPHY & MOORE
www.murphy-moorepublishing.com

Programming Languages: The Complete Guide
Bruce Goodwin
ISBN: 978-1-63987-463-7 (Hardback)

MURPHY & MOORE
Published by Murphy & Moore Publishing,
1 Rockefeller Plaza,
New York City, NY 10020, USA

Cataloging-in-Publication Data

Programming languages : the complete guide / Bruce Goodwin.
p. cm.
Includes bibliographical references and index.
ISBN 978-1-63987-463-7
1. Programming languages (Electronic computers)--Guidebooks. I. Goodwin, Bruce.
QA76.7 .P76 2022
005.13--dc23

For more information regarding Murphy & Moore Publishing and its products, please visit the publisher's website www.murphy-moorepublishing.com

Table of Contents

Preface

Programming languages are a crucial part of computer programming. They help in developing a set of instructions designed to provide a specific output. Syntax, type systems, static and dynamic semantics, and run-time systems are the most significant elements of a computer language. Some commonly used computer languages include C, C++, Java, MATLAB, etc. This textbook is a step-by-step guide to assist students in learning these programming languages. It also delves into the essential elements that constitute these languages. Those in search of information to further their knowledge will be greatly assisted by this book.

A detailed account of the significant topics covered in this book is provided below:

Chapter 1- Computer programs are written using programming language. The programming language specifies the functions that are to be performed by a program. Syntax, semantics, type system and core libraries are the main elements of computer languages. This chapter has been carefully written to provide an easy understanding of the varied facets of programming Languages.

Chapter 2- The best way to understand programming is to learn its various components such as algorithms, flowcharts, etc. Programming languages are primarily used to built software. The aspects elucidated in this chapter are of vital importance, and provide a better understanding of programming languages.

Chapter 3- Algorithms are self-contained sequences that instruct how an action or a set of actions are to be performed. They allow computers to compute and provide a required output. This chapter on computer algorithms offers an insightful focus, keeping in mind the complex subject matter.

Chapter 4- Object oriented programing is the programing where each object has a set of variables that can store relevant data. The programs designed by this programming paradigm consists of objects which can interact with each other. The topics discussed in the chapter are of great importance to broaden the existing knowledge on programming languages.

Chapter 5- C and C++ are complex computer languages that are very popular. They are also compiled languages which require compilers to run them. C and C++ programming languages are best understood in confluence with the major topics listed in the following chapter.

Chapter 6- HTML, Fortran and Java are popular web programming languages. They can be used to make web applications and web pages. Java is a very easy language to use for web programming. This chapter is an overview of the subject matter incorporating all the major aspects of programming languages with respect to web programming.

I would like to make a special mention of my publisher who considered me worthy of this opportunity and also supported me throughout the process. I would also like to thank the editing team at the back-end who extended their help whenever required.

Bruce Goodwin

Chapter 1

An Introduction to Programming Languages

Computer programs are written using programming language. The programming language specifies the functions that are to be performed by a program. Syntax, semantics, type system and core libraries are the main elements of computer languages. This chapter has been carefully written to provide an easy understanding of the varied facets of programming Languages.

Computer Programming

Computer programming (often shortened to programming) is a process that leads from an original formulation of a computing problem to executable computer programs. Programming involves activities such as analysis, developing understanding, generating algorithms, verification of requirements of algorithms including their correctness and resources consumption, and implementation (commonly referred to as coding) of algorithms in a target programming language. Source code is written in one or more programming languages. The purpose of programming is to find a sequence of instructions that will automate performing a specific task or solving a given problem. The process of programming thus often requires expertise in many different subjects, including knowledge of the application domain, specialized algorithms, and formal logic.

Related tasks include testing, debugging, and maintaining the source code, implementation of the build system, and management of derived artifacts such as machine code of computer programs. These might be considered part of the programming process, but often the term *software development* is used for this larger process with the term *programming, implementation*, or *coding* reserved for the actual writing of source code. Software engineering combines engineering techniques with software development practices.

Modern Programming

Quality Requirements

Whatever the approach to development may be, the final program must satisfy some fundamental properties. The following properties are among the most important:

- Reliability: how often the results of a program are correct. This depends on conceptual correctness of algorithms, and minimization of programming mistakes, such as mistakes in resource management (e.g., buffer overflows and race conditions) and logic errors (such as division by zero or off-by-one errors).
- Robustness: how well a program anticipates problems due to errors (not bugs). This

includes situations such as incorrect, inappropriate or corrupt data, unavailability of needed resources such as memory, operating system services and network connections, user error, and unexpected power outages.

- Usability: the ergonomics of a program: the ease with which a person can use the program for its intended purpose or in some cases even unanticipated purposes. Such issues can make or break its success even regardless of other issues. This involves a wide range of textual, graphical and sometimes hardware elements that improve the clarity, intuitiveness, cohesiveness and completeness of a program's user interface.
- Portability: the range of computer hardware and operating system platforms on which the source code of a program can be compiled/interpreted and run. This depends on differences in the programming facilities provided by the different platforms, including hardware and operating system resources, expected behavior of the hardware and operating system, and availability of platform specific compilers (and sometimes libraries) for the language of the source code.
- Maintainability: the ease with which a program can be modified by its present or future developers in order to make improvements or customizations, fix bugs and security holes, or adapt it to new environments. Good practices during initial development make the difference in this regard. This quality may not be directly apparent to the end user but it can significantly affect the fate of a program over the long term.
- Efficiency/performance: Measure of system resources a program consumes (processor time, memory space, slow devices such as disks, network bandwidth and to some extent even user interaction): the less, the better. This also includes careful management of resources, for example cleaning up temporary files and eliminating memory leaks.

Readability of Source Code

In computer programming, readability refers to the ease with which a human reader can comprehend the purpose, control flow, and operation of source code. It affects the aspects of quality above, including portability, usability and most importantly maintainability.

Readability is important because programmers spend the majority of their time reading, trying to understand and modifying existing source code, rather than writing new source code. Unreadable code often leads to bugs, inefficiencies, and duplicated code. A study found that a few simple readability transformations made code shorter and drastically reduced the time to understand it.

Following a consistent programming style often helps readability. However, readability is more than just programming style. Many factors, having little or nothing to do with the ability of the computer to efficiently compile and execute the code, contribute to readability. Some of these factors include:

- Different indent styles (whitespace)
- Comments

- Decomposition
- Naming conventions for objects (such as variables, classes, procedures, etc.)

The presentation aspects of this (such as indents, line breaks, color highlighting, and so on) are often handled by the source code editor, but the content aspects reflect the programmer's talent and skills.

Various visual programming languages have also been developed with the intent to resolve readability concerns by adopting non-traditional approaches to code structure and display. Integrated development environments (IDEs) aim to integrate all such help. Techniques like Code refactoring can enhance readability.

Algorithmic Complexity

The academic field and the engineering practice of computer programming are both largely concerned with discovering and implementing the most efficient algorithms for a given class of problem. For this purpose, algorithms are classified into *orders* using so-called Big O notation, which expresses resource use, such as execution time or memory consumption, in terms of the size of an input. Expert programmers are familiar with a variety of well-established algorithms and their respective complexities and use this knowledge to choose algorithms that are best suited to the circumstances.

Methodologies

The first step in most formal software development processes is requirements analysis, followed by testing to determine value modeling, implementation, and failure elimination (debugging). There exist a lot of differing approaches for each of those tasks. One approach popular for requirements analysis is Use Case analysis. Many programmers use forms of Agile software development where the various stages of formal software development are more integrated together into short cycles that take a few weeks rather than years. There are many approaches to the Software development process.

Popular modeling techniques include Object-Oriented Analysis and Design (OOAD) and Model-Driven Architecture (MDA). The Unified Modeling Language (UML) is a notation used for both the OOAD and MDA.

A similar technique used for database design is Entity-Relationship Modeling (ER Modeling).

Implementation techniques include imperative languages (object-oriented or procedural), functional languages, and logic languages.

Measuring Language Usage

It is very difficult to determine what are the most popular of modern programming languages. Methods of measuring programming language popularity include: counting the number of job advertisements that mention the language, the number of books sold and courses teaching the language (this overestimates the importance of newer languages), and estimates of the number of existing lines of code written in the language (this underestimates the number of users of business languages such as COBOL).

Some languages are very popular for particular kinds of applications, while some languages are regularly used to write many different kinds of applications. For example, COBOL is still strong in corporate data centers often on large mainframe computers, Fortran in engineering applications, scripting languages in Web development, and C in embedded software. Many applications use a mix of several languages in their construction and use. New languages are generally designed around the syntax of a prior language with new functionality added, (for example C++ adds object-orientation to C, and Java adds memory management and bytecode to C++, but as a result, loses efficiency and the ability for low-level manipulation).

Debugging

Debugging is a very important task in the software development process since having defects in a program can have significant consequences for its users. Some languages are more prone to some kinds of faults because their specification does not require compilers to perform as much checking as other languages. Use of a static code analysis tool can help detect some possible problems. Normally the first step in debugging is to attempt to reproduce the problem. This can be a non-trivial task, for example as with parallel processes or some unusual software bugs. Also, specific user environment and usage history can make it difficult to reproduce the problem.

After the bug is reproduced, the input of the program may need to be simplified to make it easier to debug. For example, a bug in a compiler can make it crash when parsing some large source file. However, after simplification of the test case, only few lines from the original source file can be sufficient to reproduce the same crash. Such simplification can be done manually, using a divide-and-conquer approach. The programmer will try to remove some parts of original test case and check if the problem still exists. When debugging the problem in a GUI, the programmer can try to skip some user interaction from the original problem description and check if remaining actions are sufficient for bugs to appear.

Debugging is often done with IDEs like Eclipse, Visual Studio, Xcode, Kdevelop, NetBeans and Code::Blocks. Standalone debuggers like GDB are also used, and these often provide less of a visual environment, usually using a command line. Some text editors such as Emacs allow GDB to be invoked through them, to provide a visual environment.

Programming Languages

Different programming languages support different styles of programming (called *programming paradigms*). The choice of language used is subject to many considerations, such as company policy, suitability to task, availability of third-party packages, or individual preference. Ideally, the programming language best suited for the task at hand will be selected. Trade-offs from this ideal involve finding enough programmers who know the language to build a team, the availability of compilers for that language, and the efficiency with which programs written in a given language execute. Languages form an approximate spectrum from "low-level" to "high-level"; "low-level" languages are typically more machine-oriented and faster to execute, whereas "high-level" languages are more abstract and easier to use but execute less quickly. It is usually easier to code in "high-level" languages than in "low-level" ones.

Allen Downey, in his book *How To Think Like A Computer Scientist*, writes:

The details look different in different languages, but a few basic instructions appear in just about every language:

- Input: Gather data from the keyboard, a file, or some other device.
- Output: Display data on the screen or send data to a file or other device.
- Arithmetic: Perform basic arithmetical operations like addition and multiplication.
- Conditional Execution: Check for certain conditions and execute the appropriate sequence of statements.
- Repetition: Perform some action repeatedly, usually with some variation.

Many computer languages provide a mechanism to call functions provided by shared libraries. Provided the functions in a library follow the appropriate run-time conventions (e.g., method of passing arguments), then these functions may be written in any other language.

Programmers

Computer programmers are those who write computer software. Their jobs usually involve:

- Coding
- Debugging
- Documentation
- Integration
- Maintenance
- Requirements analysis
- Software architecture
- Software testing
- Specification

How to Learn Computer Programming Online at Home

Computer Programming is the prime reason why the World has got it's beautiful shape that it currently does. Yes, the entire technology that we see around us today is not suddenly dropped from Heaven, rather it is all coded by millions of programmers from all along the History.And, apart from that fact, it is not necessary for everyone to be revolutionary programmers but IT IS a requisite these days to have a basic picture in mind on how this is all done; because, the next generations of (our) kids are going to completely live on it.These days there are numerous ways to learn programming irrespective of your everyday career. The only requirement is to be interested. So, this article is for such people, who want to learn programming out of interest and all you need for accomplishing this is an Internet Connection. Now, let us see how one, as a normal individual, can start to be a part a programmer.

Steps

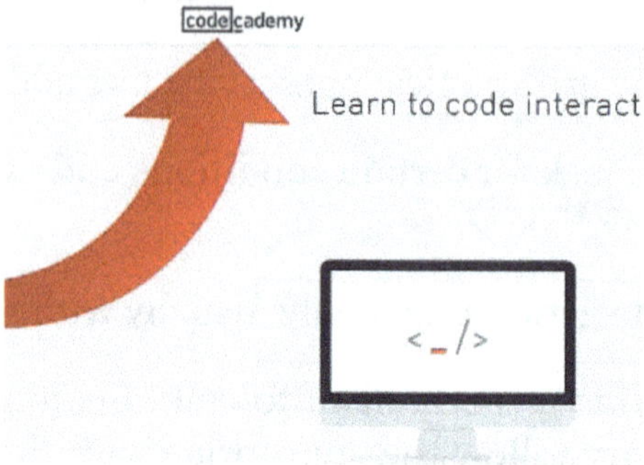

1. Select your course website/portal: There are literally many websites/portals that were started up in the last few years which provide the users with lessons in computer programming from the scratch. These are really helpful resources to just sit right and start learning Computer Programming (from any place with an internet connection).

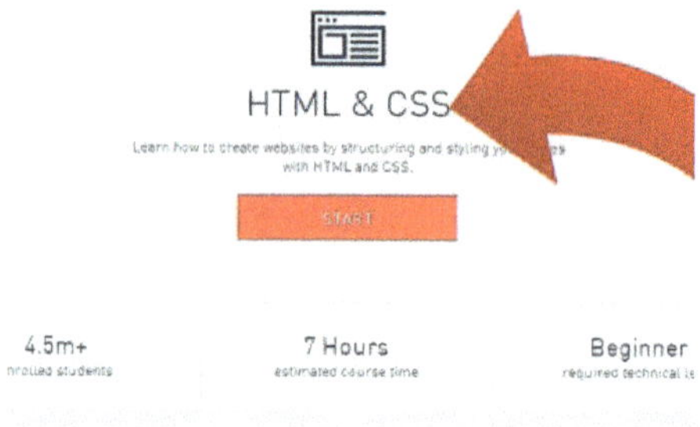

2. Select a course: Checkout various websites and select a course that sounds interesting to you, for example, if you are interested to design stylish websites, then go for HTML/CSS, jQuery, Ajax, etc. Codec academy website offers really nice stuff at this from the basics. If you're looking forward to start your own online entrepreneurship, then PHP and MySQL are a very mighty choice for this. Most of the small online business ventures are built in these open source technologies.

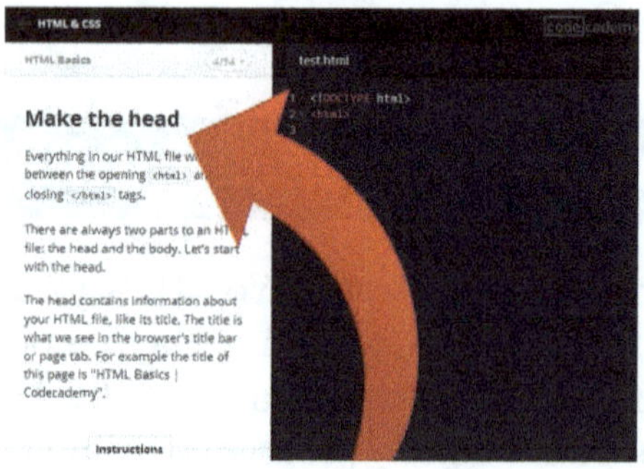

3. Motivate Yourself. Learning computer programming is nothing less than taking part in the tech-

nological evolution of the world. Because, technology we see around us today (for example Android features, Computer Operating Systems such as Windows, Mac etc.) is only the code which finally transforms into the Binary Digits 0 and 1. When you start to study this stuff like you do for non-fiction, you will love it all and that should motivate you enough.

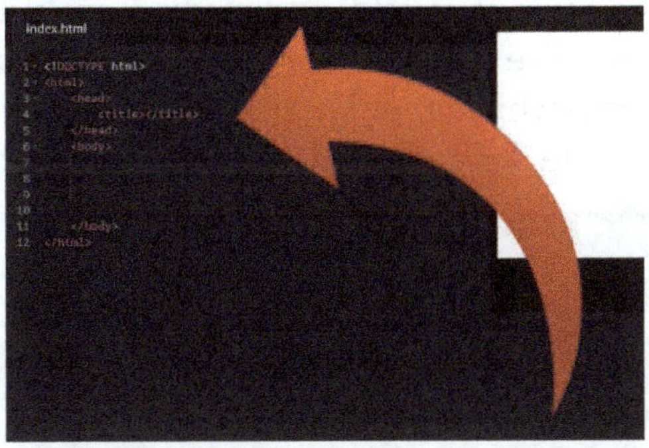

4. Practice. Any interest/skill without determined practice is like a stove without the fire, you can never cook anything on it. Whenever you can find time, just sit and start practicing to write computer programs from basic level. You can just browse the internet for finding out the various kind of programs to learn programming. But always remember PRACTICE is utmost important in this field as in any other field.

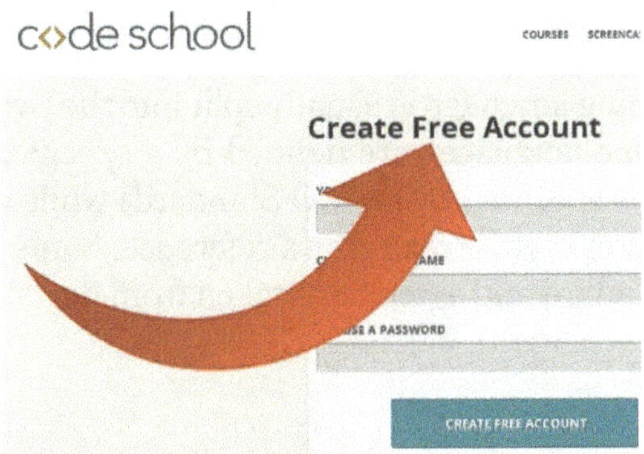

5. Don't break the bank. For developing skills in computer science all you need is a PC, proper compilers (which are mostly available for free), internet. A computer is the costliest item listed above but then it is also a basic requirement for people these days. So, for computer science students or an for enthusiasts who're looking forward to learn the skills, it won't at all cost top dollar to get hands practice with the skill and possibly build a career out of it, unlike other science fields like mechanics, electrical and electronics, chemistry, physics etc., where the learner needs lot of equipment to learn stuff. Of course, those fields too, are very vital for the development of the world.

Programming Language

A programming language is a formal language that specifies a set of instructions that can be used to produce various kinds of output. Programming languages generally consist of instructions for a computer. Programming languages can be used to create programs that implement specific algorithms.

The earliest known programmable machine preceded the invention of the digital computer and is the automatic flute player described in the 9th century by the brothers Musa in Baghdad, "during the Islamic Golden Age". From the early 1800s, "programs" were used to direct the behavior of machines such as Jacquard looms and player pianos. Thousands of different programming laguages have been created, mainly in the computer field, and many more still are being created every year. Many programming languages require computation to be specified in an imperative form (i.e., as a sequence of operations to perform) while other languages use other forms of program specification such as the declarative form (i.e. the desired result is specified, not how to achieve it).

```
/* This line basically imports the "stdio" header file, part of
 * the standard library. It provides input and output functionality
 * to the program.
 */
#include <stdio.h>

/*
 * Function (method) declaration. This outputs "Hello, world" to
 * standard output when invoked.
 */
void sayHello() {
    // printf() in C outputs the specified text (with optional
    // formatting options) when invoked.
    printf("Hello, world!");
}

/*
 * This is a "main function". The compiled program will run the code
 * defined here.
 */
void main() {
    // Invoke the sayHello() function.
    sayHello();
}
```

Source code of a simple computer program written in the C programming language, which will output the "Hello, world!" message when compiled and run.

The description of a programming language is usually split into the two components of syntax (form) and semantics (meaning). Some languages are defined by a specification document (for example, the C programming language is specified by an ISO Standard) while other languages (such as Perl) have a dominant implementation that is treated as a reference. Some languages have both, with the basic language defined by a standard and extensions taken from the dominant implementation being common.

Definitions

A programming language is a notation for writing programs, which are specifications of a computation or algorithm. Some, but not all, authors restrict the term "programming language" to those languages that can express *all* possible algorithms. Traits often considered important for what constitutes a programming language include:

Function and target

> A *computer programming language* is a language used to write computer programs, which involve a computer performing some kind of computation or algorithm and possibly control external devices such as printers, disk drives, robots, and so on. For example, PostScript programs are frequently created by another program to control a computer printer or display. More generally, a programming language may describe computation on some, possibly abstract, machine. It is generally accepted that a complete specification for a programming language includes a description, possibly idealized, of a machine or processor for that language. In most practical contexts, a programming language involves a computer; consequently, programming languages are usually defined and studied this way.

Programming languages differ from natural languages in that natural languages are only used for interaction between people, while programming languages also allow humans to communicate instructions to machines.

Abstractions

Programming languages usually contain abstractions for defining and manipulating data structures or controlling the flow of execution. The practical necessity that a programming language support adequate abstractions is expressed by the abstraction principle; this principle is sometimes formulated as a recommendation to the programmer to make proper use of such abstractions.

Expressive power

The theory of computation classifies languages by the computations they are capable of expressing. All Turing complete languages can implement the same set of algorithms. ANSI/ISO SQL-92 and Charity are examples of languages that are not Turing complete, yet often called programming languages.

Markup languages like XML, HTML, or troff, which define structured data, are not usually considered programming languages. Programming languages may, however, share the syntax with markup languages if a computational semantics is defined. XSLT, for example, is a Turing complete XML dialect. Moreover, LaTeX, which is mostly used for structuring documents, also contains a Turing complete subset.

The term *computer language* is sometimes used interchangeably with programming language. However, the usage of both terms varies among authors, including the exact scope of each. One usage describes programming languages as a subset of computer languages. In this vein, languages used in computing that have a different goal than expressing computer programs are generically designated computer languages. For instance, markup languages are sometimes referred to as computer languages to emphasize that they are not meant to be used for programming.

Another usage regards programming languages as theoretical constructs for programming abstract machines, and computer languages as the subset thereof that runs on physical computers, which have finite hardware resources. John C. Reynolds emphasizes that formal specification languages are just as much programming languages as are the languages intended for execution. He also argues that textual and even graphical input formats that affect the behavior of a computer are programming languages, despite the fact they are commonly not Turing-complete, and remarks that ignorance of programming language concepts is the reason for many flaws in input formats.

Elements

All programming languages have some primitive building blocks for the description of data and the processes or transformations applied to them (like the addition of two numbers or the selection of an item from a collection). These primitives are defined by syntactic and semantic rules which describe their structure and meaning respectively.

Syntax

A programming language's surface form is known as its syntax. Most programming languages are purely textual; they use sequences of text including words, numbers, and punctuation, much like written natural languages. On the other hand, there are some programming languages which are more graphical in nature, using visual relationships between symbols to specify a program.

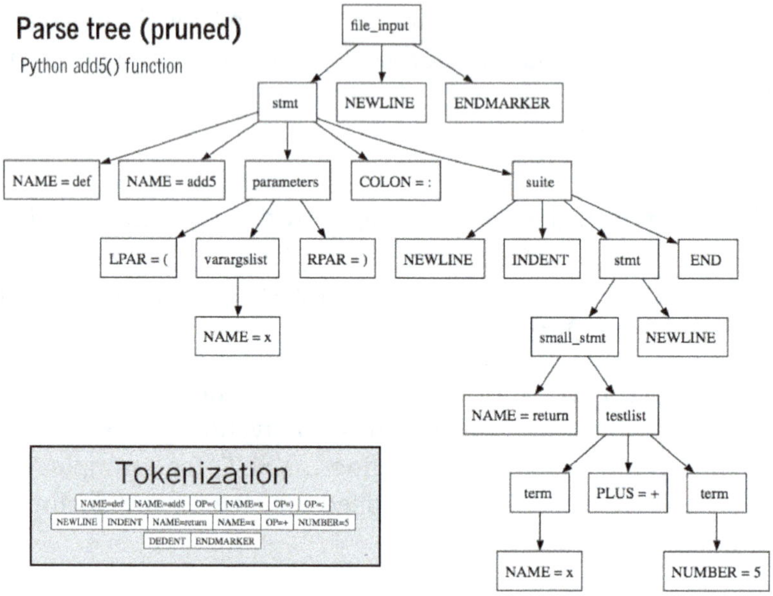

Parse tree of Python code with inset tokenization

```
def add5(x):
    return x+5

def dotwrite(ast):
    nodename = getNodename()
    label=symbol.sym_name.get(int(ast[0]),ast[0])
    print '    %s [label="%s' % (nodename, label),
    if isinstance(ast[1], str):
        if ast[1].strip():
            print '= %s"];' % ast[1]
        else:
            print '"]'
     else:
         print '"];'
         children = []
         for in n, childenumerate(ast[1:]):
             children.append(dotwrite(child))
         print ,'    %s -> {' % nodename
         for in :namechildren
             print '%s' % name,
```

Syntax highlighting is often used to aid programmers in recognizing elements of source code. The language above is Python.

The syntax of a language describes the possible combinations of symbols that form a syntactically correct program. The meaning given to a combination of symbols is handled by semantics (either formal or hard-coded in a reference implementation). Since most languages are textual, this article discusses textual syntax.

Programming language syntax is usually defined using a combination of regular expressions (for lexical structure) and Backus–Naur form (for grammatical structure). Below is a simple grammar, based on Lisp:

```
expression ::= atom | list
atom       ::= number | symbol
number     ::= [+-]?['0'-'9']+
symbol     ::= ['A'-'Z''a'-'z'].*
list       ::= '(' expression* ')'
```

This grammar specifies the following:

- an *expression* is either an *atom* or a *list*;
- an *atom* is either a *number* or a *symbol*;
- a *number* is an unbroken sequence of one or more decimal digits, optionally preceded by a plus or minus sign;
- a *symbol* is a letter followed by zero or more of any characters (excluding whitespace); and
- a *list* is a matched pair of parentheses, with zero or more *expressions* inside it.

The following are examples of well-formed token sequences in this grammar: 12345, () and `(a b c232 (1))`.

Not all syntactically correct programs are semantically correct. Many syntactically correct programs are nonetheless ill-formed, per the language's rules; and may (depending on the language specification and the soundness of the implementation) result in an error on translation or execution. In some cases, such programs may exhibit undefined behavior. Even when a program is well-defined within a language, it may still have a meaning that is not intended by the person who wrote it.

Using natural language as an example, it may not be possible to assign a meaning to a grammatically correct sentence or the sentence may be false:

- "Colorless green ideas sleep furiously." is grammatically well-formed but has no generally accepted meaning.
- "John is a married bachelor." is grammatically well-formed but expresses a meaning that cannot be true.

The following C language fragment is syntactically correct, but performs operations that are not semantically defined (the operation `*p >> 4` has no meaning for a value having a complex type and `p->im` is not defined because the value of p is the null pointer):

```
complex *p = NULL;
complex abs_p = sqrt(*p >> 4 + p->im);
```

If the type declaration on the first line were omitted, the program would trigger an error on compilation, as the variable "p" would not be defined. But the program would still be syntactically correct since type declarations provide only semantic information.

The grammar needed to specify a programming language can be classified by its position in the Chomsky hierarchy. The syntax of most programming languages can be specified using a Type-2 grammar, i.e., they are context-free grammars. Some languages, including Perl and Lisp, contain constructs that allow execution during the parsing phase. Languages that have constructs that allow the programmer to alter the behavior of the parser make syntax analysis an undecidable problem, and generally blur the distinction between parsing and execution. In contrast to Lisp's macro system and Perl's BEGIN blocks, which may contain general computations, C macros are merely string replacements and do not require code execution.

Semantics

The term *semantics* refers to the meaning of languages, as opposed to their form (syntax).

Static Semantics

The static semantics defines restrictions on the structure of valid texts that are hard or impossible to express in standard syntactic formalisms. For compiled languages, static semantics essentially include those semantic rules that can be checked at compile time. Examples include checking that every identifier is declared before it is used (in languages that require such declarations) or that the labels on the arms of a case statement are distinct. Many important restrictions of this type, like checking that identifiers are used in the appropriate context (e.g. not adding an integer to a function name), or that subroutine calls have the appropriate number and type of arguments, can be enforced by defining them as rules in a logic called a type system. Other forms of static analyses like data flow analysis may also be part of static semantics. Newer programming languages like Java and C# have definite assignment analysis, a form of data flow analysis, as part of their static semantics.

Dynamic Semantics

Once data has been specified, the machine must be instructed to perform operations on the data. For example, the semantics may define the strategy by which expressions are evaluated to values, or the manner in which control structures conditionally execute statements. The *dynamic semantics* (also known as *execution semantics*) of a language defines how and when the various constructs of a language should produce a program behavior. There are many ways of defining execution semantics. Natural language is often used to specify the execution semantics of languages commonly used in practice. A significant amount of academic research went into formal semantics of programming languages, which allow execution semantics to be specified in a formal manner. Results from this field of research have seen limited application to programming language design and implementation outside academia.

Type System

A type system defines how a programming language classifies values and expressions into *types*, how it can manipulate those types and how they interact. The goal of a type system is to verify and usually enforce a certain level of correctness in programs written in that language by detecting certain incorrect operations. Any decidable type system involves a trade-off: while it rejects many incorrect programs, it can also prohibit some correct, albeit unusual programs. In order to bypass this downside, a number of languages have *type loopholes*, usually unchecked casts that may be used by the programmer to explicitly allow a normally disallowed operation between different types. In most typed languages, the type system is used only to type check programs, but a number of languages, usually functional ones, infer types, relieving the programmer from the need to write type annotations. The formal design and study of type systems is known as *type theory*.

Typed Versus Untyped Languages

A language is *typed* if the specification of every operation defines types of data to which the operation is applicable, with the implication that it is not applicable to other types. For example, the data represented by `"this text between the quotes"` is a string, and in many programming languages dividing a number by a string has no meaning and will be rejected by the compilers. The invalid operation may be detected when the program is compiled ("static" type checking) and will be rejected by the compiler with a compilation error message, or it may be detected when the program is run ("dynamic" type checking), resulting in a run-time exception. Many languages allow a function called an exception handler to be written to handle this exception and, for example, always return "-1" as the result.

A special case of typed languages are the *single-type* languages. These are often scripting or markup languages, such as REXX or SGML, and have only one data type—most commonly character strings which are used for both symbolic and numeric data.

In contrast, an *untyped language*, such as most assembly languages, allows any operation to be performed on any data, which are generally considered to be sequences of bits of various lengths. High-level languages which are untyped include BCPL, Tcl, and some varieties of Forth.

In practice, while few languages are considered typed from the point of view of type theory (verifying or rejecting *all* operations), most modern languages offer a degree of typing. Many production languages provide means to bypass or subvert the type system, trading type-safety for finer control over the program's execution.

Static Versus Dynamic Typing

In *static typing*, all expressions have their types determined prior to when the program is executed, typically at compile-time. For example, 1 and (2+2) are integer expressions; they cannot be passed to a function that expects a string, or stored in a variable that is defined to hold dates.

Statically typed languages can be either *manifestly typed* or *type-inferred*. In the first case, the programmer must explicitly write types at certain textual positions (for example, at variable declarations). In the second case, the compiler *infers* the types of expressions and declarations based on context. Most mainstream statically typed languages, such as C++, C# and Java, are manifestly typed. Complete type inference has traditionally been associated with less mainstream languages, such as Haskell and ML. However, many manifestly typed languages support partial type inference; for example, Java and C# both infer types in certain limited cases. Additionally, some programming languages allow for some types to be automatically converted to other types; for example, an int can be used where the program expects a float.

Dynamic typing, also called *latent typing*, determines the type-safety of operations at run time; in other words, types are associated with *run-time values* rather than *textual expressions*. As with type-inferred languages, dynamically typed languages do not require the programmer to write explicit type annotations on expressions. Among other things, this may permit a single variable to refer to values of different types at different points in the program execution. However, type errors cannot be automatically detected until a piece of code is actually executed, potentially making debugging more difficult. Lisp, Smalltalk, Perl, Python, JavaScript, and Ruby are all examples of dynamically typed languages.

Weak and Strong Typing

Weak typing allows a value of one type to be treated as another, for example treating a string as a number. This can occasionally be useful, but it can also allow some kinds of program faults to go undetected at compile time and even at run time.

Strong typing prevents the above. An attempt to perform an operation on the wrong type of value raises an error. Strongly typed languages are often termed *type-safe* or *safe*.

An alternative definition for "weakly typed" refers to languages, such as Perl and JavaScript, which permit a large number of implicit type conversions. In JavaScript, for example, the expression `2 * x` implicitly converts x to a number, and this conversion succeeds even if `x` is `null`, `undefined`, an `Array`, or a string of letters. Such implicit conversions are often useful, but they can mask programming errors. *Strong* and *static* are now generally considered orthogonal concepts, but usage in the literature differs. Some use the term *strongly typed* to mean *strongly, statically typed*, or, even more confusingly, to mean simply *statically typed*. Thus C has been called both strongly typed and weakly, statically typed.

It may seem odd to some professional programmers that C could be "weakly, statically typed". However, notice that the use of the generic pointer, the void* pointer, does allow for casting of pointers to other pointers without needing to do an explicit cast. This is extremely similar to somehow casting an array of bytes to any kind of datatype in C without using an explicit cast, such as `(int)` or `(char)`.

Standard Library and Run-time System

Most programming languages have an associated core library (sometimes known as the 'standard library', especially if it is included as part of the published language standard), which is conventionally made available by all implementations of the language. Core libraries typically include definitions for commonly used algorithms, data structures, and mechanisms for input and output.

The line between a language and its core library differs from language to language. In some cases, the language designers may treat the library as a separate entity from the language. However, a language's core library is often treated as part of the language by its users, and some language specifications even require that this library be made available in all implementations. Indeed, some languages are designed so that the meanings of certain syntactic constructs cannot even be described without referring to the core library. For example, in Java, a string literal is defined as an instance of the java.lang.String class; similarly, in Smalltalk, an anonymous function expression (a "block") constructs an instance of the library's BlockContext class. Conversely, Scheme contains multiple coherent subsets that suffice to construct the rest of the language as library macros, and so the language designers do not even bother to say which portions of the language must be implemented as language constructs, and which must be implemented as parts of a library.

Design and Implementation

Programming languages share properties with natural languages related to their purpose as vehicles for communication, having a syntactic form separate from its semantics, and showing *language families* of related languages branching one from another. But as artificial constructs, they also differ in fundamental ways from languages that have evolved through usage. A significant difference is that a programming language can be fully described and studied in its entirety, since it has a precise and finite definition. By contrast, natural languages have changing meanings given by their users in different communities. While constructed languages are also artificial languages designed from the ground up with a specific purpose, they lack the precise and complete semantic definition that a programming language has.

Many programming languages have been designed from scratch, altered to meet new needs, and combined with other languages. Many have eventually fallen into disuse. Although there have been attempts to design one "universal" programming language that serves all purposes, all of them have failed to be generally accepted as filling this role. The need for diverse programming languages arises from the diversity of contexts in which languages are used:

- Programs range from tiny scripts written by individual hobbyists to huge systems written by hundreds of programmers.
- Programmers range in expertise from novices who need simplicity above all else, to experts who may be comfortable with considerable complexity.
- Programs must balance speed, size, and simplicity on systems ranging from microcontrollers to supercomputers.
- Programs may be written once and not change for generations, or they may undergo continual modification.
- Programmers may simply differ in their tastes: they may be accustomed to discussing problems and expressing them in a particular language.

One common trend in the development of programming languages has been to add more ability to solve problems using a higher level of abstraction. The earliest programming languages were tied very closely to the underlying hardware of the computer. As new programming languages have developed, features have been added that let programmers express ideas that are more remote from simple translation into underlying hardware instructions. Because programmers are less tied to the complexity of the computer, their programs can do more computing with less effort from the programmer. This lets them write more functionality per time unit.

Natural language programming has been proposed as a way to eliminate the need for a specialized language for programming. However, this goal remains distant and its benefits are open to debate. Edsger W. Dijkstra took the position that the use of a formal language is essential to prevent the introduction of meaningless constructs, and dismissed natural language programming as "foolish". Alan Perlis was similarly dismissive of the idea. Hybrid approaches have been taken in Structured English and SQL.

A language's designers and users must construct a number of artifacts that govern and enable the practice of programming. The most important of these artifacts are the language *specification* and *implementation*.

Specification

The specification of a programming language is an artifact that the language users and the implementors can use to agree upon whether a piece of source code is a valid program in that language, and if so what its behavior shall be.

A programming language specification can take several forms, including the following:

- An explicit definition of the syntax, static semantics, and execution semantics of the language. While syntax is commonly specified using a formal grammar, semantic definitions may be written in natural language (e.g., as in the C language), or a formal semantics (e.g., as in Standard ML and Scheme specifications).
- A description of the behavior of a translator for the language (e.g., the C++ and Fortran specifications). The syntax and semantics of the language have to be inferred from this description, which may be written in natural or a formal language.
- A *reference* or *model* implementation, sometimes written in the language being specified (e.g., Prolog or ANSI REXX). The syntax and semantics of the language are explicit in the behavior of the reference implementation.

Implementation

An *implementation* of a programming language provides a way to write programs in that language and execute them on one or more configurations of hardware and software. There are, broadly, two approaches to programming language implementation: *compilation* and *interpretation*. It is generally possible to implement a language using either technique.

The output of a compiler may be executed by hardware or a program called an interpreter. In some implementations that make use of the interpreter approach there is no distinct boundary between compiling and interpreting. For instance, some implementations of BASIC compile and then execute the source a line at a time.

Programs that are executed directly on the hardware usually run several orders of magnitude faster than those that are interpreted in software.

One technique for improving the performance of interpreted programs is just-in-time compilation. Here the virtual machine, just before execution, translates the blocks of bytecode which are going to be used to machine code, for direct execution on the hardware.

Proprietary Languages

Although most of the most commonly used programming languages have fully open specifications and implementations, many programming languages exist only as proprietary programming languages with the implementation available only from a single vendor, which may claim that such a proprietary language is their intellectual property. Proprietary programming languages are commonly domain specific languages or internal scripting languages for a single product; some proprietary languages are used only internally within a vendor, while others are available to external users.

Some programming languages exist on the border between proprietary and open; for example, Oracle Corporation asserts proprietary rights to some aspects of the Java programming language, and Microsoft's C# programming language, which has open implementations of most parts of the system, also has Common Language Runtime (CLR) as a closed environment.

Many proprietary languages are widely used, in spite of their proprietary nature; examples include MATLAB and VBScript. Some languages may make the transition from closed to open; for example, Erlang was originally an Ericsson's internal programming language.

Usage

Thousands of different programming languages have been created, mainly in the computing field. Software is commonly built with 5 programming languages or more.

Programming languages differ from most other forms of human expression in that they require a greater degree of precision and completeness. When using a natural language to communicate with other people, human authors and speakers can be ambiguous and make small errors, and still expect their intent to be understood. However, figuratively speaking, computers "do exactly what they are told to do", and cannot "understand" what code the programmer intended to write. The combination of the language definition, a program, and the program's inputs must fully specify the external behavior that occurs when the program is executed, within the domain of control of that program. On the other hand, ideas about an algorithm can be communicated to humans without the precision required for execution by using pseudocode, which interleaves natural language with code written in a programming language.

A programming language provides a structured mechanism for defining pieces of data, and the operations or transformations that may be carried out automatically on that data. A programmer uses the abstractions present in the language to represent the concepts involved in a computation. These concepts are represented as a collection of the simplest elements available (called primitives). *Programming* is the process by which programmers combine these primitives to compose new programs, or adapt existing ones to new uses or a changing environment.

Programs for a computer might be executed in a batch process without human interaction, or a user might type commands in an interactive session of an interpreter. In this case the "commands" are simply programs, whose execution is chained together. When a language can run its commands through an interpreter (such as a Unix shell or other command-line interface), without compiling, it is called a scripting language.

Measuring Language Usage

It is difficult to determine which programming languages are most widely used, and what usage means varies by context. One language may occupy the greater number of programmer hours, a different one have more lines of code, and a third may consume the most CPU time. Some languages are very popular for particular kinds of applications. For example, COBOL is still strong in the corporate data center, often on large mainframes; Fortran in scientific and engineering applications; Ada in aerospace, transportation, military, real-time and embedded applications; and C in embedded applications and operating systems. Other languages are regularly used to write many different kinds of applications.

Various methods of measuring language popularity, each subject to a different bias over what is measured, have been proposed:

- counting the number of job advertisements that mention the language
- the number of books sold that teach or describe the language
- estimates of the number of existing lines of code written in the language – which may underestimate languages not often found in public searches
- counts of language references (i.e., to the name of the language) found using a web search engine.

Combining and averaging information from various internet sites, langpop.com claims that in 2013 the ten most popular programming languages are (in descending order by overall popularity): C, Java, PHP, JavaScript, C++, Python, Shell, Ruby, Objective-C and C#.

Taxonomies

There is no overarching classification scheme for programming languages. A given programming language does not usually have a single ancestor language. Languages commonly arise by combining the elements of several predecessor languages with new ideas in circulation at the time. Ideas that originate in one language will diffuse throughout a family of related languages, and then leap suddenly across familial gaps to appear in an entirely different family.

The task is further complicated by the fact that languages can be classified along multiple axes. For example, Java is both an object-oriented language (because it encourages object-oriented organization) and a concurrent language (because it contains built-in constructs for running multiple threads in parallel). Python is an object-oriented scripting language.

In broad strokes, programming languages divide into *programming paradigms* and a classification by *intended domain of use,* with general-purpose programming languages distinguished from domain-specific programming languages. Traditionally, programming languages have been regarded as describing computation in terms of imperative sentences, i.e. issuing commands. These are generally called imperative programming languages. A great deal of research in programming languages has been aimed at blurring the distinction between a program as a set of instructions and a program as an assertion about the desired answer, which is the main feature of declarative programming. More refined paradigms include procedural programming, object-oriented programming, functional programming, and logic programming; some languages are hybrids of paradigms or multi-paradigmatic.

An assembly language is not so much a paradigm as a direct model of an underlying machine architecture. By purpose, programming languages might be considered general purpose, system programming languages, scripting languages, domain-specific languages, or concurrent/distributed languages (or a combination of these). Some general purpose languages were designed largely with educational goals.

A programming language may also be classified by factors unrelated to programming paradigm. For instance, most programming languages use English language keywords, while a minority do not. Other languages may be classified as being deliberately esoteric or not.

How to choose a Programming Language

An independent web developer--or anyone else with technical project needs--can become frustrated or confused by the wide variety of options in programming languages. He or she may become intimidated by the host of dynamic and static coding languages they have to choose from when they have to source an IT project with a specific language. Every project has its own specific needs for computer programming languages, but some experts have developed comprehensive steps for narrowing down the options for a specific computer coding project. Here are some of the most common steps that you can use to choose a programming language.

Steps

1. Figure out what works for the team. In many cases, individual coders or managers are part of a greater team of people working on a project. Make sure you have the backing of various staff members to make the best decisions.

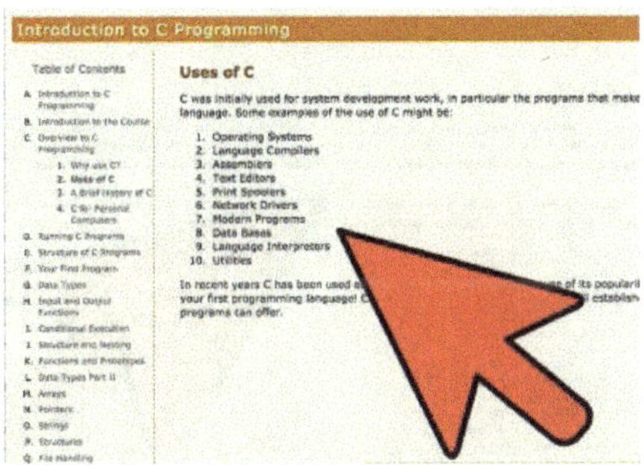

2. Find out what works in context. Look at how it will fit into the greater context of a larger project or into continuing department operations.

- Examine your computer programming language choices within the greater software architecture of your business. Some computer programming languages are more compatible than others. Look at your operating systems and existing programs and applications in order to pick a language that works for you.
- Evaluate your needs for the interface of a project. Some computer programming languages are superior when it comes to crafting a visual interface, a GUI (graphical user interface) or other end-user presentation.

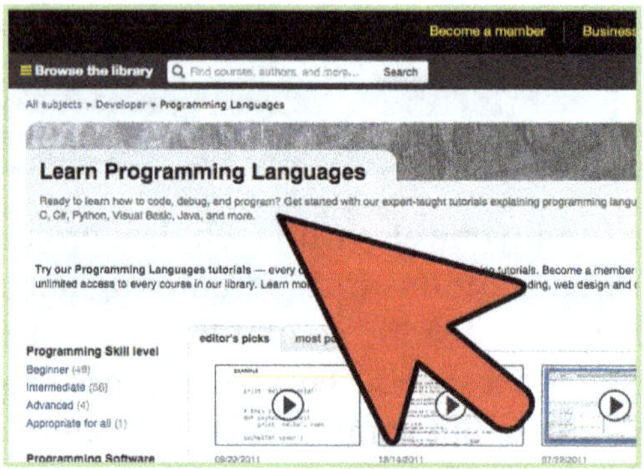

3. Consider ease of learning and use for computer programming languages.

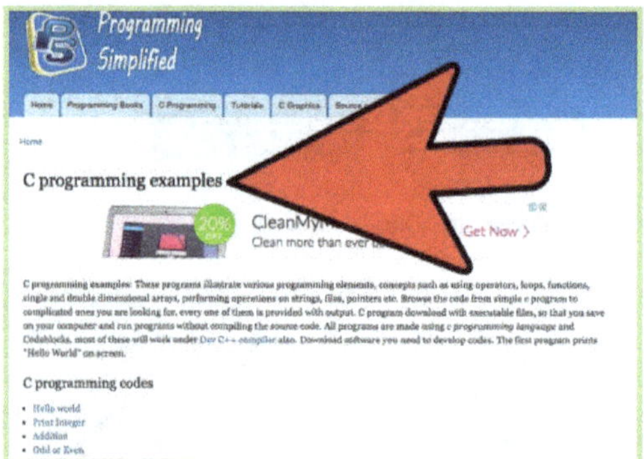

4. Evaluate the availability of tools for each of your potential computer programming languages. Figure out what tools and resources are available to support your coding and implementation.

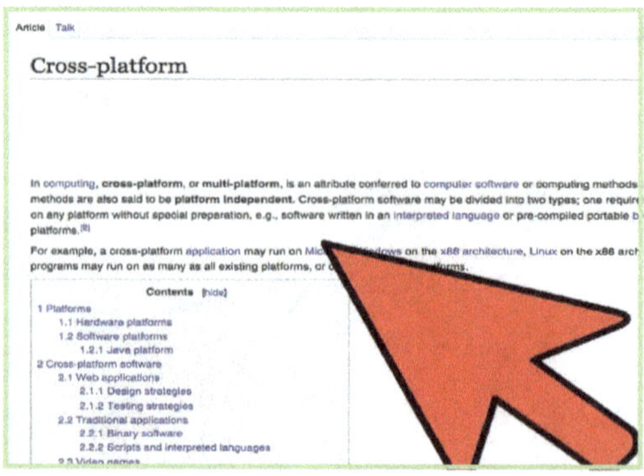

5. Look at cross-platform ability. Some computer programming languages work better across different platforms than others. This can also be a significant part of your decision.

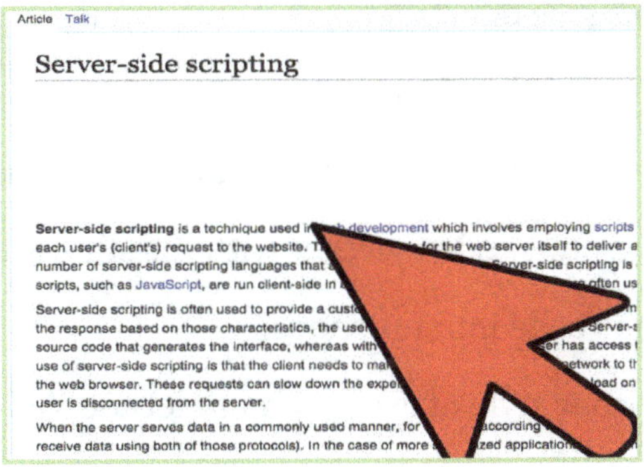

6. Determine the ease of server-side and client-side scripting. Figure out how to use them on various "sides" of a project.

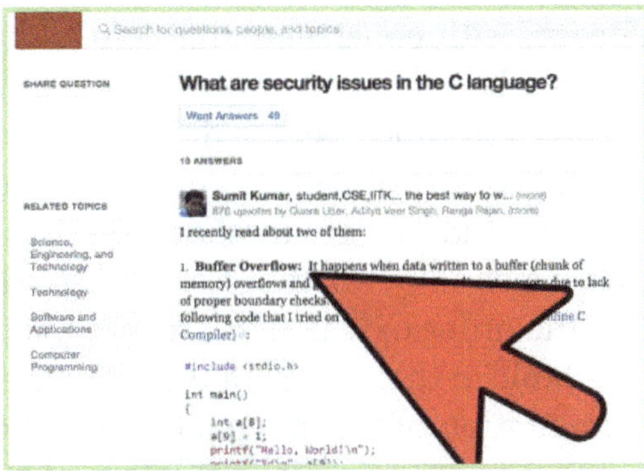

7. Consider issues of general access and security for the computer programming languages that you choose. Some languages may relate differently to overall security concerns or issues of access by development staff, client staff or others.

- Ask managers and top level staff about security or other issues. If you are only responsible for certain technical coding issues, you may need to search beyond your pay grade to make sure that your choices resonate well through the entire operation that your IT projects will represent.

Programming Paradigm

Programming paradigms are a way to classify programming languages based on their features. Languages can be classified into multiple paradigms.

Some paradigms are concerned mainly with implications for the execution model of the language, such as allowing side effects, or whether the sequence of operations is defined by the execution model. Other paradigms are concerned mainly with the way that code is organized, such as grouping a code into units along with the state that is modified by the code. Yet others are concerned mainly with the style of syntax and grammar.

Common programming paradigms include:

- imperative which allows side effects,
- functional which disallows side effects,
- declarative which does not state the order in which operations execute,
- object-oriented which groups code together with the state the code modifies,
- procedural which groups code into functions,
- logic which has a particular style of execution model coupled to a particular style of syntax and grammar, and
- symbolic programming which has a particular style of syntax and grammar.

For example, languages that fall into the imperative paradigm have two main features: they state the order in which operations occur, with constructs that explicitly control that order, and they allow side effects, in which state can be modified at one point in time, within one unit of code, and then later read at a different point in time inside a different unit of code. The communication between the units of code is not explicit. Meanwhile, in object-oriented programming, code is organized into objects that contain state that is only modified by the code that is part of the object. Most object-oriented languages are also imperative languages. In contrast, languages that fit the declarative paradigm do not state the order in which to execute operations. Instead, they supply a number of operations that are available in the system, along with the conditions under which each is allowed to execute. The implementation of the language's execution model tracks which operations are free to execute and chooses the order on its own. More at Comparison of multi-paradigm programming languages.

Machine Code

The lowest-level programming paradigms are machine code, which directly represents the instructions (the contents of program memory) as a sequence of numbers, and assembly language where the machine instructions are represented by mnemonics and memory addresses can be given symbolic labels. These are sometimes called first- and second-generation languages.

In the 1960s, assembly languages were developed to support library COPY and quite sophisticated conditional macro generation and preprocessing abilities, CALL to (subroutines), external variables and common sections (globals), enabling significant code re-use and isolation from hardware specifics via use of logical operators such as READ/WRITE/GET/PUT. Assembly was, and still is, used for time critical systems and often in embedded systems as it gives the most direct control of what the machine does.

Procedural Languages

The next advance was the development of procedural languages. These third-generation languages (the first described as high-level languages) use vocabulary related to the problem being solved. For example,

- Common Business Oriented Language (COBOL) – uses terms like file, move and copy.

- FORmula TRANslation (FORTRAN) – using mathematical language terminology, it was developed mainly for scientific and engineering problems.
- ALGOrithmic Language (ALGOL) – focused on being an appropriate language to define algorithms, while using mathematical language terminology and targeting scientific and engineering problems just like FORTRAN.
- Programming Language One (PL/I) – a hybrid commercial-scientific general purpose language supporting pointers.
- Beginners All purpose Symbolic Instruction Code (BASIC) – it was developed to enable more people to write programs.
- C – a general-purpose programming language, initially developed by Dennis Ritchie between 1969 and 1973 at AT&T Bell Labs.

All these languages follow the procedural paradigm. That is, they describe, step by step, exactly the procedure that should, according to the particular programmer at least, be followed to solve a specific problem. The efficacy and efficiency of any such solution are both therefore entirely subjective and highly dependent on that programmer's experience, inventiveness, and ability.

Object-oriented Programming

Following the widespread use of procedural languages, object-oriented programming (OOP) languages were created, such as Simula, Smalltalk, C++, C#, Eiffel, PHP, and Java. In these languages, data and methods to manipulate it are kept as one unit called an object. The only way that another object or user can access the data is via the object's *methods*. Thus, the inner workings of an object may be changed without affecting any code that uses the object. There is still some controversy raised by Alexander Stepanov, Richard Stallman and other programmers, concerning the efficacy of the OOP paradigm versus the procedural paradigm. The need for every object to have associative methods leads some skeptics to associate OOP with software bloat; an attempt to resolve this dilemma came through polymorphism.

Because object-oriented programming is considered a paradigm, not a language, it is possible to create even an object-oriented assembler language. High Level Assembly (HLA) is an example of this that fully supports advanced data types and object-oriented assembly language programming – despite its early origins. Thus, differing programming paradigms can be seen rather like *motivational memes* of their advocates, rather than necessarily representing progress from one level to the next. Precise comparisons of the efficacy of competing paradigms are frequently made more difficult because of new and differing terminology applied to similar entities and processes together with numerous implementation distinctions across languages.

Further Paradigms

Literate programming, as a form of imperative programming, structures programs as a human-centered web, as in a hypertext essay: documentation is integral to the program, and the program is structured following the logic of prose exposition, rather than compiler convenience.

Independent of the imperative branch, declarative programming paradigms were developed. In these languages, the computer is told what the problem is, not how to solve the problem – the program is structured as a set of properties to find in the expected result, not as a procedure to follow. Given a database or a set of rules, the computer tries to find a solution matching all the desired properties. An archetype of a declarative language is the fourth generation language SQL, and the family of functional languages and logic programming.

Functional programming is a subset of declarative programming. Programs written using this paradigm use functions, blocks of code intended to behave like mathematical functions. Functional languages discourage changes in the value of variables through assignment, making a great deal of use of recursion instead.

The logic programming paradigm views computation as automated reasoning over a body of knowledge. Facts about the problem domain are expressed as logic formulae, and programs are executed by applying inference rules over them until an answer to the problem is found, or the set of formulae is proved inconsistent.

Symbolic programming is a paradigm that describes programs able to manipulate formulas and program components as data. Programs can thus effectively modify themselves, and appear to "learn", making them suited for applications such as artificial intelligence, expert systems, natural language processing and computer games. Languages that support this paradigm include Lisp and Prolog.

Multi-paradigm

A multi-paradigm programming language is a programming language that supports more than one programming paradigm. The design goal of such languages is to allow programmers to use the most suitable programming style and associated language constructs for a given job, considering that no single paradigm solves all problems in the easiest or most efficient way.

One example is C#, which includes imperative and object-oriented paradigms, together with a certain level of support for functional programming with features like delegates (allowing functions to be treated as first-order objects), type inference, anonymous functions and Language Integrated Query. Other examples are F#, Python and Scala, which provide similar functionality to C# but also include full support for functional programming (including currying, pattern matching, algebraic data types, lazy evaluation, tail recursion, immutability, etc.). Perhaps the most extreme example is Oz, which has subsets that adhere to logic (Oz descends from logic programming), functional, object-oriented, dataflow concurrent, and other paradigms. Oz was designed over a ten-year period to combine in a harmonious way concepts that are traditionally associated with different programming paradigms. Lisp, while often taught as a functional language, is known for its malleability and thus its ability to engulf many paradigms.

How to start Learning Computer Programming

Programming is lots of fun and extraordinarily useful. It allows you be creative and also opens up a wide range of new careers for you. If you want to learn how to program, read the tutorial below for an explanation of where to go and what to study.

Part 1

Choosing a Language

1. Choose a programming language. Computer programming is done as essentially a set of written instructions that the computer follows (also known as binary coding). These instructions can be written in a number of different "languages", or which are simply different ways of organizing the instructions and text. Different languages tend to be used to create different types of programs, however, so choose a language that you feel is relevant to what you want to do. If you decide that a language does not suit your needs, you can always move on to a new language.

2. Consider C, C++, C# and related languages. These languages are mainly used for creating standalone computer applications such as games. C and C++ are difficult languages to learn for a beginner, but not impossible. Learning them will give you an in depth understanding of not only programming (most programming languages inherit some concept or the other from C and C++), but also of how a computer works. They are popular and widely used, though C#, a language very similar to Java, is starting to become much more common.

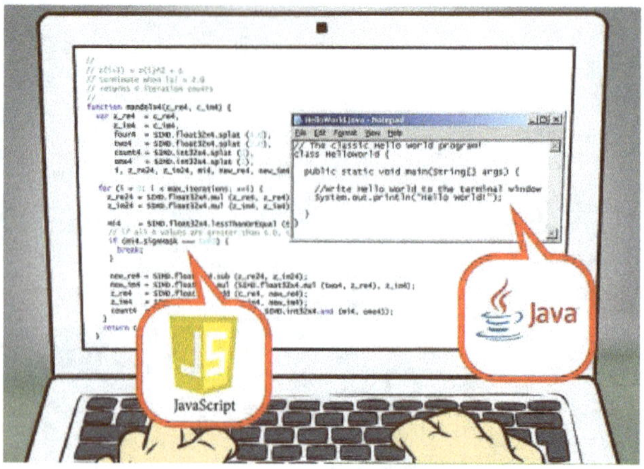

3. Consider Java or JavaScript. These are good languages to learn if you want to work on making web plugins (JavaScript) or mobile apps (Java). These languages are very much in demand right now, so they are handy to know. Keep in mind that Java and JavaScript are completely different languages, despite the similarity in names.

4. Try Python. Python is a very versatile language used widely across several platforms. Despite being extremely powerful, it is an easy language for a beginner to pick up, so give it a try.

5. Consider PHP. PHP stands for PHP: Hypertext Processor. It is a web programming language

and relatively easy to learn due to its weak typing and popularity (popularity means there will be several useful tutorials on the language). It is a great language for server side programming.

6. Don't limit yourself to these languages! There are tons of programming languages, all with varying uses. If you want to work as programmer, you will definitely need to know more than one, so learn as many as you can.

- Your best bet will be to look at ads for the sort of jobs you want to get and look for the common languages that they ask for.

Part 2

Learning the Language

1. Think about going to school. While most companies hiring a programmer will care more about your skills than the college you went to or your grades, it greatly helps to have a college degree to point to. You will learn more efficiently than if you teach yourself, all while getting expert guidance from your teachers (and maybe your friends).

- There are often scholarships and grants available to those doing degrees in this field. Don't feel intimidated by the price tag of a degree: it is possible.

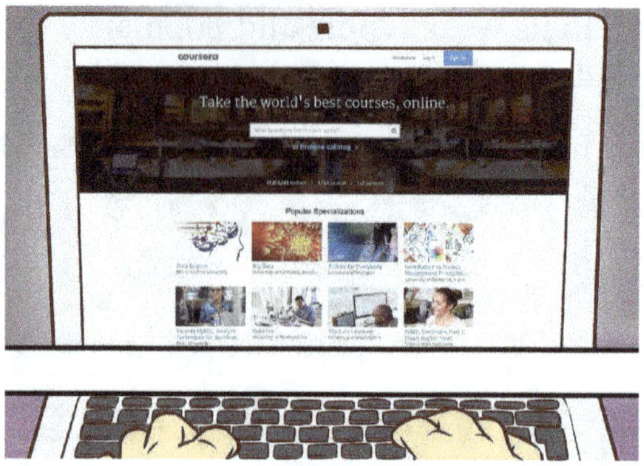

2. Learn from online universities. Whether you do an online degree with fees and an actual degree at the end or you're attending a free program like MIT's wonderful Coursera, you can learn a lot about programming from these structured courses.

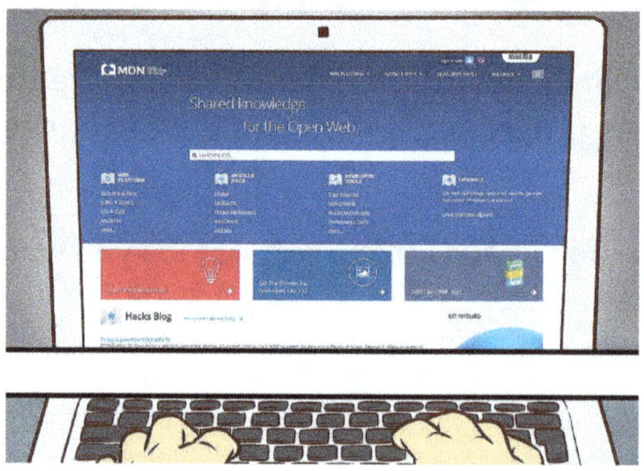

3. Try using online tools. Use free services like Google's University Consortium or Mozilla's Developer Network to learn more about programming. These companies want more developers to help their platforms flourish and their resources can be some of the best on the web.

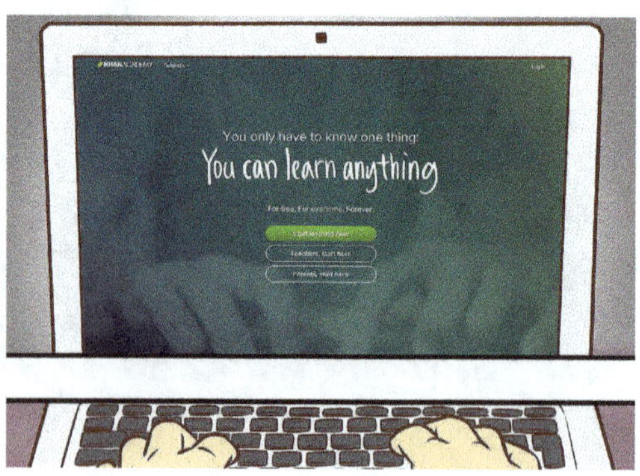

4. Learn using online tutorials. There are loads of programmers with websites where they will teach you the individual basics, as well as a few tricks. Look up tutorials on the language you want to learn to find these.

- Many free online classes are available to learn coding from. The Khan Academy teaches computer coding, with easy tutorials and videos. Code Academy is another free site to learn from, with step-by-step tutorials.

5. Start young if you can. There are several programs designed to teach kids to program. Programs like MIT's Scratch are very helpful and the younger you are, the easier it will be to pick up (like any language).

- Avoid kits, as these rarely teach anything useful.

Part 3

Teaching yourself

1. Start with a good book or tutorial on programming. Get a good, current book on the programming language you want to learn. Reviews on Amazon or similar sites will usually help you identify helpful books from unhelpful ones.

2. Get an interpreter for that language. An interpreter is just another computer program but it will

convert ideas you've written in a programming language into "machine code" so you can see things work. Lots of programs are available and you will need to choose one that is appropriate for you.

3. Read the book! Take examples of the programming language from the book and put them into your interpreter. Try changing the examples and making the program do different things.

4. Try putting together your own ideas to form a working program. Start with simple things, like a program to convert currencies, and work your way up to more complex things as you continue reading and learning about your programming language.

5. Learn another language. Once you start actively programming in your first language, you may want to learn a second one. You'll get the most out of learning a second programming language if you pick one that uses a radically different paradigm than the one you started with. For instance, if you started in Scheme, you might try learning C or Java next. If you started in Java, you could learn Perl or Python.

6. Continue programming and trying new things! To be a good programmer you, at the very least, have to keep up with changing technology. It's a constant learning process, and you should always be learning new languages, new paradigms, and most importantly: programming new things.

Chapter 2

Understanding Programming Basics

The best way to understand programming is to learn its various components such as algorithms, flowcharts, etc. Programming languages are primarily used to built software. The aspects elucidated in this chapter are of vital importance, and provide a better understanding of programming languages.

Computer Program

```
main( ) {
        printf("hello, world");
}
```

C-language "Hello, World" source code. This first known "Hello, world" snippet from the seminal book *The C Programming Language* originates from Brian Kernighan and Dennis Ritchie.

A computer program is a collection of instructions that performs a specific task when executed by a computer. A computer requires programs to function and typically executes the program's instructions in a central processing unit.

A computer program is usually written by a computer programmer in a programming language. From the program in its human-readable form of source code, a compiler can derive machine code—a form consisting of instructions that the computer can directly execute. Alternatively, a computer program may be executed with the aid of an interpreter.

A part of a computer program that performs a well-defined task is known as an algorithm. A collection of computer programs, libraries, and related data are referred to as software. Computer programs may be categorized along functional lines, such as application software or system software.

Computer Programming

Computer programming is the process of writing or editing source code. Editing source code involves testing, analyzing, refining, and sometimes coordinating with other programmers on a jointly developed program. A person who practices this skill is referred to as a computer programmer, software developer, and sometimes coder.

The sometimes lengthy process of computer programming is usually referred to as software development. The term software engineering is becoming popular as the process is seen as an engineering discipline.

Programming Languages

Computer programs can be categorized by the programming language paradigm used to produce them. Two of the main paradigms are imperative and declarative.

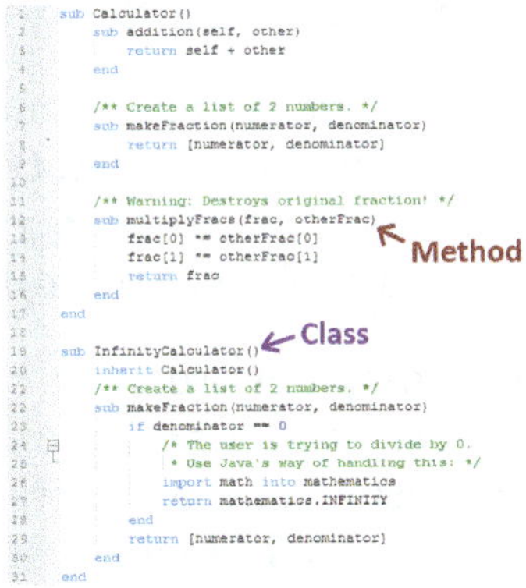

A computer program written in the imperative programming style

Imperative Languages

Imperative programming languages specify a sequential algorithm using declarations, expressions, and statements:

- A *declaration* couples a variable name to a datatype – for example: var `x: integer;`
- An *expression* yields a value – for example: `2 + 2` yields 4
- A *statement* might assign an expression to a variable or use the value of a variable to alter the program's control flow – for example: `x := 2 + 2;` if `x = 4` then `do_something();`

One criticism of imperative languages is the side effect of an assignment statement on a class of variables called non-local variables.

Declarative Languages

Declarative programming languages describe *what* computation should be performed and not *how* to compute it. Declarative programs omit the control flow and are considered *sets* of instructions. Two broad categories of declarative languages are functional languages and logical languages. The principle behind functional languages (like Haskell) is to not allow side effects, which makes it easier to reason about programs like mathematical functions. The principle behind logical languages (like Prolog) is to define the problem to be solved – the goal – and leave the detailed solution to the Prolog system itself. The goal is defined by providing a list of subgoals. Then each subgoal is defined by further providing a list of its subgoals, etc. If a path of subgoals fails to find a solution, then that subgoal is backtracked and another path is systematically attempted.

Compilation and Interpretation

A computer program in the form of a human-readable, computer programming language is called source code. Source code may be converted into an executable image by a compiler or executed immediately with the aid of an interpreter.

Compilers are used to translate source code from a programming language into either object code or machine code. Object code needs further processing to become machine code, and machine code consists of the central processing unit's native instructions, ready for execution. Compiled computer programs are commonly referred to as executables, binary images, or simply as binaries – a reference to the binary file format used to store the executable code.

Interpreters are used to execute source code from a programming language line-by-line. The interpreter decodes each statement and performs its behavior. One advantage of interpreters is that they can easily be extended to an interactive session. The programmer is presented with a prompt, and individual lines of code are typed in and performed immediately.

The main disadvantage of interpreters is computer programs run slower than when compiled. Interpreting code is slower because the interpreter must decode each statement and then perform it. However, software development may be faster using an interpreter because testing is immediate when the compiling step is omitted. Another disadvantage of interpreters is an interpreter must be present on the executing computer. By contrast, compiled computer programs need no compiler present during execution.

Just in time compilers pre-compile computer programs just before execution. For example, the Java virtual machine Hotspot contains a Just In Time Compiler which selectively compiles Java bytecode into machine code - but only code which Hotspot predicts is likely to be used many times.

Either compiled or interpreted programs might be executed in a batch process without human interaction.

Scripting languages are often used to create batch processes. One common scripting language is Unix shell, and its executing environment is called the command-line interface.

No properties of a programming language require it to be exclusively compiled or exclusively interpreted. The categorization usually reflects the most popular method of language execution. For example, Java is thought of as an interpreted language and C a compiled language, despite the existence of Java compilers and C interpreters.

Storage and Execution

Computer programs were stored on perforated paper tape

Typically, computer programs are stored in non-volatile memory until requested either directly or indirectly to be executed by the computer user. Upon such a request, the program is loaded into random-access memory, by a computer program called an operating system, where it can be accessed directly by the central processor. The central processor then executes ("runs") the program, instruction by instruction, until termination. A program in execution is called a process. Termination is either by normal self-termination or by error – software or hardware error.

Simultaneous Execution

Many operating systems support multitasking which enables many computer programs to appear to run simultaneously on one computer. Operating systems may run multiple programs through process scheduling – a software mechanism to switch the CPU among processes often so users can interact with each program while it runs. Within hardware, modern day multiprocessor computers or computers with multicore processors may run multiple programs.

Multiple lines of the same computer program may be simultaneously executed using threads. Multithreading processors are optimized to execute multiple threads efficiently.

Self-modifying Programs

A computer program in execution is normally treated as being different from the data the program operates on. However, in some cases, this distinction is blurred when a computer program modifies itself. The modified computer program is subsequently executed as part of the same program. Self-modifying code is possible for programs written in machine code, assembly language, Lisp, C, COBOL, PL/1, and Prolog.

Functional Categories

Computer programs may be categorized along functional lines. The main functional categories are application software and system software. System software includes the operating system which couples computer hardware with application software. The purpose of the operating system is to provide an environment in which application software executes in a convenient and efficient manner. In addition to the operating system, system software includes embedded programs, boot programs, and micro programs. Application software designed for end users have a user interface. Application software not designed for the end user includes middleware, which couples one application with another. Application software also includes utility programs. The distinction between system software and application software is under debate.

Application Software

There are many types of application software:

- The word app came to being in 21st century. It is a clipping of the word "application". They have been designed for many platforms, but the word was first used for smaller mobile apps. Desktop apps are traditional computer programs that run on desktop computers. Mobile apps run on mobile devices. Web apps run inside a web browser. Both mobile and desktop apps may be downloaded from the developers' website or purchased from app stores such as Windows Store, Apple App Store, Mac App Store, Google Play or Intel AppUp.

- An application suite consists of multiple applications bundled together. Examples include Microsoft Office, LibreOffice, and iWork. They bundle a word processor, spreadsheet, and other applications.

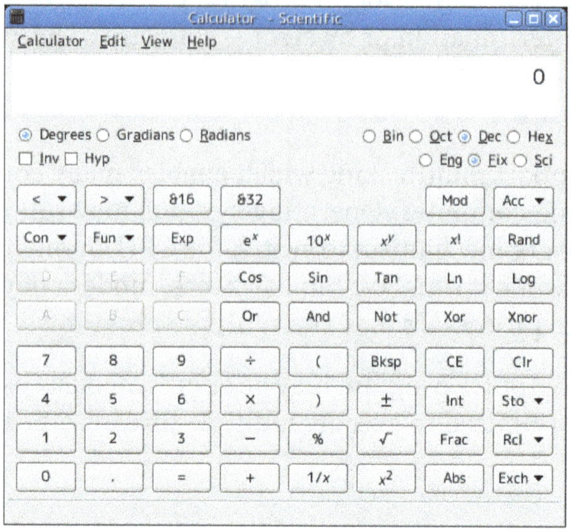

Example of an app: GCalctool, a software calculator

- Enterprise applications bundle accounting, personnel, customer, and vendor applications. Examples include enterprise resource planning, customer relationship management, and supply chain management software.
- Enterprise infrastructure software supports the enterprise's software systems. Examples include databases, email servers, and network servers.
- Information worker software are designed for workers at the departmental level. Examples include time management, resource management, analytical, collaborative and documentation tools. Word processors, spreadsheets, email and blog clients, personal information system, and individual media editors may aid in multiple information worker tasks.
- Media development software generates print and electronic media for others to consume, most often in a commercial or educational setting. These produce graphics, publications, animations, and videos.
- Product engineering software is used to help develop large machines and other application software. Examples includes computer-aided design (CAD), computer-aided engineering (CAE), and integrated development environments.
- Entertainment Software can refer to video games, movie recorders and players, and music recorders and players.

Utility Programs

Utility programs are application programs designed to aid system administrators and computer programmers.

Operating System

An operating system is a computer program that acts as an intermediary between a user of a computer and the computer hardware.

In the 1950s, the programmer, who was also the operator, would write a program and run it. After the program finished executing, the output may have been printed, or it may have been punched onto paper tape or cards for later processing. More often than not the program did not work. The programmer then looked at the console lights and fiddled with the console switches. If less fortunate, a memory printout was made for further study. In the 1960s, programmers reduced the amount of wasted time by automating the operator's job. A program called an *operating system* was kept in the computer at all times.

Originally, operating systems were programmed in assembly; however, modern operating systems are typically written in C.

Boot Program

A stored-program computer requires an initial computer program stored in its read-only memory to boot. The boot process is to identify and initialize all aspects of the system, from processor registers to device controllers to memory contents. Following the initialization process, this initial computer program loads the operating system and sets the program counter to begin normal operations.

Embedded Programs

The microcontroller on the right of this USB flash drive is controlled with embedded firmware.

Independent of the host computer, a hardware device might have embedded firmware to control its operation. Firmware is used when the computer program is rarely or never expected to change, or when the program must not be lost when the power is off.

Microcode Programs

Microcode programs control some central processing units and some other hardware. This code moves data between the registers, buses, arithmetic logic units, and other functional units in the CPU. Unlike conventional programs, microcode is not usually written by, or even visible to, the end users of systems, and is usually provided by the manufacturer, and is considered internal to the device.

How to Learn the Basics of Programming

Good programming skills aren't that hard to achieve. Programming is the reflection of the way you want your things to be done. So in order to have good programming skills follow the steps.

Steps

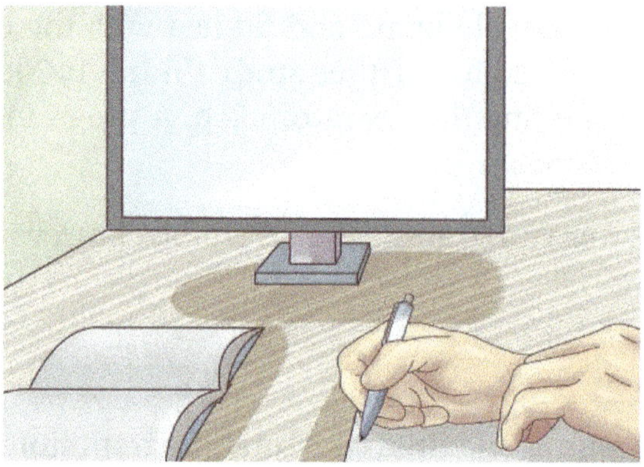

1. Learn *Algorithm* and *Flowchart* and practice designing a flowchart of as many problems as you see.

2. Get hold of a small book on the programming language you want to learn. Though the book is small it will help you to get the basics.

3. With those basics you can start programming and keep learning.

4. Before implementing, design it's flowchart and optimize it. It will make your program work more efficiently and also be debugged shortly and easily.

5. Read basics and overcome them. Learn about *Variables, Control Structures, Arrays* and their usages.

6. After it. Lead your coding into a structure oriented and object oriented world.

7. Learn about how to manage your software projects.

How to Learn a Programming Language

If you have an interest in creating computer programs, mobile apps, websites, games or any other piece of software, you'll need to learn how to program. Programs are created through the use of a programming language. This language allows the program to function with the machine it is running on, be it a computer, a mobile phone, or any other piece of hardware.

Part 1

Choosing a Language

1. Determine your area of interest. You can start learning with any programming language (though some are definitely "easier" than others), so you'll want to start by asking yourself what it is you want to accomplish by learning a programming language. This will help you determine what type of programming you should pursue, and provide you a good starting point.

- If you want to get into web development, you'll have a whole different set of languages that you'll need to learn as opposed to developing computer programs. Mobile app developing requires a different skillset than machine programming. All of these decisions will influence your direction.

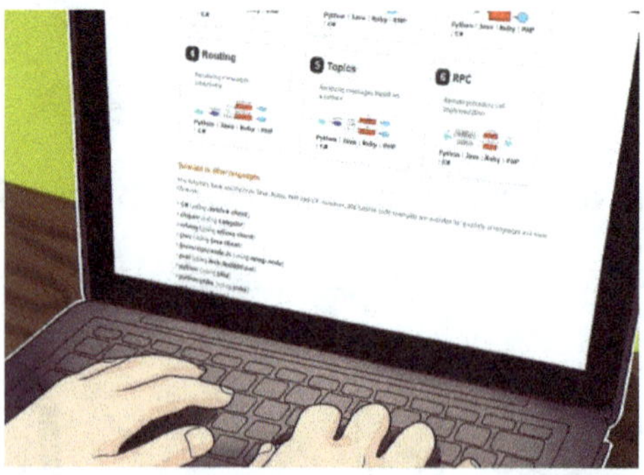

2. Consider starting with a "simpler" language. Regardless of your decision, you may want to consider starting with one of the high-level, simpler languages. These languages are especially useful for beginners, as they teach basic concepts and thought processes that can apply to virtually any language.

- The two most popular languages in this category are Python and Ruby. These are both object-oriented web application languages that use a very readable syntax.

- "Object-oriented" means that the language is built around the concepts of "objects", or collections of data, and their manipulation. This is a concept that is used in many advanced programming languages such as C++, Java, Objective-C, and PHP.

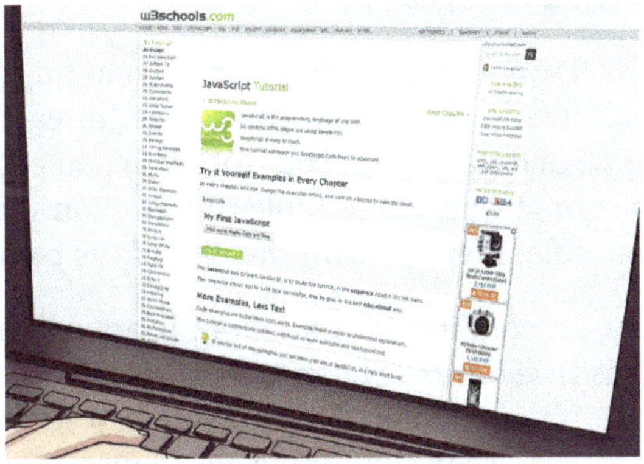

3. Read through some basic tutorials for a variety of languages. If you're still not sure which language you should start learning, read through some tutorials for a few different languages. If one language makes a bit more sense than the others, try it out for a bit to see if it clicks. There are countless tutorials for every programming available online:

- Python - A great starter language that is also quite powerful when you get familiar with it. Used for many web applications and a number of games.
- Java - Used in countless types of programs, from games to web applications to ATM software.
- HTML - An essential starting place for any web developer. Having a handle on HTML is vital before moving on to any other sort of web development.
- C - One of the older languages, C is still a powerful tool, and is the basis for the more modern C++, C#, and Objective-C.

Part 2

Starting Small

1. Learn the core concepts of the language. While the parts of this step that apply will vary depend-

ing on the language you choose, all programming languages have fundamental concepts that are essential to building useful programs. Learning and mastering these concepts early will make it easier to solve problems and create powerful and efficient code. Below are just some of the core concepts found in many different languages:

- Variables - A variable is a way to store and refer to changing pieces of data. Variables can be manipulated, and often have defined types such as "integers", "characters", and others, which determine the type of data that can be stored. When coding, variables typically have names that make them somewhat identifiable to a human reader. This makes it easier to understand how the variable interacts with the rest of the code.
- Conditional Statements - A conditional statement is an action that is performed based on whether the statement is true or not. The most common form of a conditional statement is the "If-Then" statement. If the statement is true (e.g. x = 5) then one thing happens. If the statement is false (e.g. x != 5), then something else happens.
- Functions or Subroutines - The actual name for this concept may be called something different depending on the language. It could also be "Procedure", a "Method", or a "Callable Unit". This is essentially a smaller program within a larger program. A function can be "called" by the program multiple times, allowing the programmer to efficiently create complex programs.
- Data input - This is a broad concept that is used in nearly every language. it involves handling a user's input as well as storing that data. How that data is gathered depend on the type of program and the inputs available to the user (keyboard, file, etc.). This is closely linked to Output, which is how the result is returned to the user, be it displayed on the screen or delivered in a file.

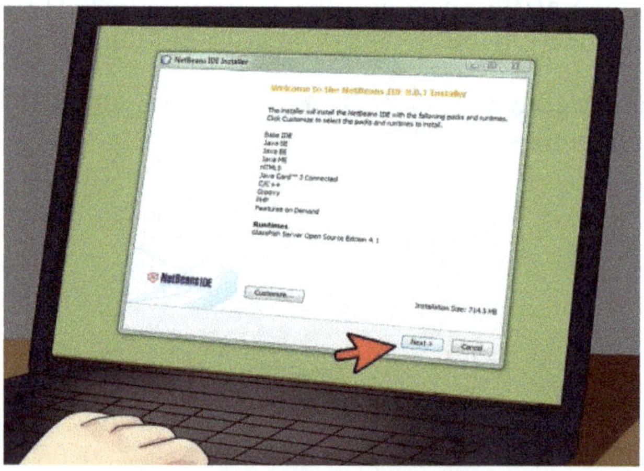

2. Install any necessary software. Many programming languages require compilers, which are programs designed to translate the code into a language that the machine can understand. Other languages, such as Python, use an interpreter which can execute the programs instantly without compiling.

- Some languages have IDEs (Integrated Development Environment) which usually contain a code editor, a compiler and/or interpreter, and a debugger. This allows the programmer to perform any necessary function in one place. IDEs may also contain visual representations of object hierarchies and directories.

- There are a variety of code editors available online. These programs offer different ways of highlighting syntax and provide other developer-friendly tools.

Part 3

Creating your first Program

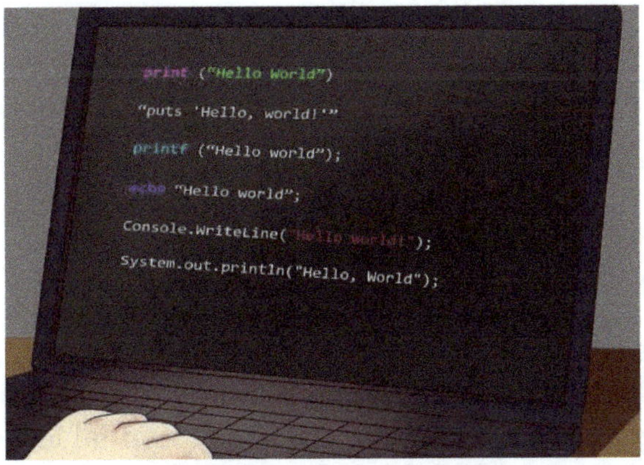

1. Focus on one concept at a time. One of the first programs taught for any language is the "Hello World" program. This is a very simple program that displays the text "Hello, World" (or some variation), on the screen. This program teaches first-time programmers the syntax to create a basic, functioning program, as well as how to handle displaying output. By changing the text, you can learn how basic data is handled by the program.

- Hello World in Python
- Hello World in Ruby
- Hello World in C
- Hello World in PHP
- Hello World in C#
- Hello World in Java

2. Learn through deconstruction of online examples. There are thousands of code examples online

for virtually every programming languages. Use these examples to examine how various aspects of the language work and how different parts interact. Take bits and pieces from various examples to create your own programs.

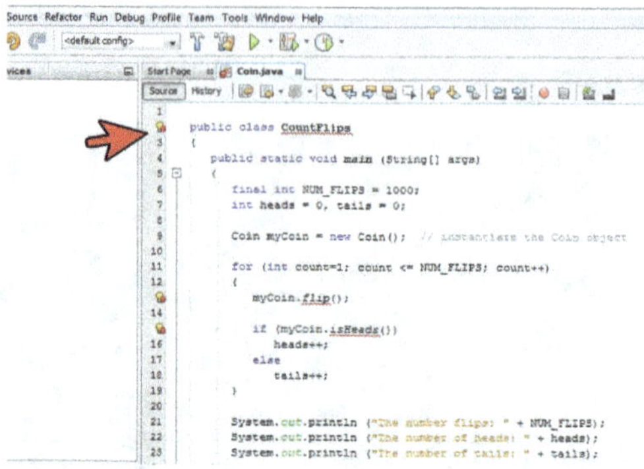

3. Examine the syntax. The syntax is the way the language is written so that the compiler or interpreter can understand it. Each language has a unique syntax, though some elements may be shared across multiple languages. Learning the syntax is essential for learning how to program in the language, and is often what people think of when they think about computer programming. In reality, it is simply the foundation upon which more advanced concepts are built.

4. Experiment with changes. Make changes to your example programs and then test the result. By experimenting, you can learn what works and what doesn't much quicker than by reading a book or guide. Don't be afraid to break your program; learning to fix errors is a major part of any development process, and new things almost never work right the first time.

5. Start practicing debugging. When you're programming, you're invariably going to come across

bugs. These are errors in the program, and can manifest virtually anywhere. Bugs can be harmless quirks in the program, or they can be major errors that keep the program from compiling or running. Hunting down and fixing these errors is a major process in the software development cycle, so get used to doing this early.

- As you experiment with changing basic programs, you're going to come across things that don't work. Figuring out how to take a different approach is one of the most valuable skills you can have as a programmer.

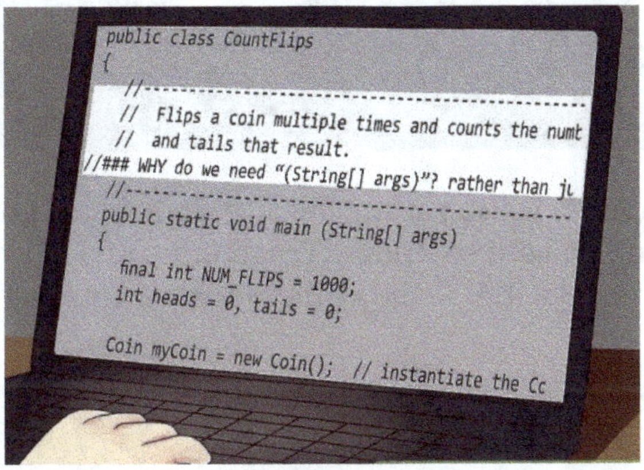

6. Comment all of your code. Nearly all programming languages have a "comment" function that allows you to include text that is not processed by the interpreter or compiler. This allows you to leave short, but clear, human-language explanations of what the code does. This will not only help you remember what your code does in a large program, it is an essential practice in a collaborative environment, as it allows others to understand what your code is doing.

Part 4

Practicing Regularly

1. Code daily. Mastering a programming language takes time above all else. Even a simpler language like Python, which may only take a day or two to understand the basic syntax, takes lots of time to become truly proficient at. Like any other skill, practice is the key to becoming more proficient. Try to spend at least some time each day coding, even if it's only for an hour between work and dinner.

2. Set goals for your programs. By setting attainable but challenging goals, you will be able to start solving problems and coming up with solutions. Try to think of a basic application, such as a calculator, and develop a way to make it. Use the syntax and concepts you've been learning and apply them to practical uses.

3. Talk with others and read other programs. There are lots of programming communities dedicated to specific languages or disciplines. Finding and participating in a community can do wonders for your learning. You will gain access to a variety of samples and tools that can aid you in your learning process. Reading other programmers' code can inspire you and help you grasp concepts that you haven't mastered yet.

- Check out programming forums and online communities for your language of choice. Make sure to participate and not just constantly ask questions. These communities are usually viewed as a place of collaboration and discussion and not simply Q&A. Feel free to ask for help, but be prepared to show your work and be open to trying different approaches.
- Once you have some experience under your belt, consider attending a hack-a-thon or programming jam. these are events where individuals or teams compete against the clock to develop a functional program, usually based around a specific theme. These events can be a lot of fun and are a great way to meet other programmers.

4. Challenge yourself to keep it fun. Try to do things that you don't know how to do yet. Research ways to accomplish the task (or a similar one), and then try to implement that in your own program. Try to avoid being content with a program that "basically" works; do everything you can to make sure every aspect works flawlessly.

Part 5

Expanding your knowledge

1. Take a few training courses. Many universities, community colleges, and community centers offer programming classes and workshops that you can attend without having to enroll in the school. These can be great for new programmers, as you can get hands-on help from an experienced programmer, as well as network with other local programmers.

2. Buy or borrow a book. There are thousands of instructional books available for every conceiv-

able programming language. While your knowledge should not come strictly from a book, they make great references and often contain a lot of good examples.

3. Study math and logic. Most programming involves basic arithmetic, but you may want to study more advanced concepts. This is especially important if you are developing complex simulations or other algorithm-heavy programs. For most day-to-day programming, you don't need much advanced math. Studying logic, especially computer logic, can help you understand how best to approach complex problem solving for more advanced programs.

4. Never stop programming. There is a popular theory that becoming an expert takes at least 10,000 hours of practice. While this is up for debate, the general principle remains true: mastery takes time and dedication. Don't expect to know everything overnight, but if you stay focused and continue to learn, you may very well end up an expert in your field.

5. Learn another programming language. While you can certainly get by with mastering one lan-

guage, many programmers help their chances of success in the field by learning multiple languages. Their second or third languages are usually complementary to their first one, allowing them to develop more complex and interesting programs. Once you have a good grasp on your first program, it may be time to start learning a new one.

- You will likely find that learning your second language goes much quicker than the first. Many core concepts of programming carry over across languages, especially if the languages are closely related.

Part 6

Applying your skills

1. Enroll in a four year program. While not strictly necessary, a four year program at a college or university can expose you to a variety of different languages, as well as help you network with professionals and other students. This method certainly isn't for everyone, and plenty of successful programmers never attended a four-year institution.

2. Create a portfolio. As you create programs and expand your knowledge, make sure that all of your best work is saved in a portfolio. You can show this portfolio to recruiters and interviewers as an example of the work you do. Make sure to include any work done on your own time, and ensure that you are allowed to include any work done with another company.

3. Do some freelance work. There is a very large freelance market for programmers, especially mobile app developers. Take on a few small freelance jobs to get a feel for how commercial programming works. Oftentimes you can use the freelance jobs to help build your portfolio and point to published work.

4. Develop your own freeware or commercial programs. You don't have to work for a company to make money programming. If you have the skills, you can develop software yourself and release it for purchase, either through your own website or through another marketplace. be prepared to be able to provide support for any software you release for commercial sale, as customers will expect their purchase to work.

- Freeware is a popular way to distribute small programs and utilities. The developer doesn't receive any money, but it's a great way to build name recognition and make yourself visible in the community.

How to start Learning to Program

Ever wanted to make a program from scratch? Programming can be a very rewarding experience. All the great computer programmers started just like you: with no knowledge but a willingness to read, study, and practice.

Steps

1. Decide what you would like to do with your programming knowledge. Do you want to learn how to create games, or is web development more your style?

2. Start reading and find out what programming languages are used. For game making, it would be beneficial to learn one of the C languages. For web development, you should start with HTML and CSS and move on to whichever server-side language you require, such as Perl or PHP.

3. Do some more research and find out what you need to test it. For example, if learning PHP, you will need to download and install a server such as Apache, as well as PHP itself. For a C language, you might have to buy a program, however there are good programs you can get for free to compile a C language.

4. Start reading. Start by the manual for your program, and work your way through the examples. You might try some beginner tutorials.

5. Decide what your first project will be. Pick something simple. If you're learning how to program games, try an easy game such as a number guessing game.

6. Start programming. You will probably find it difficult and have to reference the manual or tutorials quite often, but it's a start.

7. Move on to a slightly more difficult project.

- Eventually you will have enough of a grasp of the language and its syntax, as well as the "theory" of programming, that you can complete more difficult projects.

8. Find a good mentor. A good mentor will accelerate your learning process and help prevent you from making common mistakes.

How to create a Program

Computer programs are implemented everywhere these days, from our cars to our smartphones, and in almost every job. As the world becomes more and more digital, the need for new programs will always keep increasing. If you have the next big idea, why not make it yourself? See Step 1 below to find out how to get started learning a language, developing your idea into a testable product, and then iterating on it until it's ready for release.

Part 1

Coming up with an Idea

1. Brainstorm ideas. A good program will perform a task that makes life easier for the user. Look at the software that is currently available for the task you want to perform, and see if there are ways that the process could be easier or smoother. A successful program is one that users will find a lot of utility in.

- Examine your daily tasks on your computer. Is there some way that you could automate a portion of those tasks with a program?
- Write down every idea. Even if it seems silly or outlandish at the time, it could change into something useful or even brilliant.

2. Examine other programs. What do they do? How could they do it better? What are they missing? Answering these questions can help you come up with ideas for your own take on it.

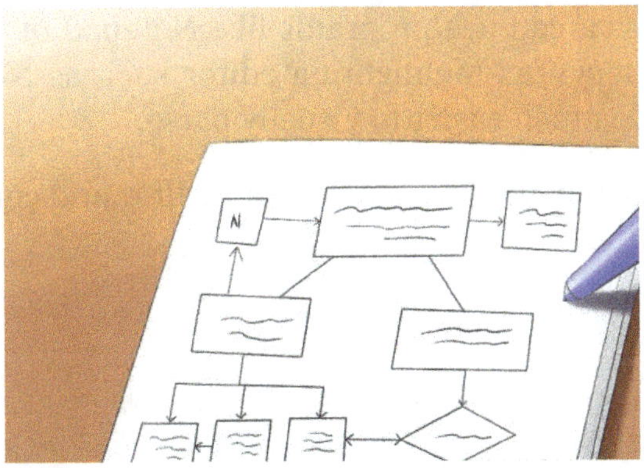

3. Write a design document. This document will outline the features and what you intend to achieve with the project. Referring to the design document during the development process will help keep your project on track and focused. Writing the design document will also help you decide which programming language will work best for your project.

4. Start simple. When you are just getting started with computer programming, it will behoove you to start small and grow over time. You will learn a lot more if you set tangible goals that you can reach with a basic program.

Part 2

Learning a Language

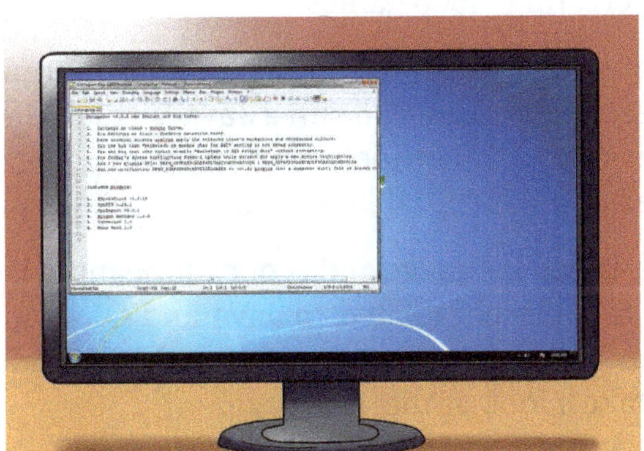

1. Download a good text editor. Almost all programs are written in text editors and then compiled

to run on computers. While you can use programs like Notepad or TextEdit, it is highly recommended that you download a syntax-highlighting editor such as Notepad++ JEdit, or Sublime Text. This will make your code much easier to visually parse.

- Some languages such as Visual Basic include an editor and compiler in one package.

2. Learn a programming language. All programs are created through coding. If you want to create your own programs, you will need to be familiar with at least one programming language. The languages you will need to learn will vary depending on the type of program you want to create. Some of the more useful and important ones include:

- C - C is a low-level language that interacts very closely with the computer's hardware. It is one of the older programming languages that still sees widespread use.
- C++ - The biggest drawback of C is that it is not object-oriented. This is where C++ comes in. C++ is currently the most popular programming language in the world. Programs such as Chrome, Firefox, Photoshop, and many others are all built with C++. It is also a very popular language for creating video games.
- Java - Java is an evolution of the C++ language, and is extremely portable. Most computers, regardless of operating system, can run a Java Virtual Machine, allowing the program to be used nearly universally. It is widely used in video games and business software, and is often recommended as an essential language.
- C# - C# is a Windows-based language and is one of the main languages used when creating Windows programs. It is closely related to Java and C++, and should be easy to learn if you're already familiar with Java. If you want to make a Windows or Windows Phone program, you'll want to take a look at this language.
- Objective-C - This is another cousin of the C language that is specifically designed for Apple systems. If you want to make iPhone or iPad apps, this is the language for you.

3. Download the compiler or interpreter. For any high-level language such as C++, Java, and many others, you will need a compiler to convert your code into a format that the computer can use. There are a variety of compilers to choose from depending on the language you are using.

- Some languages are interpreted languages, which means they don't need a compiler. Instead, they only need the language interpreter installed on the computer, and the programs can run instantly. Some examples of interpreted languages include Perl and Python.

4. Learn basic programming concepts. No matter which language you pick, you'll likely need to understand some basic common concepts. Knowing how to handle the syntax of the language will allow you to create much more powerful programs. Common concepts include:

- Declaring variables - Variables are the way your data is temporarily stored in your program. This data can then be stored, modified, manipulated, and called upon later in the program.
- Using conditional statements (if, else, when, etc.) - These are one of the basic functions of programs, and dictate how the logic works. Conditional statements revolve around "true" and "false" statements.
- Using loops (for, goto, do, etc.) - Loops allow you to repeat processes over and over until a command is given to stop.

- Using escape sequences - These commands perform functions such as create new lines, indents, quotes, and more.
- Commenting on code - Comments are essential for remembering what your code does, helping other programmers understand your code, and for temporarily disabling parts of code.
- Understand regular expressions.

5. Find some books on the language of your choice. There are books for every language and for every level of expertise. You can find programming books at your local bookstore or any online retailer. A book can be an invaluable tool as you can keep it close at hand while you're working.

- Beyond books, the internet is an endless treasure-trove of guides and tutorials. Search for guides on the language of your choice on sites such as Codecademy, Code.org, Bento, Udacity, Udemy, Khan Academy, W3Schools, and many more.

6. Take some classes. Anyone can teach themselves to make a program if they put their mind to it, but sometimes having a teacher and a classroom environment can be really beneficial. One-on-one time with an expert can greatly decrease the time it takes you to grasp programming fundamentals and concepts. Classes are also a good place to learn advanced math and logic that will be required for more complex programs.

- Classes cost money, so make sure that you are signing up for classes that will help you learn what you want to know.

7. Ask questions. The internet is a fantastic way to connect with other developers. If you find yourself stumped on one of your projects, ask for help on sites such as StackOverflow. Make sure that you ask in an intelligent manner and can prove that you have already tried several possible solutions.

Part 3

Building your Prototype

1. Start writing a basic program with your core functionality. This will be the prototype that shows off the functionality that you're aiming to achieve. A prototype is a quick program, and should be iterated on until you find a design that works. For example, if you are creating a calendar program, your prototype would be a basic calendar (with correct dates!) and a way to add events to it.

- Your prototype will change often during the development cycle as you come up with new ways to tackle problems or think of an idea later that you want to incorporate.
- The prototype doesn't have to be pretty. In fact, art and design should be one of the last things you focus on. Using the calendar example again, your prototype should most likely just be text.

- If you're making a game, your prototype should be fun! If the prototype isn't fun, then chances are the full game won't be fun either.
- If your desired mechanics just aren't working in the prototype, then it may be time to go back to the drawing board.

2. Assemble a team. If you are developing your program on your own, you can use a prototype to help build a team. A team will help you track down bugs faster, iterate features, and design the visual aspects of the program.

- A team is definitely not necessary for small projects, but will cut down development time significantly.
- Running a team is a complex and difficult process, and requires good management skills along with a good structure for the team.

3. Start over from scratch if necessary. Once you're familiar with your language, you may be able to get prototypes up and running in just a few days. Because of their quick nature, don't be afraid to scrap your idea and start over from a different angle if you're not happy with how it's turning out. It's much easier to make major changes at this stage than it is later on when the features start falling into place.

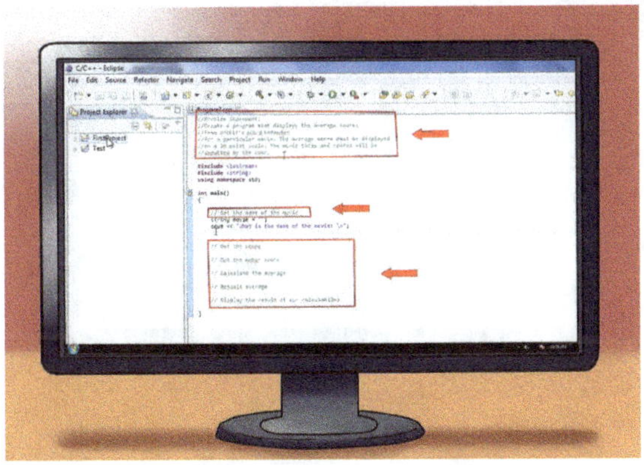

4. Comment on everything. Use the comment syntax in your programming language to leave notes on all but the most basic lines of code. This will help you remember what you were doing if you have to put the project down for awhile, and will help other developers understand your code. This is especially essential if you are working as part of a programming team.

- You can use comments to temporarily disable parts of your code during testing. Simply enclose the code you want to disable in comment syntax and it won't be compiled. You can then delete the comment syntax and the code will be restored.

Part 4

Alpha Testing

1. Gather a testing team. In the alpha stage, the testing team can and should be small. A small group will help you get focused feedback and gives you the ability to interface with testers one on one. Every time you make updates to the prototype, new builds are sent out to the alpha testers. The testers then try all of the included features and also try to break the program, documenting their results.

- If you are developing a commercial product, you will want to make sure that all of your testers sign a Non-Disclosure Agreement (NDA). This will prevent them from telling others about your program, and prevent leaks to press and other users.
- Take some time to come up with a solid testing plan. Make sure that your testers have a way to easily report bugs in the program, as well as easily access new versions of the alpha. GitHub and other code repositories are a great way to easily manage this aspect.

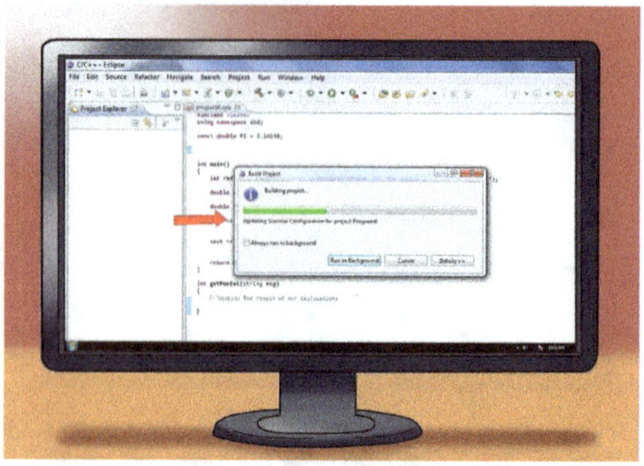

2. Test your prototype over and over. Bugs are the bane of every developer. Errors in code and unexpected usage can cause all kinds of problems in a finished product. As you continue to work on your prototype, test it as much as possible. Do everything you can to break it, and then try to keep it from breaking in the future.

- Try inputting odd dates if your program deals with dates. Really old dates or far future dates may cause odd reactions with the program.
- Input the wrong kind of variables. For example, if you have a form that asks for the user's age, enter in a word instead and see what happens to the program.
- If your program has a graphical interface, click on everything. What happens when you go back to a previous screen, or click buttons in the wrong order?

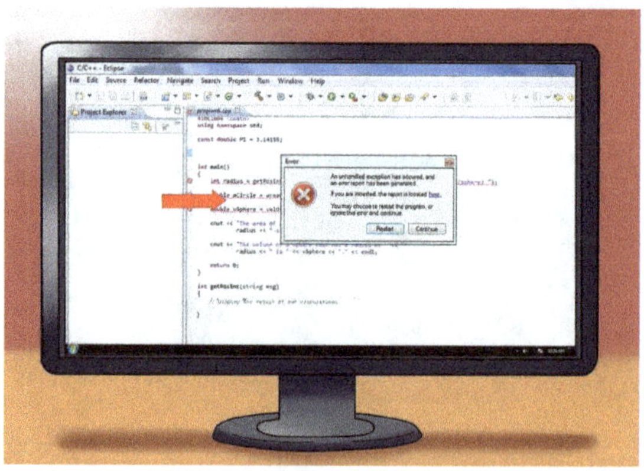

3. Address bugs in order of priority. When revising the program in the alpha, you will be spending a lot of time fixing features that do not work correctly. When organizing your bug reports from your alpha testers, they will need to be sorted based on two metrics: Severity and Priority.

- The Severity of a bug is a measure of how much damage the bug causes. Bugs that crash the program, corrupt data, keep the program from running are referred to as Blockers. Features that don't work or return incorrect results are labeled Critical, while difficult to use or bad-looking features are labeled Major. There are also Normal, Minor, and Trivial bugs that affect smaller sections or less-crucial features.
- The Priority of a bug determines what order you tackle them when attempting to fix bugs.

Fixing bugs in software is a time-consuming process, and takes away from the time you have to add features and polish. As such, you have to take the priority of a bug into account to make sure that you meet deadlines. All Blocker and Critical bugs take the highest priority, sometimes referred to as P1. P2 bugs are usually Major bugs that are scheduled to be fixed, but won't hold a product back from being shipped. P3 and P4 bugs are usually not scheduled fixes, and fall into the "nice to have" category.

4. Add more features. During the alpha phase, you will be adding more features to your program to bring it closer to the program outlined in your design document. The alpha stage is where the prototype evolves into the basic for of the full program. By the end of the alpha stage, your program should have all of its features implemented.

- Don't stray too far from your original design document. A common problem in software development is "feature-creep", where new ideas keep getting added, causing the original focus to be lost and spreading development time between too many different features. You want your program to be the best at what it does, not a jack of all trades.

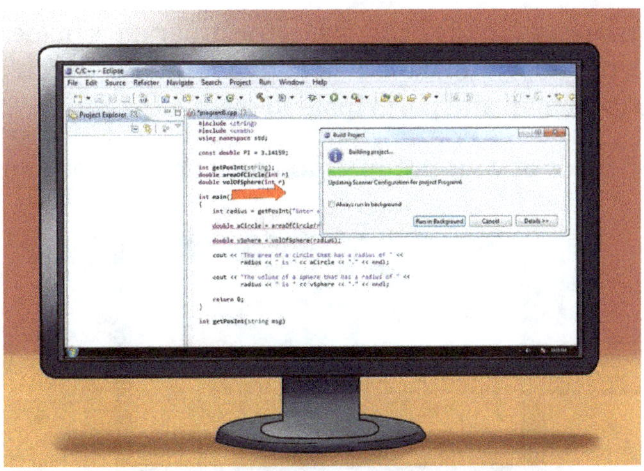

5. Test each feature as you add it. As you add features to your program during the alpha phase, send out the new build to your testers. The regularity of new builds will be entirely dependent on your team's size and how much progress you're making on the features.

6. Lock your features when the alpha is finished. Once you've implemented all of the features and functionality in your program, you can move out of the alpha phase. At this point, no further features should be added, and the included features should essentially work. Now you can move onto wider testing and polish, known as the beta phase.

Part 5

Beta Testing

1. Increase your testing group size. In the beta phase, the program is made available to a much larger group of testers. Some developers make the beta phase public, which is referred to as an open beta. This allows anyone to sign up and participate in testing the product.

- Depending on the needs of your product, you may or may not want to do an open beta.

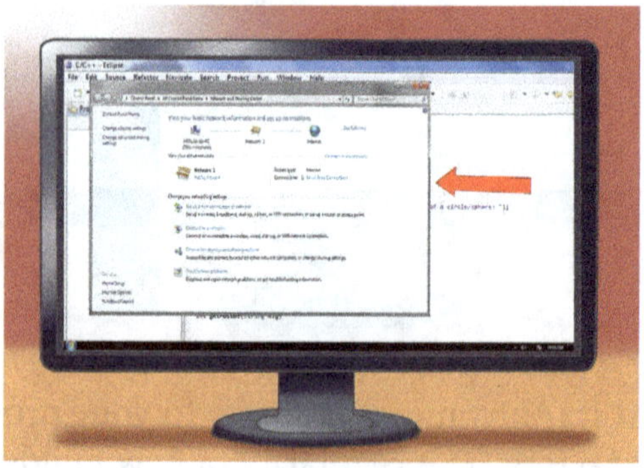

2. Test connectivity. As programs become more and more interconnected, there's a good chance

that your program will rely on connections to other products or connections to servers. Beta testing allows you to ensure that these connections work under a larger load, which will ensure that your program is usable by the public when it releases.

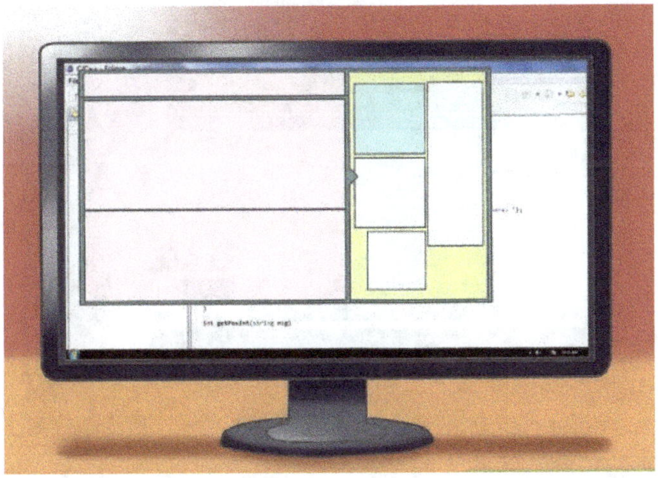

3. Polish your software. In the beta phase, no more features are being added, so focus can be turned to improving the program's aesthetics and usability. In this phase, UI design becomes a priority, ensuring that the users will have no difficulty navigating the program and taking advantage of the features.

- UI design and functionality can be very difficult and complex. People make whole careers out of designing UIs. Just make sure that your personal project is easy to use and easy on the eyes. A professional UI may not be possible without a budget and a team.
- If you have the budget, there are lots of freelance graphics designers who could potentially design a UI on contract for you. If you have a solid project that you're hoping will become the next big thing, find a good UI designer and make them part of your team.

4. Continue bug hunting. Throughout the beta phase, you should still be cataloging and prioritizing bug reports from your user base. Since more testers will have access to the product, chances are new bugs will be discovered. Eliminate bugs based on their priority, keeping your final deadlines in mind.

Part 6

Releasing the Program

1. Market your program. If you want to get users, you'll want to make sure that they know your program exists. Just like any product, you'll need to do a bit of advertising in order to make people aware. The extent and depth of your marketing campaign will be dictated by your program's function as well as your available budget. Some easy ways to raise awareness of you program include:

- Posting about your program on related message boards. Make sure that you follow the posting rules of whichever forum you choose so that your posts don't get marked as spam.
- Send out press releases to tech sites. Find some tech blogs and sites that fit your program's genre. Send the editors a press release detailing your program and what it does. Include a few screenshots.
- Make some YouTube videos. If your program is designed to complete a specific task, make some YouTube videos showing your program in action. Structure them as "How-To" videos.
- Create social media pages. You can create free Facebook and Google+ pages for your program, and can use Twitter for both company and program-specific news.

2. Host your program on your website. For small programs, you can most likely host the file on

your own website. You may want to include a payment system if you are going to be charging for your software. If your program becomes very popular, you may need to host the file on a server that can handle more downloads.

3. Set up a support service. Once your program is released in the wild, you will invariably have users with technical problems or who don't understand how the program works. Your website should have thorough documentation available, as well as some sort of support service. This can include a technical support forum, a support email, live help, or any combination of those. What you can provide will be dependent on your available budget.

4. Keep your product up to date. Almost all programs these days are patched and updated long after their initial release. These patches may fix critical or non-critical bugs, update security protocols, improve stability, or even add functionality or redo the aesthetics. Keeping your program updated will help keep in competitive.

How to make a Program using Notepad

Want to start learning a programming language? You don't need any fancy software; Notepad is capable of writing in any programming language. It doesn't offer many options, but is great for quick Batch files or for testing other small programs. You can have a simple program ready in just a minute, though you may want to consider another editor for more complex programs.

Part 1

Basics

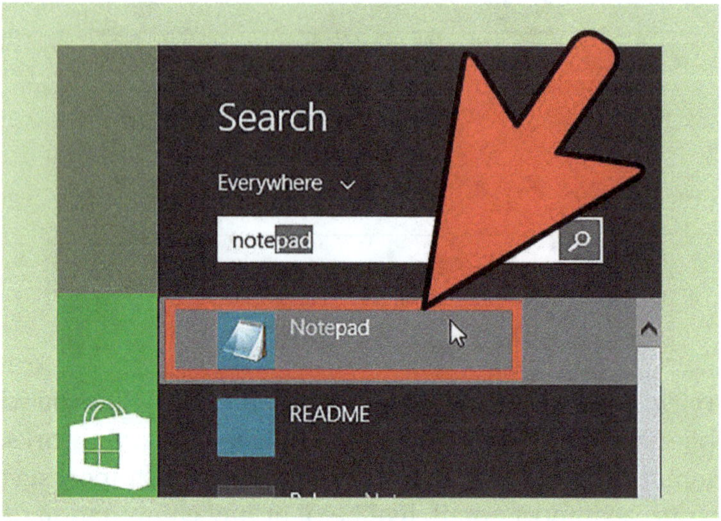

1. Write code for any language. Since Notepad is a plain text editor, you can use it to write code for any language, from C to HTML. You can open Notepad from the Accessories folder in your Start menu, or by searching for "notepad".

- In the sections below, you will find some basic examples for a few different programming languages.

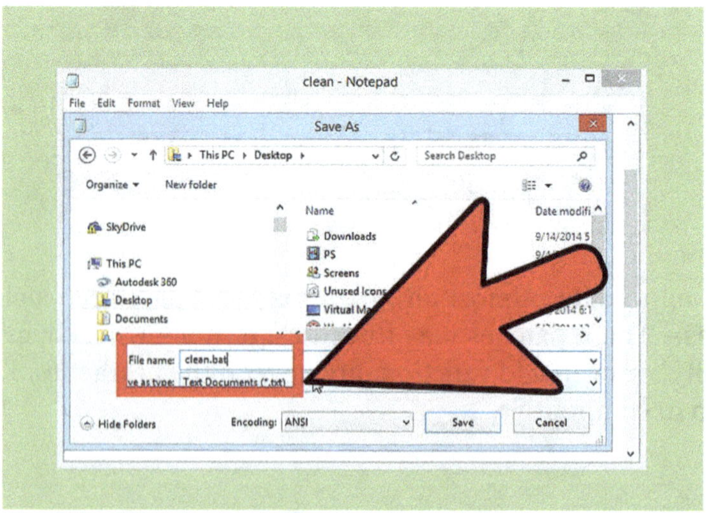

2. Save the file in the correct format. If you want to use your code in the compiler or interpreter for the language you are programming in, you will need to save the file in the language's format. Click File → Save As. In the "Save as type" drop-down menu, select "All files (*.*)". Enter the extension for the language you are writing.

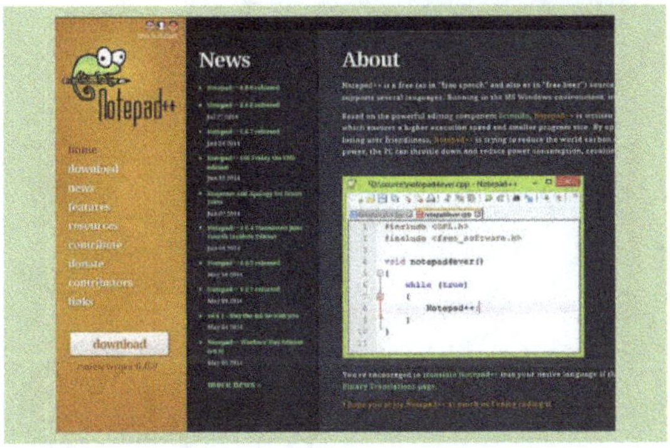

3. Consider a more robust editor. While you can certainly write entire programs in Notepad, it's definitely not the easiest way. Notepad doesn't contain any syntax highlighting or indentation options, making it difficult to use for writing larger pieces of code. Consider a program such as Notepad++, which is designed around programming syntax and is also free.

Part 2

Batch File

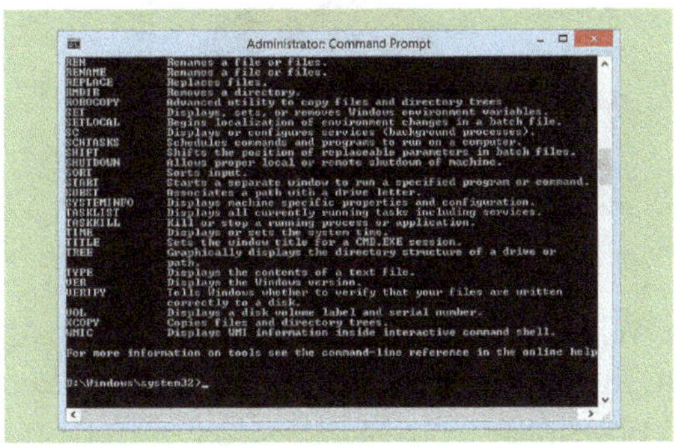

1. Learn basic Batch commands. Notepad is most commonly used to create Batch files. Batch files are programs used to automate functions through the command prompt. You can use batch files to apply changes to a number of files at once, create backup systems, and more.

- Below are a few basic Batch file examples.

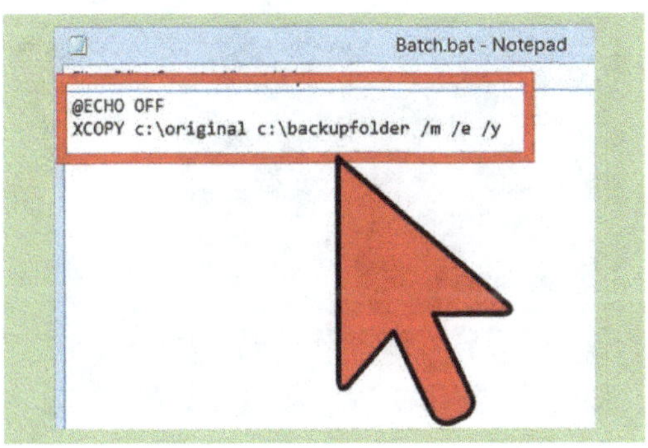

2. Write a basic backup program. This is a simple program that can backup files from one folder to another, only backing up files that have been modified since the last backup.

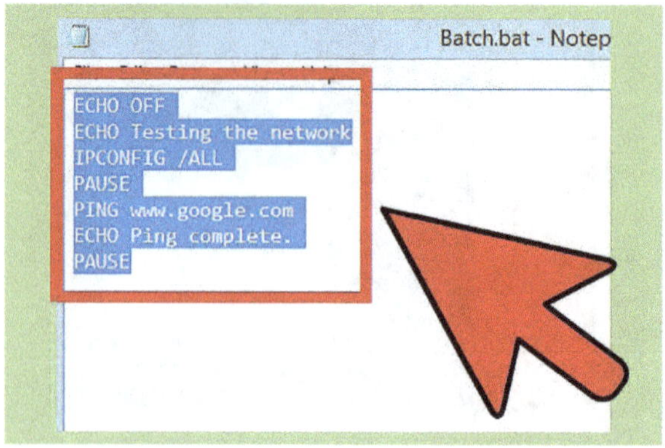

3. Write a batch file to test your network. If you find yourself testing networks and internet connectivity often, this batch file will quickly display the IPConfig and Ping information for you.

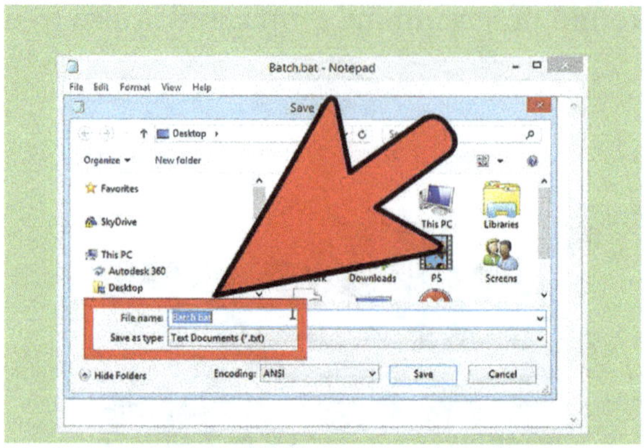

4. Save your file as a BAT file. When writing a Batch file in Notepad, you will want to save it as a .BAT file. This will change the file into a Batch file that can be executed by double-clicking it or running it from the command prompt.

- Click File → Save As. In the "Save as type" drop-down menu, select "All files (*.*)". Enter the extension ".bat" at the end of the file. When you save it, the file will turn into a Batch file, allowing you to run it.

5. Create your own Batch files. There is a lot that you can do with Batch files. You can add delays, make a program for compressing files, add a password, and much more.

Part 3

Python Program

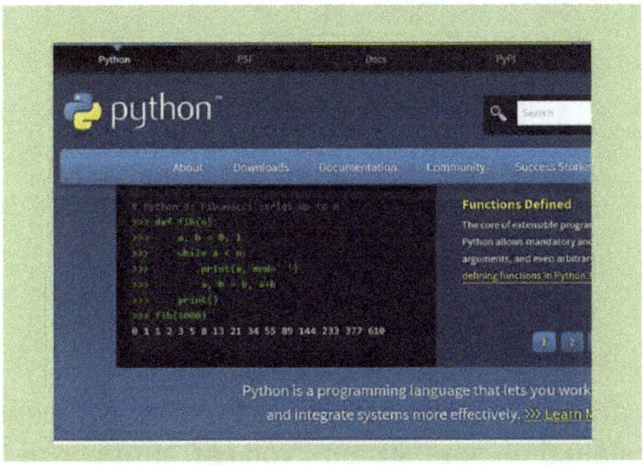

1. Learn basic Python scripting. Python is a popular programming language for web scripting, and is one of the easier languages to learn. Python programs don't need to be compiled; you just need the interpreter installed on your system. Most Python programs are run through the command line interface.

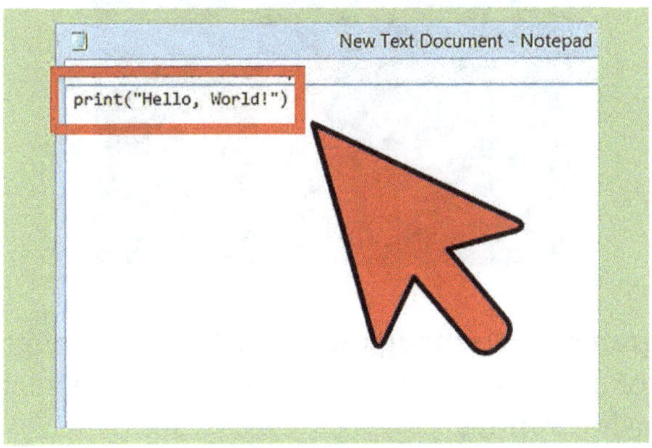

2. Create a "Hello, World" program. This is one of the easiest programs to create and teaches you the basics of constructing programs in Python. It simply displays the phrase "Hello, World!" on the user's screen.

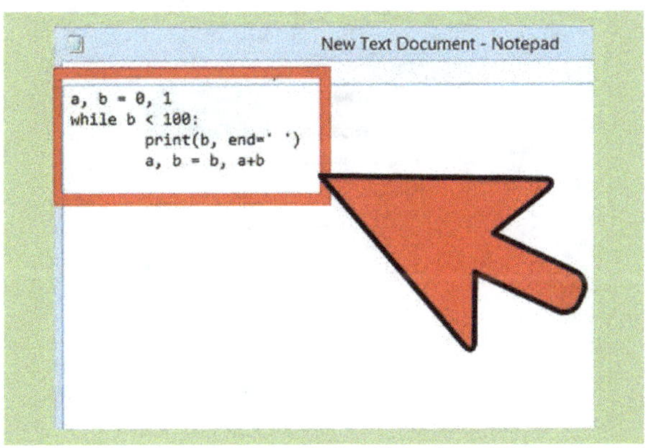

3. Print the Fibonacci sequence. This simple program will calculate Fibonacci numbers up to 100.

You can change the 100 value in the second line to whatever you'd like to change the number of results you get. Make sure to include the indentations, as that is how Python designates functions.

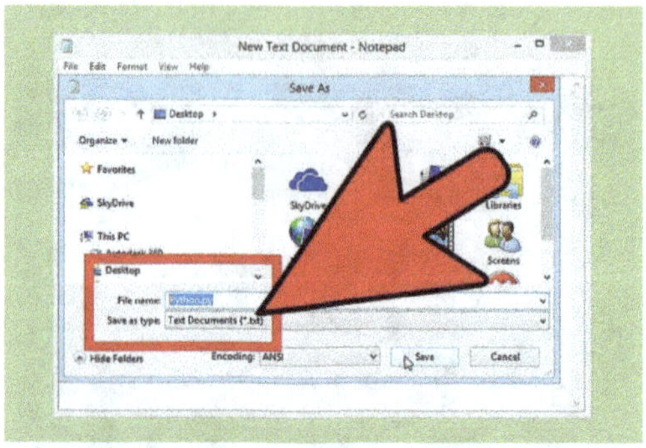

4. Run your programs. You do not need to compile Python programs in order to run them. If you have a Python interpreter installed on your system, you can simply run the saved Python file to execute the program. Click File → Save As. In the "Save as type" drop-down menu, select "All files (*.*)". Enter the extension ".py" and save the file. This will allow your Python interpreter to open the file.

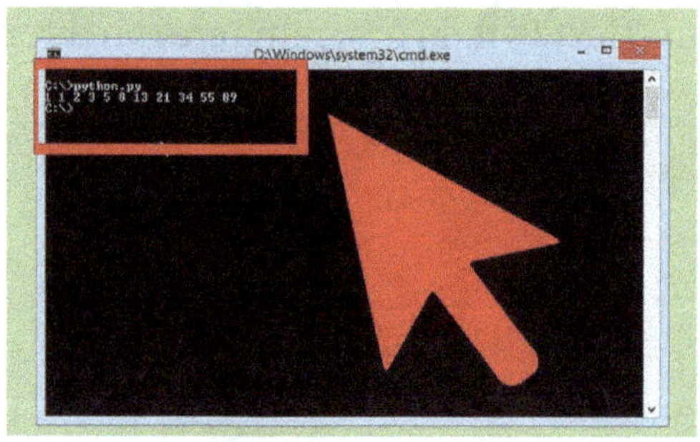

5. Create more Python programs. Even though it's a fairly simple language, Python is very powerful and you can make a lot of useful stuff with it. You can create lists, loops, and graphing charts. You can even make games using Python.

Part 4

C Program

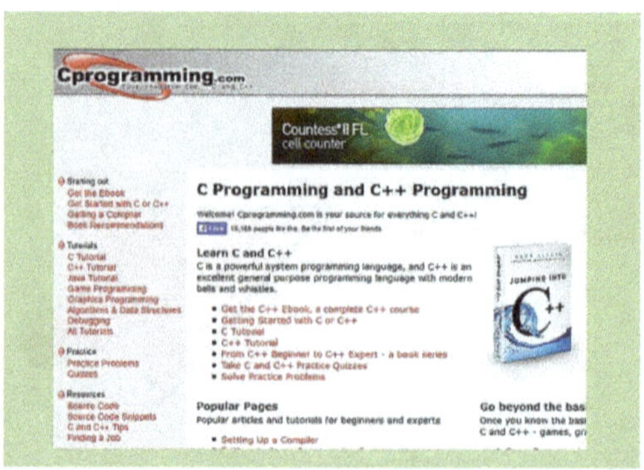

1. Learn basic C coding. C is one of the older programming languages around, and is the base for many of the more popular languages being used currently, such as C++ and Objective-C.

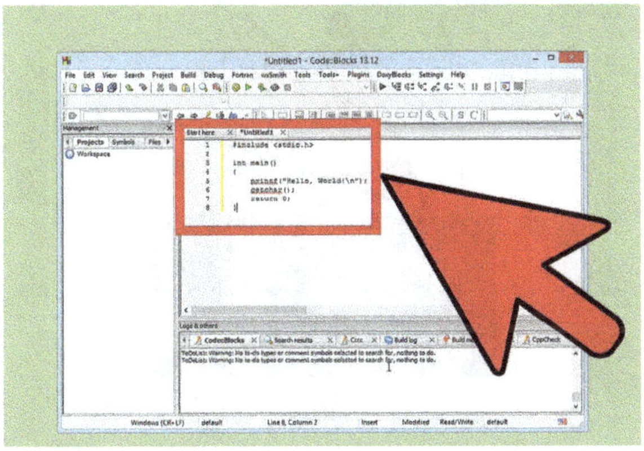

2. Create a "Hello, World" program. This is one of the easiest programs to create and teaches you the basics of constructing programs in C. It simply displays the phrase "Hello, World!" on the user's screen. Make sure to include the indentations, as they denote functions.

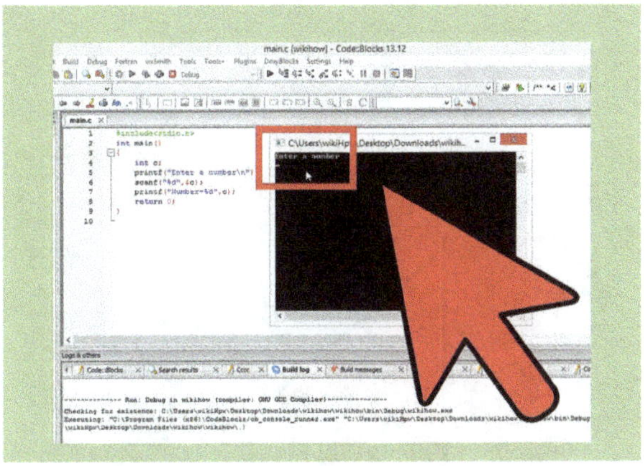

3. Create a program that stores user input. Much of what you'll be doing in C involves taking and manipulating user input. This basic program allows you to take a number and store it as a variable, which is the first step towards constructing larger programs.

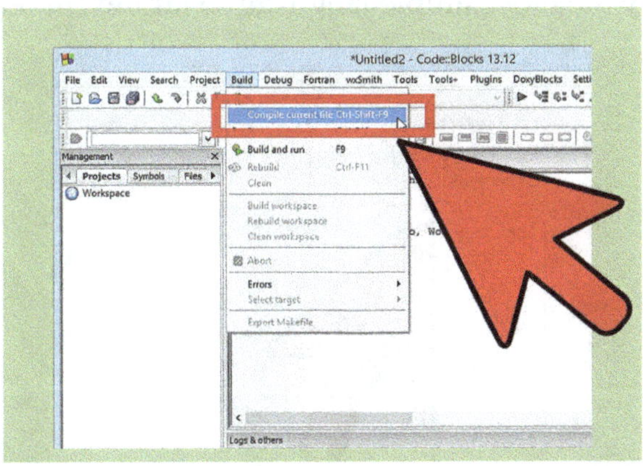

4. Compile your programs. C requires a compiler in order to turn the code into a working program. Click File → Save As. In the "Save as type" drop-down menu, select "All files (*.*)". Enter the extension ".c" and then save the file. This will allow you to open it in your compiler.

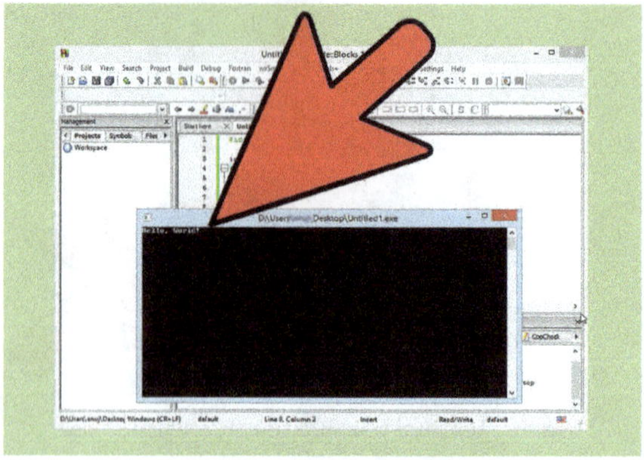

5. Create more programs. This is the very tip of the iceberg when it comes to C, which is a very powerful programming language. There is a lot you can do with C programs: you can compare strings, delay the program, make an alert, and much more.

Part 5

Krake Program

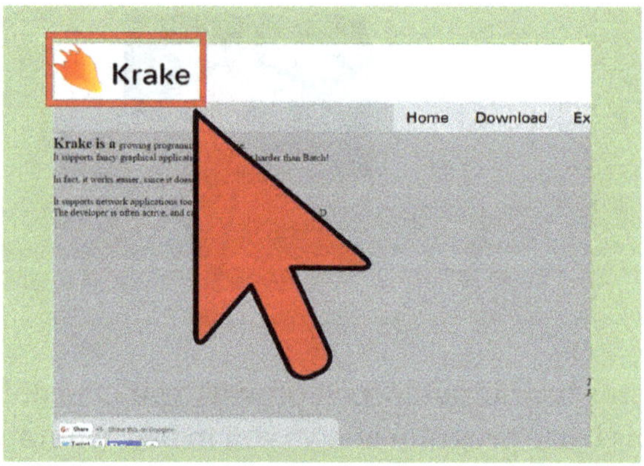

1. Learn Krake. It's probably the most simple language so far out there.

2. Print "Hello World" to the screen.

- As it sounds, it's literally "print Hello World" (without quotes) you type.

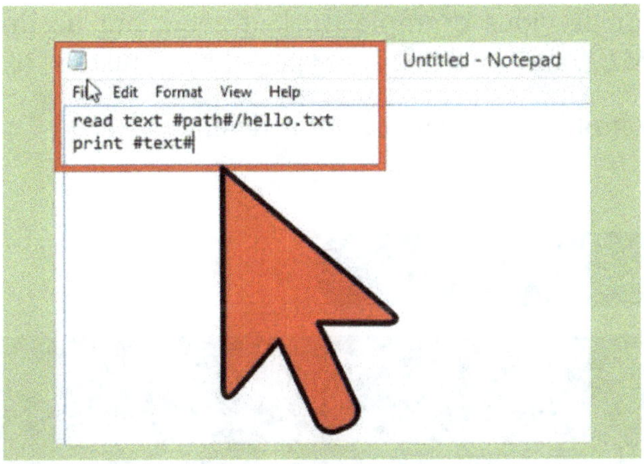

3. Print out the contents of a file!

- Read it first, and save it to a variable,then extract the value of the variable and print it.

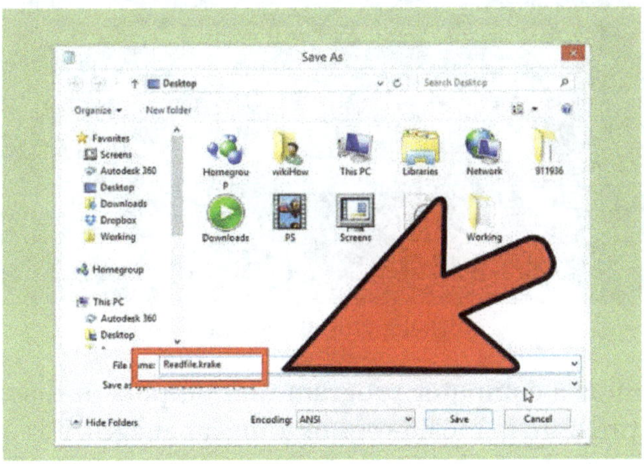

4. Run the program.

- Krake doesn't require any compiling. Just save and run it.

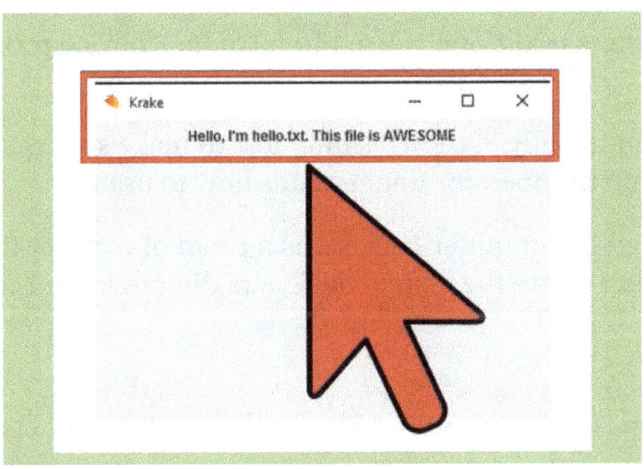

5. Create more.

- As you can see our previous example worked good, but no line breaks. That's because "print" prints HTML4, and we'd need to type "<br />" instead of lines.
- Learn Krake at their official website or our article.

"Hello, World!" Program

"Hello, World!" Program

A "Hello, World!" program is a computer program that outputs or displays "Hello, World!" to a user. Being a very simple program in most programming languages, it is often used to illustrate the basic syntax of a programming language for a working program. It is often the very first program people write when they are new to a language.

Purpose

A "Hello, World!" program is traditionally used to introduce novice programmers to a programming language.

"Hello, world!" is also traditionally used in a sanity test to make sure that a computer language is correctly installed, and that the operator understands how to use it.

"Hello, world!" is also used by computer hackers as a proof of concept that arbitrary code can be executed through an exploit where the system designers did not intend code to be executed.

Variations

A "Hello, world!" program running on Sony's PlayStation Portable as a proof of concept.

There are many variations on the punctuation and casing of the phrase. Variations include the presence or absence of the comma and exclamation mark, and the capitalization of the 'H', both the 'H' and the 'W', or neither. Some languages are forced to implement different forms, such as "HELLO WORLD", on systems that support only capital letters, while many "hello, world" programs in esoteric languages print out a slightly modified string. For example, the first non-trivial Malbolge program printed "HEllO WORld", this having been determined to be good enough.

There are variations in spirit, as well. Functional programming languages, like Lisp, ML and Haskell, tend to substitute a factorial program for Hello, World, as functional programming emphasizes recursive techniques, whereas the original examples emphasize I/O, which violates the spirit of pure functional programming by producing side effects. Languages otherwise capable of Hello, World (Assembly, C, VHDL) may also be used in embedded systems, where text output is either difficult (requiring additional components or communication with another computer) or nonexistent. For devices such as microcontrollers, field-programmable gate arrays, and CPLD's, "Hello, World" may thus be substituted with a blinking LED, which demonstrates timing and interaction between components.

The Debian and Ubuntu Linux distributions provide the "hello, world" program through the apt packaging system; this allows users to simply type "apt-get install hello" for the program to be installed, along with any software dependencies. While of itself useless, it serves as a sanity check and a simple example to newcomers of how to install a package. It is significantly more useful for developers, however, as it provides an example of how to create a .deb package, either traditionally or using debhelper, and the version of hello used, GNU Hello, serves as an example of how to write a GNU program.

How to write the Hello World Program in CPP

The best way to learn programming is by writing the programs. Hello World! is the first program most programmers have to write before they start the lesson. If you want to learn CPP, and you don't know how to write Hello World yet, read on.

Steps

1. Get a CPP compiler. If you're using Windows OS, I'd suggest you to get the latest Microsoft Visual CPP. If you're running a linux distribution or Mac OS, get Code::Blocks or Bloodshed Dev CPP. You can obviously get them on windows too and use whichever you feel most comfortable with.

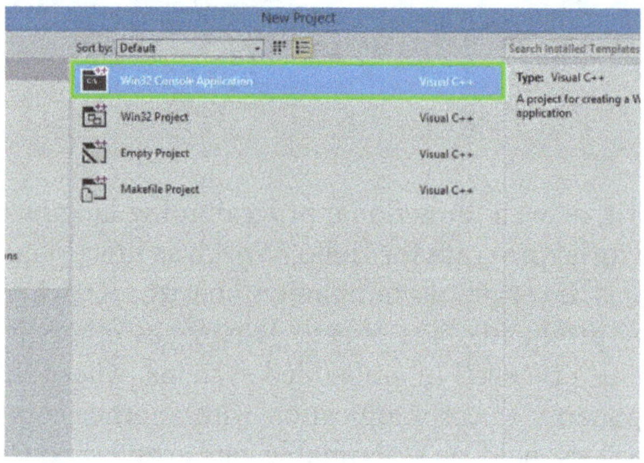

2. Open a new project file, and choose "console application" on your compiler. This means your "Hello World!" application would be running on the console and not your operating system.

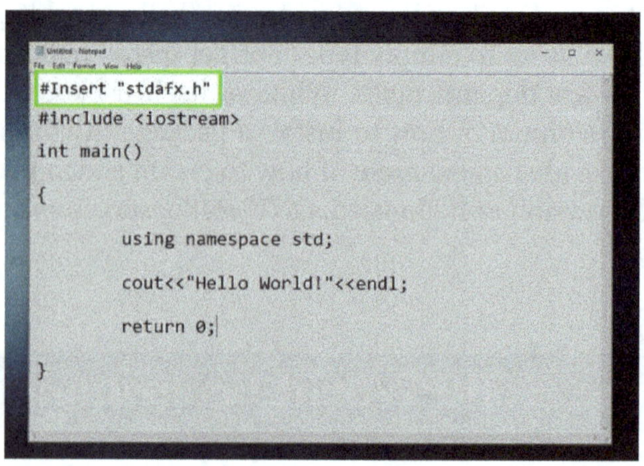

3. If your compiler is a Microsoft Visual CPP, then first enter the following on the first line - #Insert "stdafx.h". Ignore this step if your compiler is not a Microsoft Visual CPP.

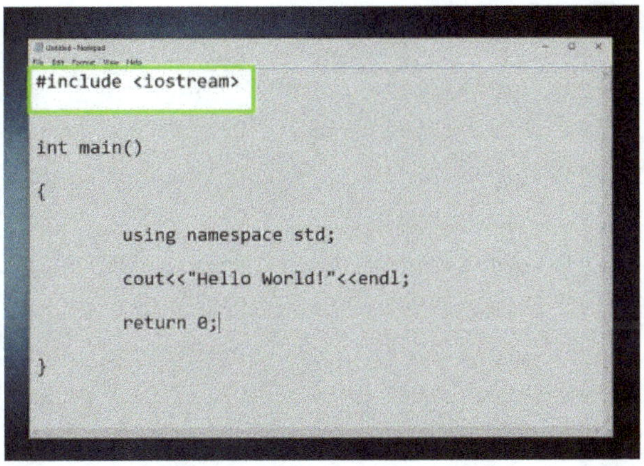

4. On the next line (if you've entered the previous statement, otherwise this would be the first line), enter #include <iostream> . This statement declares that the terms we are going to use to write the program are included in the CPP library known as "iostream".

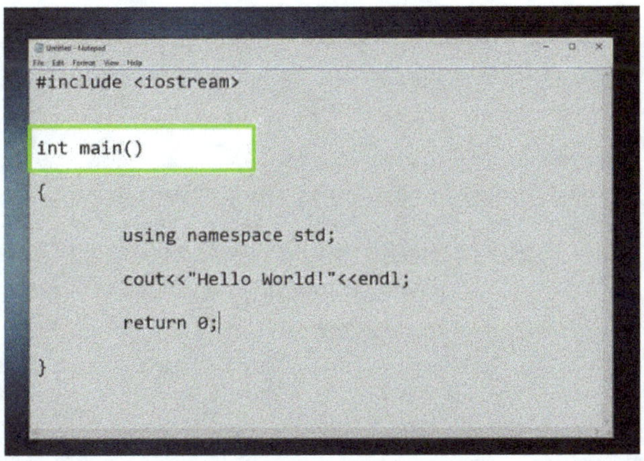

5. Go to the next line to enter your function, the set of instructions that defines the structure of your program and tells the compiler what to do, in this case to display the message "Hello World!" from your console. Type "int main ()" .

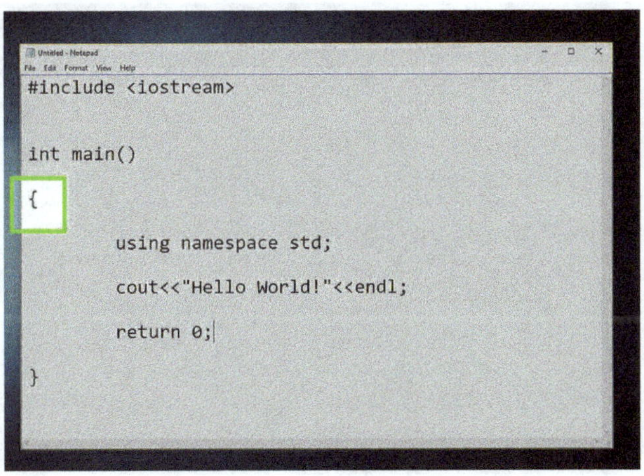

6. Go to the next line and use a flower bracket "{", to mark the beginning of this main () function.

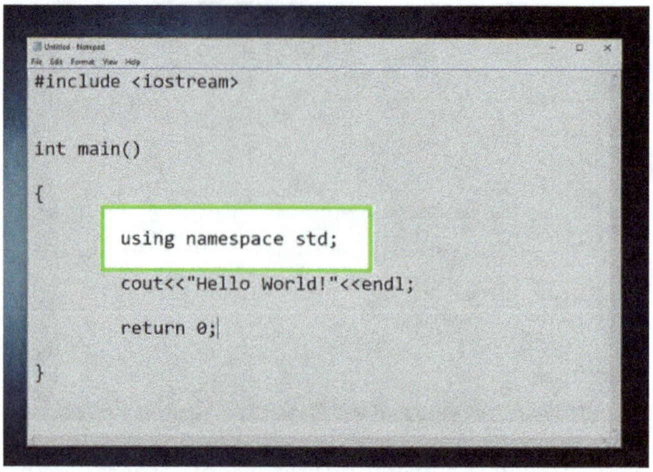

7. On the next line, you have to write statements, the group of which is the function. First statement in this program is - using namespace std;.

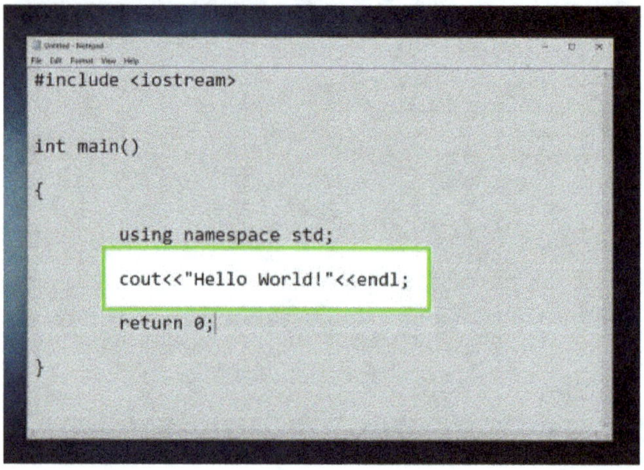

8. Each statements inside a function ends with a semi-colon ";". The last statement ends with "endl" and semi-colon. Now go to the next line and type cout << "Hello World!" endl;

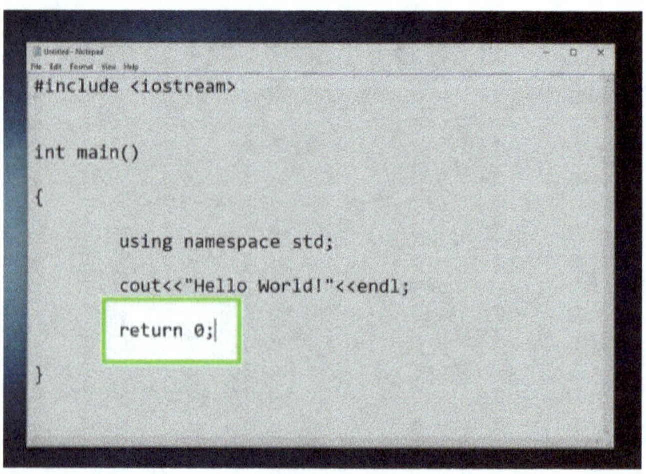

9. Go to the next line and declare the return value of this function - return 0;

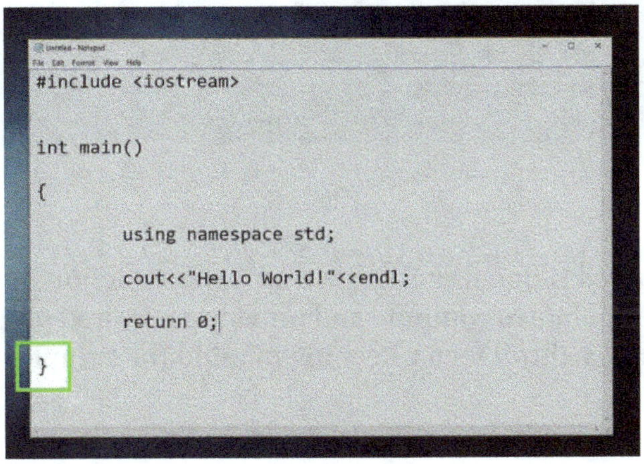

10. Go to the next line and use the ending flower bracket "}" to denote the end of your main function. While complicated programs would include numerous functions, this is the simplest program possible and your first program ever so it just contains the main function.

11. Press "F7" or click on the compile icon or option from the drop down menu to compile your program.

12. Press "CTRL" and "F5" together to run your program.

Chapter 3

Computer Algorithms: An Overview

Algorithms are self-contained sequences that instruct how an action or a set of actions are to be performed. They allow computers to compute and provide a required output. This chapter on computer algorithms offers an insightful focus, keeping in mind the complex subject matter.

Algorithm

In mathematics and computer science, an algorithm is a self-contained sequence of actions to be performed. Algorithms can perform calculation, data processing and automated reasoning tasks.

An algorithm is an effective method that can be expressed within a finite amount of space and time and in a well-defined formal language for calculating a function. Starting from an initial state and initial input (perhaps empty), the instructions describe a computation that, when executed, proceeds through a finite number of well-defined successive states, eventually producing "output" and terminating at a final ending state. The transition from one state to the next is not necessarily deterministic; some algorithms, known as randomized algorithms, incorporate random input.

The concept of *algorithm* has existed for centuries; however, a partial formalization of what would become the modern *algorithm* began with attempts to solve the Entscheidungsproblem (the "dcision problem") posed by David Hilbert in 1928. Subsequent formalizations were framed as attempts to define "effective calculability" or "effective method"; those formalizations included the Gödel–Herbrand–Kleene recursive functions of 1930, 1934 and 1935, Alonzo Church's lambda calculus of 1936, Emil Post's "Formulation 1" of 1936, and Alan Turing's Turing machines of 1936–7 and 1939. Giving a formal definition of algorithms, corresponding to the intuitive notion, remains a challenging problem.

Implementation

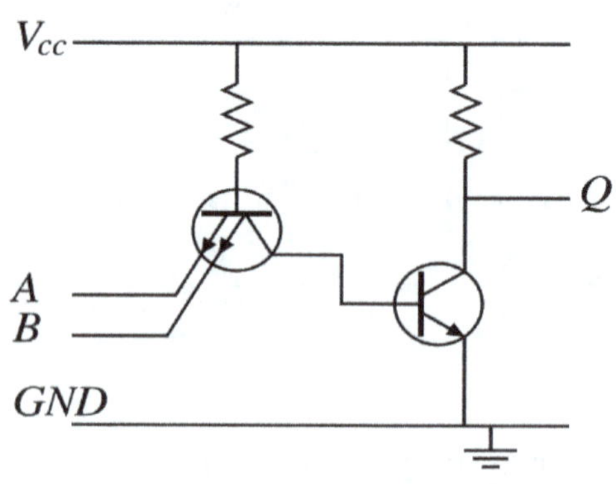

Logical NAND algorithm implemented electronically in 7400 chip

Most algorithms are intended to be implemented as computer programs. However, algorithms are also implemented by other means, such as in a biological neural network (for example, the human brain implementing arithmetic or an insect looking for food), in an electrical circuit, or in a mechanical device.

Computer Algorithms

In computer systems, an algorithm is basically an instance of logic written in software by software developers to be effective for the intended "target" computer(s) to produce *output* from given (perhaps null) *input*. An optimal algorithm, even running in old hardware, would produce faster results than a non-optimal (higher time complexity) algorithm for the same purpose, running in more efficient hardware; that is why algorithms, like computer hardware, are considered technology.

"Elegant" (compact) programs, "good" (fast) programs : The notion of "simplicity and elegance" appears informally in Knuth and precisely in Chaitin:

> Knuth: "...we want *good* algorithms in some loosely defined aesthetic sense. One criterion ... is the length of time taken to perform the algorithm ... Other criteria are adaptability of the algorithm to computers, its simplicity and elegance, etc"
>
> Chaitin: " ... a program is 'elegant,' by which I mean that it's the smallest possible program for producing the output that it does"

Chaitin prefaces his definition with: "I'll show you can't prove that a program is 'elegant'"—such a proof would solve the Halting problem (ibid).

Algorithm versus function computable by an algorithm: For a given function multiple algorithms may exist. This is true, even without expanding the available instruction set available to the programmer. Rogers observes that "It is ... important to distinguish between the notion of *algorithm*, i.e. procedure and the notion of *function computable by algorithm*, i.e. mapping yielded by procedure. The same function may have several different algorithms".

Unfortunately there may be a tradeoff between goodness (speed) and elegance (compactness)—an elegant program may take more steps to complete a computation than one less elegant. An example that uses Euclid's algorithm appears below.

Computers (and computors), mode*ls of computation*: A computer (or human "computor") is a restricted type of machine, a "discrete deterministic mechanical device" that blindly follows its instructions. Melzak's and Lambek's primitive models reduced this notion to four elements: (i) discrete, distinguishable *locations*, (ii) discrete, indistinguishable *counters* (iii) an agent, and (iv) a list of instructions that are *effective* relative to the capability of the agent.

Minsky describes a more congenial variation of Lambek's "abacus" model in his "Very Simple Bases for Computability". Minsky's machine proceeds sequentially through its five (or six, depending on how one counts) instructions, unless either a conditional IF–THEN GOTO or an unconditional GOTO changes program flow out of sequence. Besides HALT, Minsky's machine includes three *assignment* (replacement, substitution) operations: ZERO (e.g. the contents of location replaced by 0: L ← 0), SUCCESSOR (e.g. L ← L+1), and DECREMENT (e.g. L ← L – 1). Rarely must a programmer write "code" with such a limited instruction set. But Minsky shows (as do Melzak and Lambek) that his machine is Turing complete with only four general *types* of instructions: conditional GOTO, unconditional GOTO, assignment/replacement/substitution, and HALT.

Simulation of an algorithm: computer (computor) language: Knuth advises the reader that "the best way to learn an algorithm is to try it . . . immediately take pen and paper and work through an example". But what about a simulation or execution of the real thing? The programmer must translate the algorithm into a language that the simulator/computer/computor can *effectively* execute. Stone gives an example of this: when computing the roots of a quadratic equation the computor must know how to take a square root. If they don't, then the algorithm, to be effective, must provide a set of rules for extracting a square root.

This means that the programmer must know a "language" that is effective relative to the target computing agent (computer/computor).

But what model should be used for the simulation? Van Emde Boas observes "even if we base complexity theory on abstract instead of concrete machines, arbitrariness of the choice of a model remains. It is at this point that the notion of *simulation* enters". When speed is being measured, the instruction set matters. For example, the subprogram in Euclid's algorithm to compute the remainder would execute much faster if the programmer had a "modulus" instruction available rather than just subtraction (or worse: just Minsky's "decrement").

Structured programming, canonical structures: Per the Church–Turing thesis, any algorithm can be computed by a model known to be Turing complete, and per Minsky's demonstrations, Turing completeness requires only four instruction types—conditional GOTO, unconditional GOTO, assignment, HALT. Kemeny and Kurtz observe that, while "undisciplined" use of unconditional GOTOs and conditional IF-THEN GOTOs can result in "spaghetti code", a programmer can write structured programs using only these instructions; on the other hand "it is also possible, and not too hard, to write badly structured programs in a structured language". Tausworthe augments the three Böhm-Jacopini canonical structures: SEQUENCE, IF-THEN-ELSE, and WHILE-DO, with two more: DO-WHILE and CASE. An additional benefit of a structured program is that it lends itself to proofs of correctness using mathematical induction.

Canonical flowchart symbols: The graphical aide called a flowchart offers a way to describe and document an algorithm (and a computer program of one). Like program flow of a Minsky machine, a flowchart always starts at the top of a page and proceeds down. Its primary symbols are only four: the directed arrow showing program flow, the rectangle (SEQUENCE, GOTO), the diamond (IF-THEN-ELSE), and the dot (OR-tie). The Böhm–Jacopini canonical structures are made of these primitive shapes. Sub-structures can "nest" in rectangles, but only if a single exit occurs from the superstructure. The symbols, and their use to build the canonical structures, are shown in the diagram.

Examples

Algorithm Example

One of the simplest algorithms is to find the largest number in a list of numbers of random order. Finding the solution requires looking at every number in the list. From this follows a simple algorithm, which can be stated in a high-level description English prose, as:

High-level description:

1. If there are no numbers in the set then there is no highest number.
2. Assume the first number in the set is the largest number in the set.
3. For each remaining number in the set: if this number is larger than the current largest number, consider this number to be the largest number in the set.
4. When there are no numbers left in the set to iterate over, consider the current largest number to be the largest number of the set.

(Quasi-)formal description: Written in prose but much closer to the high-level language of a computer program, the following is the more formal coding of the algorithm in pseudocode or pidgin code:

```
Algorithm LargestNumber
  Input: A list of numbers L.
  Output: The largest number in the list L.
  if L.size = 0 return null
  largest ← L
  for each item in L, do
    if item > largest, then
      largest ← item
  return largest
```

- "←" is a shorthand for "changes to". For instance, "*largest* ← *item*" means that the value of *largest* changes to the value of *item*.
- "return" terminates the algorithm and outputs the value that follows.

Euclid's Algorithm

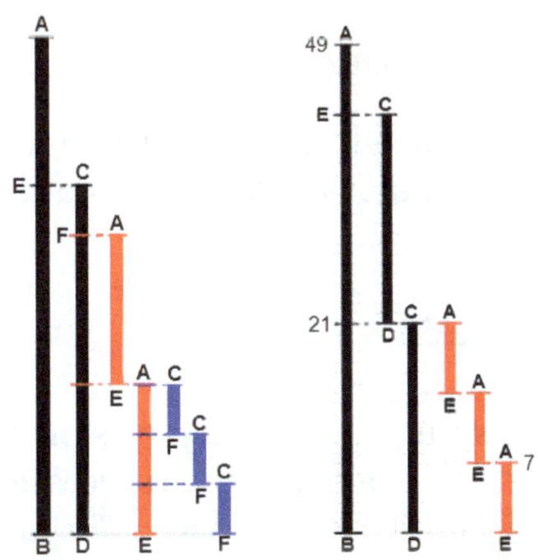

Euclid's example Nicomachus' example

The example-diagram of Euclid's algorithm from T.L. Heath , with more detail added. Euclid does not go beyond a third measuring, and gives no numerical examples. Nicomachus gives the example of 49 and 21: "I subtract the less from the greater; 28 is left; then again I subtract from this the same 21 (for this is possible); 7 is left; I subtract this from 21, 14 is left; from which I again subtract 7 (for this is possible); 7 is left, but 7 cannot be subtracted from 7." Heath comments that, "The last phrase is curious, but the meaning of it is obvious enough, as also the meaning of the phrase about ending 'at one and the same number'."

Euclid's algorithm to compute the greatest common divisor (GCD) to two numbers appears as Proposition II in Book VII ("Elementary Number Theory") of his *Elements*. Euclid poses the problem thus: "Given two numbers not prime to one another, to find their greatest common measure". He defines "A number [to be] a multitude composed of units": a counting number, a positive integer not including zero. To "measure" is to place a shorter measuring length s successively (q times) along longer length l until the remaining portion r is less than the shorter length s. In modern words, remainder $r = l - q \times s$, q being the quotient, or remainder r is the "modulus", the integer-fractional part left over after the division.

For Euclid's method to succeed, the starting lengths must satisfy two requirements: (i) the lengths must not be zero, AND (ii) the subtraction must be "proper"; i.e., a test must guarantee that the smaller of the two numbers is subtracted from the larger (alternately, the two can be equal so their subtraction yields zero).

Euclid's original proof adds a third requirement: the two lengths must not be prime to one another. Euclid stipulated this so that he could construct a reductio ad absurdum proof that the two numbers' common measure is in fact the *greatest*. While Nicomachus' algorithm is the same as Euclid's, when the numbers are prime to one another, it yields the number "1" for their common measure. So, to be precise, the following is really Nicomachus' algorithm.

```
1599 = 650×2 + 299
 650 = 299×2 + 52
 299 = 52×5 + 39
 52 = 39×1 + 13
 39 = 13×3 + 0
```

Computer Language for Euclid's Algorithm

Only a few instruction *types* are required to execute Euclid's algorithm—some logical tests (conditional GOTO), unconditional GOTO, assignment (replacement), and subtraction.

- A *location* is symbolized by upper case letter(s), e.g. S, A, etc.
- The varying quantity (number) in a location is written in lower case letter(s) and (usually) associated with the location's name. For example, location L at the start might contain the number $l = 3009$.

An Inelegant Program for Euclid's Algorithm

The following algorithm is framed as Knuth's four-step version of Euclid's and Nicomachus', but, rather than using division to find the remainder, it uses successive subtractions of the shorter length s from the remaining length r until r is less than s. The high-level description, shown in boldface, is adapted from Knuth 1973:2–4:

INPUT:

```
1 [Into two locations L and S put the numbers l and s that represent the two lengths]:
  INPUT L, S
2 [Initialize R: make the remaining length r equal to the starting/initial/input length
```

```
l]:
  R ← L
```

E0: [Ensure $r \geq s$.]

```
3 [Ensure the smaller of the two numbers is in S and the larger in R]:
  IF R > S THEN
    the contents of L is the larger number so skip over the exchange-steps 4, 5 and 6:
    GOTO step 6
  ELSE
    swap the contents of R and S.
4   L ← R (this first step is redundant, but is useful for later discussion).
5   R ← S
6   S ← L
```

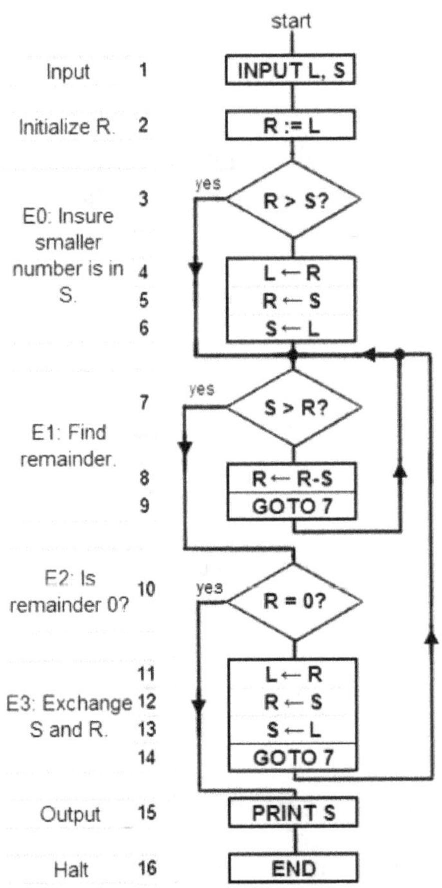

"Inelegant"

"Inelegant" is a translation of Knuth's version of the algorithm with a subtraction-based remainder-loop replacing his use of division (or a "modulus" instruction). Derived from Knuth 1973:2–4. Depending on the two numbers "Inelegant" may compute the g.c.d. in fewer steps than "Elegant".

E1: [Find remainder]: Until the remaining length r in R is less than the shorter length s in S, repeatedly subtract the measuring number s in S from the remaining length r in R.

```
7 IF S > R THEN
```

```
    done measuring so
    GOTO 10
  ELSE
    measure again,
8   R ← R - S
9   [Remainder-loop]:
    GOTO 7.
```

E2: [Is the remainder zero?]: EITHER (i) the last measure was exact, the remainder in R is zero, and the program can halt, OR (ii) the algorithm must continue: the last measure left a remainder in R less than measuring number in S.

```
10 IF R = 0 THEN
     done so
     GOTO step 15
   ELSE
     CONTINUE TO step 11,
```

E3: [Interchange *s* and *r*]: The nut of Euclid's algorithm. Use remainder *r* to measure what was previously smaller number *s*; L serves as a temporary location.

```
11  L ← R
12  R ← S
13  S ← L
14  [Repeat the measuring process]:
    GOTO 7
```

OUTPUT:

```
15 [Done. S contains the greatest common divisor]:
   PRINT S
```

DONE:

```
16 HALT, END, STOP.
```

An Elegant Program for Euclid's Algorithm

The following version of Euclid's algorithm requires only six core instructions to do what thirteen are required to do by "Inelegant"; worse, "Inelegant" requires more *types* of instructions. The flowchart of "Elegant" can be found at the top of this article. In the (unstructured) Basic language, the steps are numbered, and the instruction LET [] = [] is the assignment instruction symbolized by ←.

```
 5 REM Euclid's algorithm for greatest common divisor
 6 PRINT "Type two integers greater than 0"
10 INPUT A,B
```

```
20 IF B=0 THEN GOTO 80

30 IF A > B THEN GOTO 60

40 LET B=B-A

50 GOTO 20

60 LET A=A-B

70 GOTO 20

80 PRINT A

90 END
```

The following version can be used with Object Oriented languages:

```
// Euclid's algorithm for greatest common divisor
integer euclidAlgorithm (int A, int B){
     A=Math.abs(A);
     B=Math.abs(B);
     while (B!=0){
          if (A>B) A=A-B;
          else B=B-A;
     }
     return A;
}
```

How "Elegant" works: In place of an outer "Euclid loop", "Elegant" shifts back and forth between two "co-loops", an A > B loop that computes A ← A − B, and a B ≤ A loop that computes B ← B − A. This works because, when at last the minuend M is less than or equal to the subtrahend S (Difference = Minuend − Subtrahend), the minuend can become *s* (the new measuring length) and the subtrahend can become the new *r* (the length to be measured); in other words the "sense" of the subtraction reverses.

Testing the Euclid Algorithms

Does an algorithm do what its author wants it to do? A few test cases usually suffice to confirm core functionality. One source uses 3009 and 884. Knuth suggested 40902, 24140. Another interesting case is the two relatively prime numbers 14157 and 5950.

But exceptional cases must be identified and tested. Will "Inelegant" perform properly when R > S, S > R, R = S? Ditto for "Elegant": B > A, A > B, A = B? (Yes to all). What happens when one number is zero, both numbers are zero? ("Inelegant" computes forever in all cases; "Elegant" computes forever when A = 0.) What happens if *negative* numbers are entered? Fractional numbers? If the input numbers, i.e. the domain of the function computed by the algorithm/program, is to include only positive integers including zero, then the failures at zero indicate that the algorithm (and the program that instantiates it) is a partial function rather than a total function. A notable failure due to exceptions is the Ariane 5 Flight 501 rocket failure (4 June 1996).

Proof of program correctness by use of mathematical induction: Knuth demonstrates the application of mathematical induction to an "extended" version of Euclid's algorithm, and he proposes "a general method applicable to proving the validity of any algorithm". Tausworthe proposes that a measure of the complexity of a program be the length of its correctness proof.

Measuring and Improving the Euclid Algorithms

Elegance (compactness) versus goodness (speed): With only six core instructions, "Elegant" is the clear winner, compared to "Inelegant" at thirteen instructions. However, "Inelegant" is *faster* (it arrives at HALT in fewer steps). Algorithm analysis indicates why this is the case: "Elegant" does *two* conditional tests in every subtraction loop, whereas "Inelegant" only does one. As the algorithm (usually) requires many loop-throughs, *on average* much time is wasted doing a "B = 0?" test that is needed only after the remainder is computed.

Can the algorithms be improved?: Once the programmer judges a program "fit" and "effective"—that is, it computes the function intended by its author—then the question becomes, can it be improved?

The compactness of "Inelegant" can be improved by the elimination of five steps. But Chaitin proved that compacting an algorithm cannot be automated by a generalized algorithm; rather, it can only be done heuristically; i.e., by exhaustive search (examples to be found at Busy beaver), trial and error, cleverness, insight, application of inductive reasoning, etc. Observe that steps 4, 5 and 6 are repeated in steps 11, 12 and 13. Comparison with "Elegant" provides a hint that these steps, together with steps 2 and 3, can be eliminated. This reduces the number of core instructions from thirteen to eight, which makes it "more elegant" than "Elegant", at nine steps.

The speed of "Elegant" can be improved by moving the "B=0?" test outside of the two subtraction loops. This change calls for the addition of three instructions (B = 0?, A = 0?, GOTO). Now "Elegant" computes the example-numbers faster; whether this is always the case for any given A, B and R, S would require a detailed analysis.

Algorithmic Analysis

It is frequently important to know how much of a particular resource (such as time or storage) is theoretically required for a given algorithm. Methods have been developed for the analysis of algorithms to obtain such quantitative answers (estimates); for example, the sorting algorithm above has a time requirement of $O(n)$, using the big O notation with n as the length of the list. At all times the algorithm only needs to remember two values: the largest number found so far, and its current position in the input list. Therefore, it is said to have a space requirement of $O(1)$, if the space required to store the input numbers is not counted, or $O(n)$ if it is counted.

Different algorithms may complete the same task with a different set of instructions in less or more time, space, or 'effort' than others. For example, a binary search algorithm (with cost $O(\log n)$) outperforms a sequential search (cost $O(n)$) when used for table lookups on sorted lists or arrays.

Formal Versus Empirical

The analysis and study of algorithms is a discipline of computer science, and is often practiced abstractly without the use of a specific programming language or implementation. In this sense, algorithm analysis resembles other mathematical disciplines in that it focuses on the underlying properties of the algorithm and not on the specifics of any particular implementation. Usually pseudocode is used for analysis as it is the simplest and most general representation. However, ultimately, most algorithms are usually implemented on particular hardware / software platforms and their algorithmic efficiency is eventually put to the test using real code. For the solution of a "one off" problem, the efficiency of a particular algorithm may not have significant consequences (unless n is extremely large) but for algorithms designed for fast interactive, commercial or long life scientific usage it may be critical. Scaling from small n to large n frequently exposes inefficient algorithms that are otherwise benign.

Empirical testing is useful because it may uncover unexpected interactions that affect performance. Benchmarks may be used to compare before/after potential improvements to an algorithm after program optimization.

Execution Efficiency

To illustrate the potential improvements possible even in well established algorithms, a recent significant innovation, relating to FFT algorithms (used heavily in the field of image processing), can decrease processing time up to 1,000 times for applications like medical imaging. In general, speed improvements depend on special properties of the problem, which are very common in practical applications. Speedups of this magnitude enable computing devices that make extensive use of image processing (like digital cameras and medical equipment) to consume less power.

Classification

There are various ways to classify algorithms, each with its own merits.

By Implementation

One way to classify algorithms is by implementation means.

Recursion

> A recursive algorithm is one that invokes (makes reference to) itself repeatedly until a certain condition (also known as termination condition) matches, which is a method common to functional programming. Iterative algorithms use repetitive constructs like loops and sometimes additional data structures like stacks to solve the given problems. Some problems are naturally suited for one implementation or the other. For example, towers of Hanoi is well understood using recursive implementation. Every recursive version has an equivalent (but possibly more or less complex) iterative version, and vice versa.

Logical

> An algorithm may be viewed as controlled logical deduction. This notion may be expressed as: *Algorithm = logic + control*. The logic component expresses the axioms that may be used in the computation and the control component determines the way in which deduction is applied to the axioms. This is the basis for the logic programming paradigm. In pure

logic programming languages the control component is fixed and algorithms are specified by supplying only the logic component. The appeal of this approach is the elegant semantics: a change in the axioms has a well-defined change in the algorithm.

Serial, parallel or distributed

Algorithms are usually discussed with the assumption that computers execute one instruction of an algorithm at a time. Those computers are sometimes called serial computers. An algorithm designed for such an environment is called a serial algorithm, as opposed to parallel algorithms or distributed algorithms. Parallel algorithms take advantage of computer architectures where several processors can work on a problem at the same time, whereas distributed algorithms utilize multiple machines connected with a network. Parallel or distributed algorithms divide the problem into more symmetrical or asymmetrical subproblems and collect the results back together. The resource consumption in such algorithms is not only processor cycles on each processor but also the communication overhead between the processors. Some sorting algorithms can be parallelized efficiently, but their communication overhead is expensive. Iterative algorithms are generally parallelizable. Some problems have no parallel algorithms, and are called inherently serial problems.

Deterministic or non-deterministic

Deterministic algorithms solve the problem with exact decision at every step of the algorithm whereas non-deterministic algorithms solve problems via guessing although typical guesses are made more accurate through the use of heuristics.

Exact or approximate

While many algorithms reach an exact solution, approximation algorithms seek an approximation that is closer to the true solution. Approximation can be reached by either using a deterministic or a random strategy. Such algorithms have practical value for many hard problems. One of the examples of an approximate algorithm is the Knapsack problem. The Knapsack problem is a problem where there is a set of given items. The goal of the problem is to pack the knapsack to get the maximum total value. Each item has some weight and some value. Total weight that we can carry is no more than some fixed number X. So, we must consider weights of items as well as their value.

Quantum algorithm

They run on a realistic model of quantum computation. The term is usually used for those algorithms which seem inherently quantum, or use some essential feature of quantum computation such as quantum superposition or quantum entanglement.

By Design Paradigm

Another way of classifying algorithms is by their design methodology or paradigm. There is a certain number of paradigms, each different from the other. Furthermore, each of these categories include many different types of algorithms. Some common paradigms are:

Brute-force or exhaustive search

This is the naive method of trying every possible solution to see which is best.

Divide and conquer

A divide and conquer algorithm repeatedly reduces an instance of a problem to one or more smaller instances of the same problem (usually recursively) until the instances are small enough to solve easily. One such example of divide and conquer is merge sorting. Sorting can be done on each segment of data after dividing data into segments and sorting of entire data can be obtained in the conquer phase by merging the segments. A simpler variant of divide and conquer is called a *decrease and conquer algorithm*, that solves an identical subproblem and uses the solution of this subproblem to solve the bigger problem. Divide and conquer divides the problem into multiple subproblems and so the conquer stage is more complex than decrease and conquer algorithms. An example of decrease and conquer algorithm is the binary search algorithm.

Search and enumeration

Many problems (such as playing chess) can be modeled as problems on graphs. A graph exploration algorithm specifies rules for moving around a graph and is useful for such problems. This category also includes search algorithms, branch and bound enumeration and backtracking.

Randomized algorithm

Such algorithms make some choices randomly (or pseudo-randomly). They can be very useful in finding approximate solutions for problems where finding exact solutions can be impractical. For some of these problems, it is known that the fastest approximations must involve some randomness. Whether randomized algorithms with polynomial time complexity can be the fastest algorithms for some problems is an open question known as the P versus NP problem. There are two large classes of such algorithms:

1. Monte Carlo algorithms return a correct answer with high-probability. E.g. RP is the subclass of these that run in polynomial time.
2. Las Vegas algorithms always return the correct answer, but their running time is only probabilistically bound, e.g. ZPP.

Reduction of complexity

This technique involves solving a difficult problem by transforming it into a better known problem for which we have (hopefully) asymptotically optimal algorithms. The goal is to find a reducing algorithm whose complexity is not dominated by the resulting reduced algorithm's. For example, one selection algorithm for finding the median in an unsorted list involves first sorting the list (the expensive portion) and then pulling out the middle element in the sorted list (the cheap portion). This technique is also known as *transform and conquer*.

Optimization Problems

For optimization problems there is a more specific classification of algorithms; an algorithm for such problems may fall into one or more of the general categories described above as well as into one of the following:

Linear programming

When searching for optimal solutions to a linear function bound to linear equality and inequality constraints, the constraints of the problem can be used directly in producing the optimal solutions. There are algorithms that can solve any problem in this category, such as the popular simplex algorithm. Problems that can be solved with linear programming include the maximum flow problem for directed graphs. If a problem additionally requires that one or more of the unknowns must be an integer then it is classified in integer programming. A linear programming algorithm can solve such a problem if it can be proved that all restrictions for integer values are superficial, i.e., the solutions satisfy these restrictions anyway. In the general case, a specialized algorithm or an algorithm that finds approximate solutions is used, depending on the difficulty of the problem.

Dynamic programming

When a problem shows optimal substructures – meaning the optimal solution to a problem can be constructed from optimal solutions to subproblems – and overlapping subproblems, meaning the same subproblems are used to solve many different problem instances, a quicker approach called *dynamic programming* avoids recomputing solutions that have already been computed. For example, Floyd–Warshall algorithm, the shortest path to a goal from a vertex in a weighted graph can be found by using the shortest path to the goal from all adjacent vertices. Dynamic programming and memoization go together. The main difference between dynamic programming and divide and conquer is that subproblems are more or less independent in divide and conquer, whereas subproblems overlap in dynamic programming. The difference between dynamic programming and straightforward recursion is in caching or memoization of recursive calls. When subproblems are independent and there is no repetition, memoization does not help; hence dynamic programming is not a solution for all complex problems. By using memoization or maintaining a table of subproblems already solved, dynamic programming reduces the exponential nature of many problems to polynomial complexity.

The greedy method

A greedy algorithm is similar to a dynamic programming algorithm in that it works by examining substructures, in this case not of the problem but of a given solution. Such algorithms start with some solution, which may be given or have been constructed in some way, and improve it by making small modifications. For some problems they can find the optimal solution while for others they stop at local optima, that is, at solutions that cannot be improved by the algorithm but are not optimum. The most popular use of greedy algorithms is for finding the minimal spanning tree where finding the optimal solution is possible with this method. Huffman Tree, Kruskal, Prim, Sollin are greedy algorithms that can solve this optimization problem.

The heuristic method

> In optimization problems, heuristic algorithms can be used to find a solution close to the optimal solution in cases where finding the optimal solution is impractical. These algorithms work by getting closer and closer to the optimal solution as they progress. In principle, if run for an infinite amount of time, they will find the optimal solution. Their merit is that they can find a solution very close to the optimal solution in a relatively short time. Such algorithms include local search, tabu search, simulated annealing, and genetic algorithms. Some of them, like simulated annealing, are non-deterministic algorithms while others, like tabu search, are deterministic. When a bound on the error of the non-optimal solution is known, the algorithm is further categorized as an approximation algorithm.

By Field of Study

Every field of science has its own problems and needs efficient algorithms. Related problems in one field are often studied together. Some example classes are search algorithms, sorting algorithms, merge algorithms, numerical algorithms, graph algorithms, string algorithms, computational geometric algorithms, combinatorial algorithms, medical algorithms, machine learning, cryptography, data compression algorithms and parsing techniques.

Fields tend to overlap with each other, and algorithm advances in one field may improve those of other, sometimes completely unrelated, fields. For example, dynamic programming was invented for optimization of resource consumption in industry, but is now used in solving a broad range of problems in many fields.

By Complexity

Algorithms can be classified by the amount of time they need to complete compared to their input size:

- Constant time: if the time needed by the algorithm is the same, regardless of the input size. E.g. an access to an array element.
- Linear time: if the time is proportional to the input size. E.g. the traverse of a list.
- Logarithmic time: if the time is a logarithmic function of the input size. E.g. binary search algorithm.
- Polynomial time: if the time is a power of the input size. E.g. the bubble sort algorithm has quadratic time complexity.
- Exponential time: if the time is an exponential function of the input size. E.g. Brute-force search.

Some problems may have multiple algorithms of differing complexity, while other problems might have no algorithms or no known efficient algorithms. There are also mappings from some problems to other problems. Owing to this, it was found to be more suitable to classify the problems themselves instead of the algorithms into equivalence classes based on the complexity of the best possible algorithms for them.

Continuous Algorithms

The adjective "continuous" when applied to the word "algorithm" can mean:

- An algorithm operating on data that represents continuous quantities, even though this data is represented by discrete approximations—such algorithms are studied in numerical analysis; or
- An algorithm in the form of a differential equation that operates continuously on the data, running on an analog computer.

How to write an Algorithm in Programming Language

This article will help how to write an algorithm for any programming language. Nowadays, programming languages play a vital role in the real world and use to develop real world applications. To design a code, one must design an algorithm first.

Steps

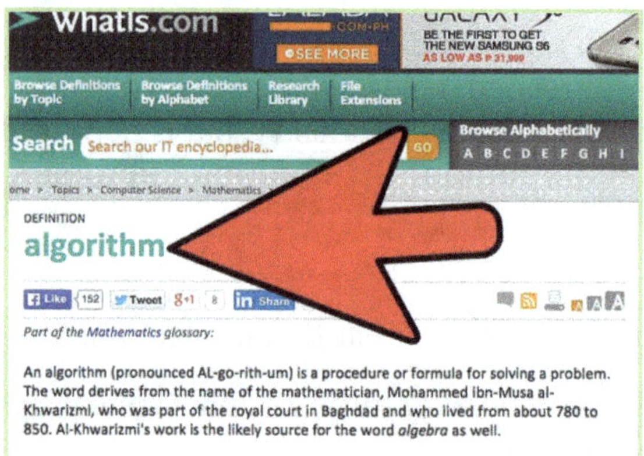

1. Keep in mind that algorithm is a step-by-step process.

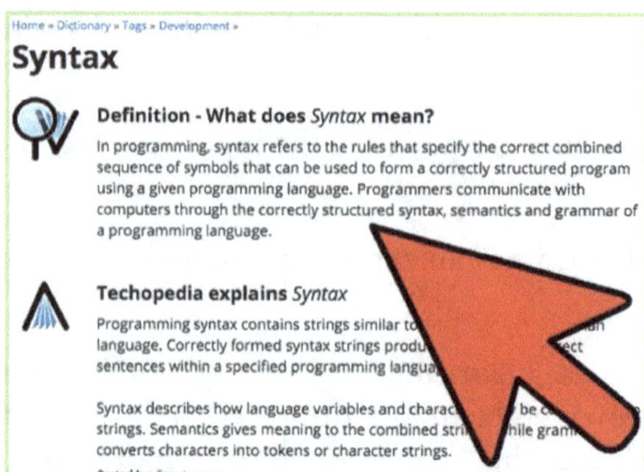

2. Depending upon programming language, include syntax where necessary.

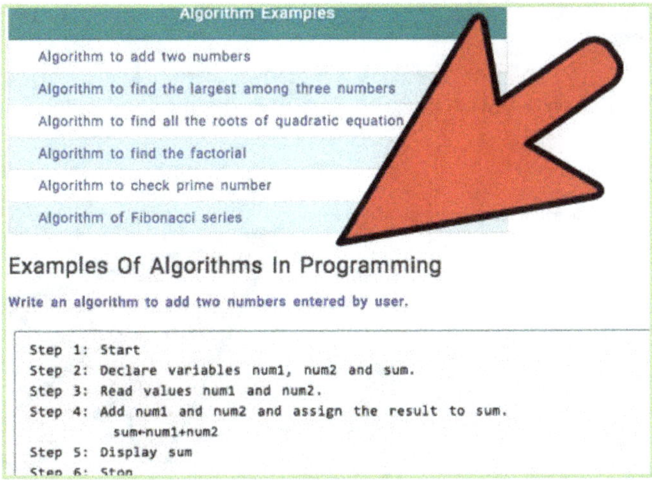

3. Begin.

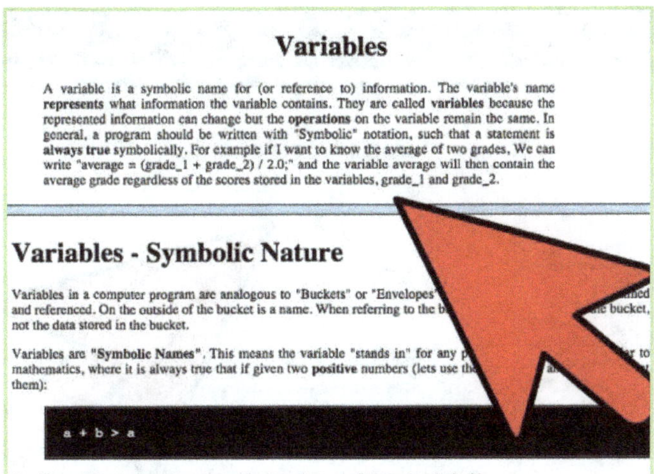

4. Include variables and their usage.

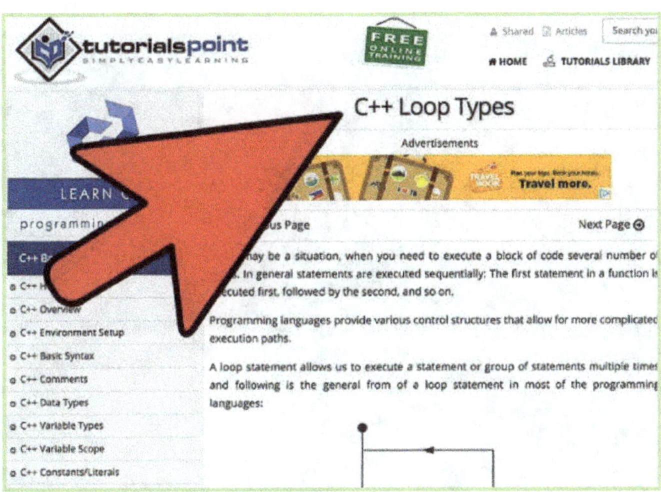

5. If they are any loops, try to give sub number lists.

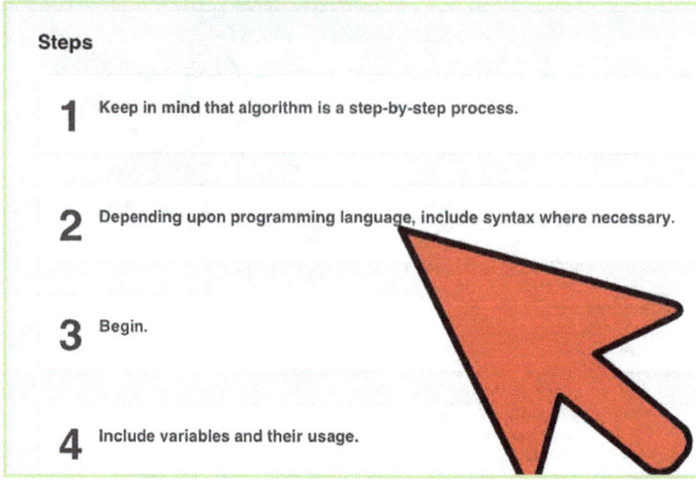

6. Try to give go back to step number if loop or condition fails.

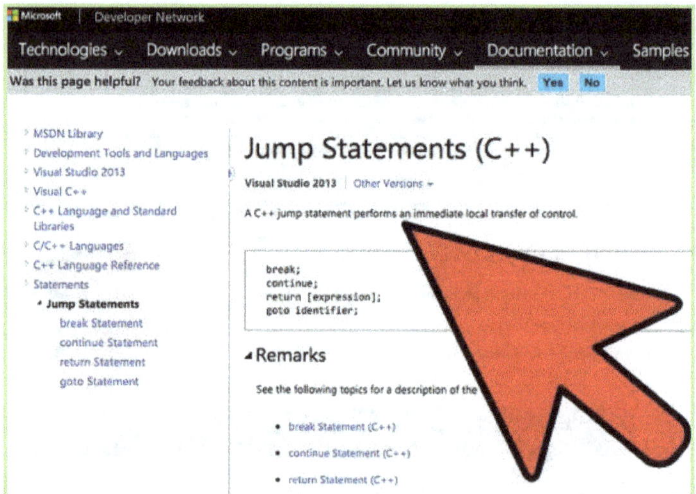

7. Use jump statement to jump from one statement to another.

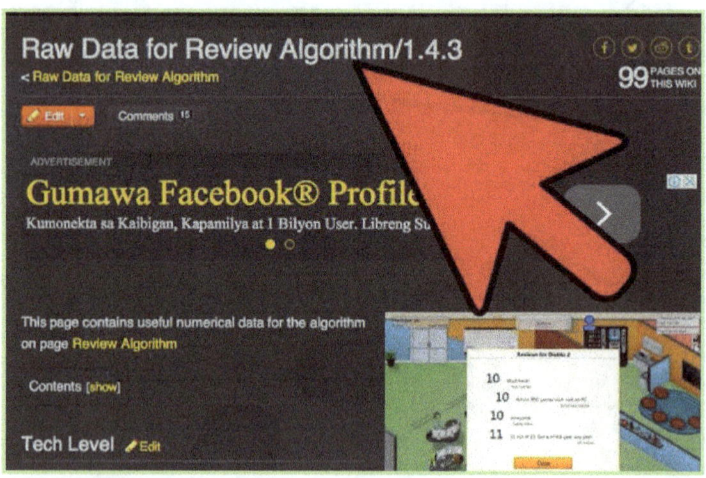

8. Try to avoid unwanted raw data in algorithm.

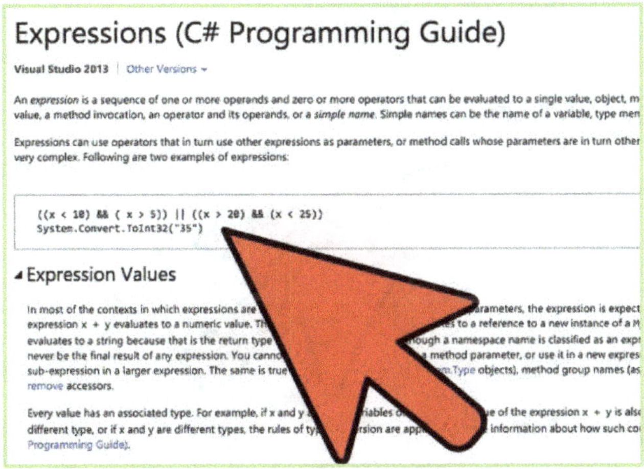

9. Define expressions.

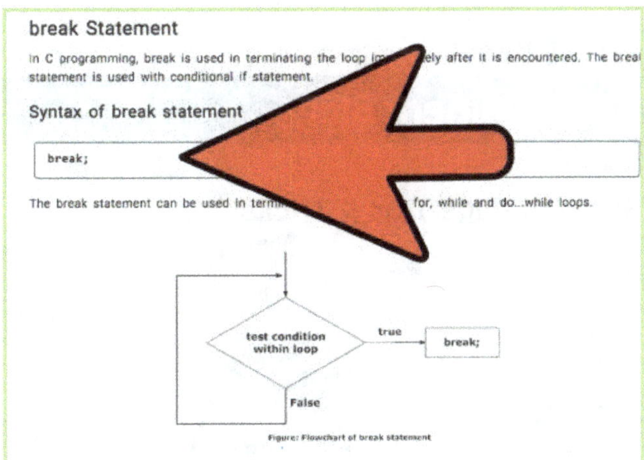

10. Use break and stop to terminate the process.

Logging in

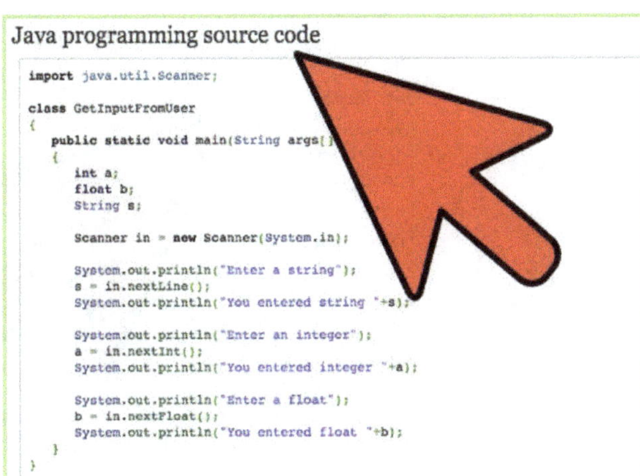

1. Get user input.

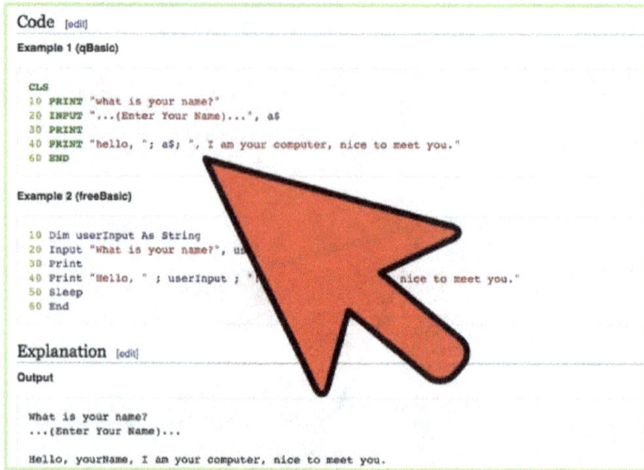

2. Check if the entered username and password match the pre-stored credentials in the database.

3. If true, set session and redirect your user to the success page.

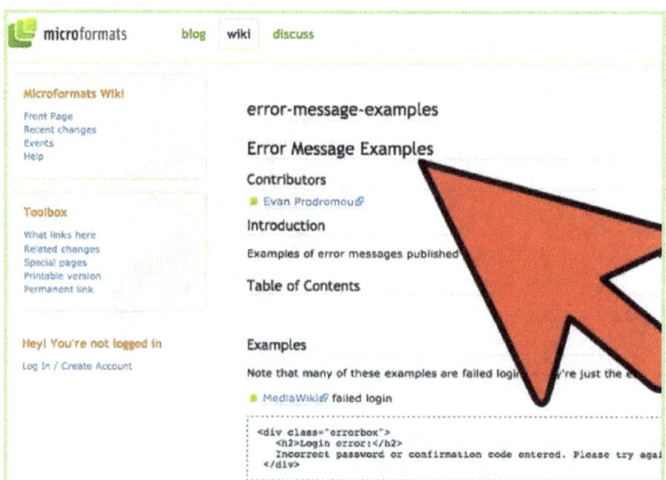

4. If false, print a failure message, redirect on the same login page and ask user to re-enter the credentials.

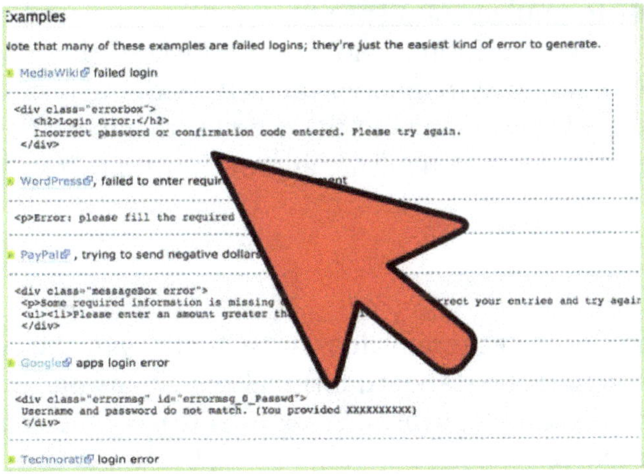

Pseudocode

Pseudocode is an informal high-level description of the operating principle of a computer program or other algorithm.

It uses the structural conventions of a normal programming language, but is intended for human reading rather than machine reading. Pseudocode typically omits details that are essential for machine understanding of the algorithm, such as variable declarations, system-specific code and some subroutines. The programming language is augmented with natural language description details, where convenient, or with compact mathematical notation. The purpose of using pseudocode is that it is easier for people to understand than conventional programming language code, and that it is an efficient and environment-independent description of the key principles of an algorithm. It is commonly used in textbooks and scientific publications that are documenting various algorithms, and also in planning of computer program development, for sketching out the structure of the program before the actual coding takes place.

No standard for pseudocode syntax exists, as a program in pseudocode is not an executable program. Pseudocode resembles, but should not be confused with skeleton programs which can be compiled without errors. Flowcharts, drakon-charts and Unified Modeling Language (UML) charts can be thought of as a graphical alternative to pseudocode, but are more spacious on paper. Languages such as HAGGIS bridge the gap between pseudocode and code written on programming languages. Its main use is to introduce students to high level languages through use of this hybrid language.

Application

Textbooks and scientific publications related to computer science and numerical computation often use pseudocode in description of algorithms, so that all programmers can understand them, even if they do not all know the same programming languages. In textbooks, there is usually an accompanying introduction explaining the particular conventions in use. The level of detail of the pseudo-code may in some cases approach that of formalized general-purpose languages.

A programmer who needs to implement a specific algorithm, especially an unfamiliar one, will often start with a pseudocode description, and then "translate" that description into the target programming language and modify it to interact correctly with the rest of the program. Programmers may also start a project by sketching out the code in pseudocode on paper before writing it in its actual language, as a top-down structuring approach, with a process of steps to be followed as a refinement.

Syntax

As the name suggests, pseudocode generally does not actually obey the syntax rules of any particular language; there is no systematic standard form, although any particular writer will generally borrow style and syntax; for example, control structures from some conventional programming language. Popular syntax sources include Fortran, Pascal, BASIC, C, C++, Java, Lisp, and ALGOL. Variable declarations are typically omitted. Function calls and blocks of code, such as code contained within a loop, are often replaced by a one-line natural language sentence.

Depending on the writer, pseudocode may therefore vary widely in style, from a near-exact imitation of a real programming language at one extreme, to a description approaching formatted prose at the other.

This is an example of pseudocode (for the mathematical game fizz buzz):

Fortran style pseudo code	Pascal style pseudo code	C style pseudo code:	Basic style pseudo code
program fizzbuzz	procedure fizzbuzz	void function fizzbuzz {	Sub fizzbuzz()
Do i = 1 to 100	For i := 1 to 100 do	for (i = 1; i <= 100; i++) {	For i = 1 to 100
set print_number to true	set print_number to true;	set print_number to true;	print_number = True
If i is divisible by 3	If i is divisible by 3 then	If i is divisible by 3	If i is divisible by 3 Then
print "Fizz"	print "Fizz";	print "Fizz";	Print "Fizz"
set print_number to false	set print_number to false;	set print_number to false;	print_number = False
			End If
If i is divisible by 5	If i is divisible by 5 then	If i is divisible by 5	If i is divisible by 5 Then
print "Buzz"	print "Buzz";	print "Buzz";	Print "Buzz"

<table>
<tr>
<td>set print_number to false

If print_number, print i

print a newline

end do</td>
<td>set print_number to false;

If print_number, print i;

print a newline;

end</td>
<td>If print_number, print i;

print a newline;

}

}</td>
<td>End If

If print_number = True Then print i

Print a newline

Next i

End Sub</td>
</tr>
</table>

Mathematical Style Pseudocode

In numerical computation, pseudocode often consists of mathematical notation, typically from set and matrix theory, mixed with the control structures of a conventional programming language, and perhaps also natural language descriptions. This is a compact and often informal notation that can be understood by a wide range of mathematically trained people, and is frequently used as a way to describe mathematical algorithms. For example, the sum operator (capital-sigma notation) or the product operator (capital-pi notation) may represent a for-loop and a selection structure in one expression:

Return $\sum_{k \in S} x_k$

Normally non-ASCII typesetting is used for the mathematical equations, for example by means of markup languages, such as TeX or MathML, or proprietary formula editors.

Mathematical style pseudocode is sometimes referred to as pidgin code, for example *pidgin ALGOL* (the origin of the concept), *pidgin Fortran*, *pidgin BASIC*, *pidgin Pascal*, *pidgin C*, and *pidgin Lisp*.

Common Mathematical Symbols

Type of operation	Symbol	Example
Assignment	← or :=	$c \leftarrow 2\pi r$, $c := 2\pi r$
Comparison	=, ≠, <, >, ≤, ≥	
Arithmetic	+, −, ×, /, mod	
Floor/ceiling	⌊, ⌋, ⌈, ⌉	$a \leftarrow \lfloor b \rfloor + \lceil c \rceil$
Logical	and, or	
Sums, products	Σ Π	$h \leftarrow \sum_{a \in A} 1/a$

Example

Here follows a longer example of mathematical-style pseudo-code, for the Ford–Fulkerson algorithm:

```
algorithm ford-fulkerson is
```

```
input: Graph G with flow capacity c,
       source node s,
       sink node t
output: Flow f such that f is maximal from s to t
```

(Note that $f_{(u,v)}$ is the flow from node u to node v, and $c_{(u,v)}$ is the flow capacity from node u to node v)

```
for each edge (u, v) in G_E do
    f_(u, v) ← 0
    f_(v, u) ← 0
while there exists a path p from s to t in the residual network G_f do
    let c_f be the flow capacity of the residual network G_f
    c_f(p) ← min{c_f(u, v) | (u, v) in p}
    for each edge (u, v) in p do
        f_(u, v) ← f_(u, v) + c_f(p)
        f_(v, u) ← -f_(u, v)
return f
```

Machine Compilation of Pseudocode Style Languages

Natural Language Grammar in Programming Languages

Various attempts to bring elements of natural language grammar into computer programming have produced programming languages such as HyperTalk, Lingo, AppleScript, SQL, Inform and to some extent Python. In these languages, parentheses and other special characters are replaced by prepositions, resulting in quite talkative code. These languages are typically dynamically typed, meaning that variable declarations and other boilerplate code can be omitted. Such languages may make it easier for a person without knowledge about the language to understand the code and perhaps also to learn the language. However, the similarity to natural language is usually more cosmetic than genuine. The syntax rules may be just as strict and formal as in conventional programming, and do not necessarily make development of the programs easier.

Mathematical Programming Languages

An alternative to using mathematical pseudocode (involving set theory notation or matrix operations) for documentation of algorithms is to use a formal mathematical programming language that is a mix of non-ASCII mathematical notation and program control structures. Then the code can be parsed and interpreted by a machine.

Several formal specification languages include set theory notation using special characters. Examples are:

- Z notation
- Vienna Development Method Specification Language (VDM-SL).

Some array programming languages include vectorized expressions and matrix operations as non-ASCII formulas, mixed with conventional control structures. Examples are:

- A programming language (APL), and its dialects APLX and A+.
- MathCAD.

How to write Pseudocode

Pseudocode is an informal tool that you can use to plan out your algorithms. As you begin to write more complex code, it can be hard to keep an entire program in your head before coding it. Think of pseudocode as a step-by-step verbal outline of your code that you can later transcribe into a programming language. It is a combination of human language and programming language: it mimics the syntax of actual computer code, but it is more concerned with readability than with technical specificity.

Part 1

Understanding Pseudocode

1. Know what pseudocode is. Pseudocode is a step-by-step verbal outline of your code that you can gradually transcribe into programming language. Many programmers use it to plan out the function of an algorithm before setting themselves to the more technical task of coding. Pseudocode serves as an informal guide, a tool for thinking through program problems, and a communication device that can help you explain your ideas to other people.

2. Understand why pseudocode is useful. Pseudocode is used to show how a computing algorithm should and could work. Coders often use pseudocode as an intermediate step in programming, in between the initial planning stage and the stage of writing actual, executable code. Good pseudocode can become comments in the final program, guiding the programmer in the future when debugging the code, or revising it in the future. Pseudocode can also be useful for:

- Describing how an algorithm should work. Pseudocode can illustrate where a particular construct, mechanism, or technique could or must appear in a program. Senior programmers often use the pseudocode to quickly explain the steps their junior programmers need to follow in order to accomplish a required task.
- Explaining a computing process to less technical people. Computers need a very strict input syntax to run a program, but humans (especially non-programmers) may find it easier to understand a more fluid, subjective language that clearly states the purpose of each line of code.
- Designing code in a collaborative development group. High-level software architects will often include pseudocode into their designs to help solve a complex problem they see their

programmers running into. If you are developing a program along with other coders, you may find that pseudocode helps make your intentions clear.

3. Remember that pseudocode is subjective and nonstandard. There is no set syntax that you absolutely must use for pseudocode, but it is common professional courtesy to use standard pseudocode structures that other programmers can easily understand. If you are coding a project by yourself, then the most important thing is that the pseudocode helps you structure your thoughts and enact your plan. If you are working with others on a project—whether they are your peers, junior programmers, or non-technical collaborators—it is important to use at least some standard structures so that everyone else can easily understand your intent.

- If you are enrolled in a programming course at a university, a coding camp, or a company, you will likely be tested against a taught pseudocode "standard". This standard often varies between institutions and teachers.
- Clarity is a primary goal of pseudocode, and it may help if you work within accepted programming conventions. As you develop your pseudocode into actual code, you will need to transcribe it into a programming language – so it can help to structure your outline with this in mind.

4. Understand algorithms. An algorithm is a procedure for solving a problem in terms of the actions that a program will take and the order in which it will take those actions. An algorithm is merely the sequence of steps taken to solve a problem. The steps are normally "sequence," "selection, " "iteration," and a case-type statement.

- In C, "sequence statements" are imperatives.
- The "selection" is the "if then else" statement.
- The iteration is satisfied by a number of statements, such as the "while," " do," and the "for."
- The case-type statement is satisfied by the "switch" statement.

5. Remember the three basic constructs that control algorithm flow. If you can implement a "sequence" function, a "while" (looping) function, and an "if-then-else" (selection) function, then you have the basic tools that you need to write a "proper" algorithm.

- SEQUENCE is a linear progression where one task is performed sequentially after another. For example:
    - READ height of rectangle
    - READ width of rectangle
    - COMPUTE area as height times width
- WHILE is a loop (repetition) with a simple conditional test at its beginning. The beginning and ending of the loop are indicated by two keywords WHILE and ENDWHILE. The loop is entered only if the condition is true. For example:
    - WHILE Population < Limit

        - ◊ Compute Population as Population + Births - Deaths
    - o ENDWHILE

- IF-THEN-ELSE is a decision (selection) in which a choice is made between two alternative courses of action. A binary choice is indicated by these four keywords: IF, THEN, ELSE, and ENDIF. For example:
    - o IF HoursWorked > NormalMaximum THEN
        - ◊ Display overtime message
    - o ELSE
        - ◊ Display regular time message
    - o ENDIF

Part 2

Example Pseudocode

1. Consider an simple example program. Imagine that the program must replace all instances of the word "foo" in a text file. The program will read each line in a file, look for a certain word in each line, and then replace that word. You can see that the steps to be repeated are indented with spaces in the pseudocode, just like it would be ideally in real code. A first draft of the pseudocode might look like this:

- open the file
- for each line in the file:
    - o look for the word
    - o remove the characters of that word
    - o insert the characters of the new word
- then close the file.

2. Use pseudocode iteratively: write it once, and then revise it later. One of the strengths of pseudocode is that you can lay out the basics and leave the hard stuff for later. Notice that in the word-replacement example above, there is no detail about how to look for the word. You, the programmer, can re-write the pseudocode to include algorithms for removing the characters of the word, and inserting the characters of the new word. A second draft of the pseudocode may look like this:

- open the file
- for each line in the file:
    - o look for the word by doing this:
        - ◊ read the character in the line

- if the character matches, then:
  - ◊ if all of the following characters match,
  - ◊ then there is a true match.
  - ◊ remove the characters of that word
  - ◊ insert the characters of the new word
- then close the file.

3. Use pseudocode to add features. Pseudocode helps programmers think their way through a problem, just like intermediate steps in a math problem. When used properly, pseudocode can make a complicated programming challenge seem simple. You can improve the pseudocode little by little, one step at a time:

- open the file
- ask the user for the word to be replaced
- ask the user for the word with which to replace it
- for each line in the file:
  - look for the word by doing this:
    - ◊ read the character in the line
    - ◊ if the character matches, then:
      - if all of the following characters match,
      - then there is a true match.
  - Count the occurrence of that word.
  - remove the characters of that word
  - insert the characters of the new word
  - display the amount of occurrences of the word,
- then close the file.

Part 3

Standard Pseudocode Procedure

1. Write only one statement per line. Each statement in your pseudocode should express just one action for the computer. In most cases, if the task list is properly drawn, then each task will correspond to one line of pseudocode. Consider writing out your task list, then translating that list into pseudocode, then gradually developing that pseudocode into actual, computer-readable code.

- Task list:
  - Read name, hourly rate, hours worked, deduction rate
  - Perform calculations
  - gross = hourly rate * hours worked
  - deduction = gross pay * deduction rate
  - net pay = gross pay – deduction
  - Write name, gross, deduction, net pay
- Pseudocode:
  - READ name, hourlyRate, hoursWorked, deductionRate
  - grossPay = hourlyRate * hoursWorked
  - deduction = grossPay * deductionRate
  - netPay = grossPay – deduction
  - WRITE name, grossPay, deduction, netPay

2. Capitalize the initial keyword of each main direction. In the above example, READ and WRITE are capitalized to indicate that they are the primary functions of the program. Relevant keywords might include: READ, WRITE, IF, ELSE, ENDIF, WHILE, ENDWHILE, REPEAT, and UNTIL.

3. Write what you mean, not how to program it. Some programmers write pseudocode like a computer program: they write something like "if a % 2 == 1 then". However, most readers must stop to reason through lines that are so abstractly symbolic. It is easier to understand a verbal line like "if an odd then". The clearer you are, the more easily people will be able to understand what you mean.

4. Leave nothing to the imagination. Everything that is happening in the process must be described completely. Pseudocode statements are close to simple English statements. Pseudocode does not typically use variables, but instead describes what the program should do with close-to-real-world objects such as account numbers, names, or transaction amounts.

- Some examples of valid pseudocode are:
  - If the account number and password are valid then display the basic account information.
  - Prorate the total cost proportional to the invoice amount for each shipment.
- Some examples of invalid pseudocode are:
  - let g=54/r *(Why: Do not use variables. Instead, you should describe the real-world meaning.)*

- o do the main processing until it is done *(Why: You should be specific about what 'main processing' means, and what qualifies the process as 'done'.)*

5. Use standard programming structures. Even if there is no standard for pseudocode, it will be easier for other programmers to understand your steps if you use structures from existing (sequential) programming languages. Use terms like "if", "then", "while", "else", and "loop" the same way that you would in your preferred programming language. Consider the following structures:

- if CONDITION then INSTRUCTION – This means that a given instruction will only conducted if a given condition is true. "Instruction", in this case, means a step that the program will perform. "Condition" means that the data must meet a certain set of criteria before the program takes action.
- while CONDITION do INSTRUCTION – This means that the instruction should be repeated again and again until the condition is no longer true.
- do INSTRUCTION while CONDITION – This is very similar to "while CONDITION do INSTRUCTION". In the first case, the condition is checked before the instruction is conducted, but in the second case the instruction will be conducted first. So in the second case, INSTRUCTION will be conducted at least one time.
- for a = NUMBER1 to NUMBER2 do INSTRUCTION – This means that "a", a variable, will be automatically set to NUMBER1. "a" will be increased by one in every step until the value of the variable reaches NUMBER2. You can use any name for the variable that you think fits better than "a".
- function NAME (ARGUMENTS): INSTRUCTION – This means that every time a certain name is used in the code, it is an abbreviation for a certain instruction. "Arguments" are lists of variables that you can use to clarify the instruction.

6. Use blocks to structure steps. Blocks are syntactic tools that tie several instructions together into one instruction. You can use blocks to order information (say, steps in Block 1 always come before steps in Block 2) or simply to wrap information (say, Instruction1 and Instruction2 are thematically related). In general, indent all statements that show "dependency" on another statement. There are two ways to do this.

- Using curled brackets:
  - o {
  - o INSTRUCTION1
  - o INSTRUCTION2
  - o ...}
- Or using spaces. When using spaces, every instruction of the same block has to start at the same position. Blocks within blocks have more spaces than the parent block. An instruction from a parent block ends the child block, even if there is an instruction later with the same amount of spaces in front.

- o BLOCK1
- o BLOCK1
  - ◊ BLOCK2
  - ◊ BLOCK2
    - • BLOCK3
  - ◊ BLOCK2
    - • BLOCK3
- o BLOCK1

Part 4

Practicing Pseudocode

1. Start by writing down the purpose of the process. This gives you a way to judge whether the pseudocode is complete: in short, if the pseudocode accomplishes the purpose, it is complete. Continue by writing down the process. If the process is simple, this may take only one pass. Look at what you have written down and ask the following questions:

- Would this pseudocode be understood by someone who is at least somewhat familiar with the process?
- Is the pseudocode written in such a way that it will be easy to translated it into a computing language?
- Does the pseudocode describe the complete process without leaving anything out?
- Is every object name used in the pseudocode clearly understood by the target audience?

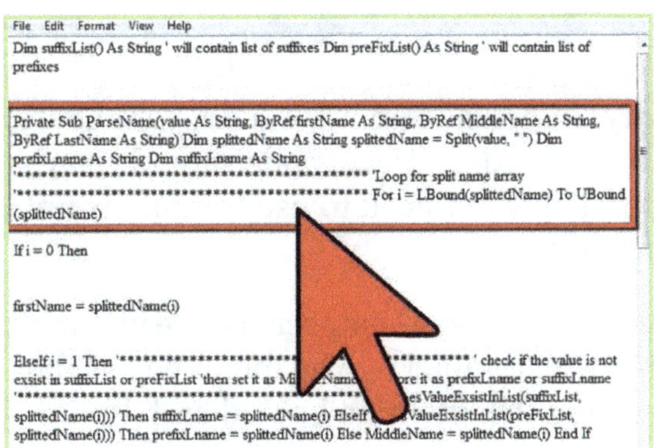

2. Write initial steps of pseudocode that set the stage for functions. The first parts of a code typically define the variables and other elements that you will use to make the algorithm functional.

- Include dimension variables. Write code that shows how each variable or data element will be used.

- Set up controls. You will need to define your controls in pseudocode—from text and image boxes in object-oriented programming (OOP) languages to basic controls in simpler codes—much as you would in a regular project.

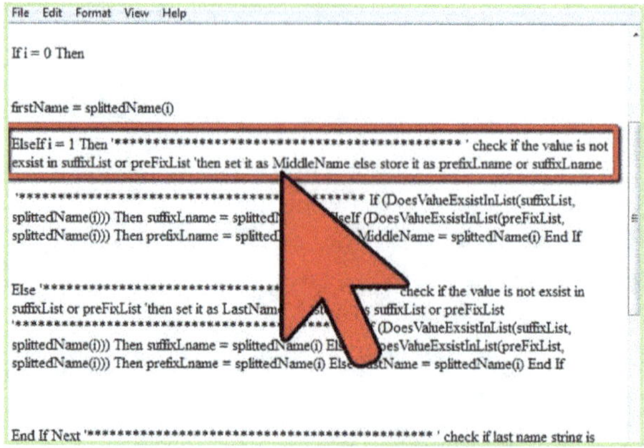

3. Write functional pseudocode. Use pseudocode principles to add specific "event-driven" or "object-driven" code when you have completed the "setting" for your project. Each line of your code should describe a sequence function, a looping function, a selection function, or another distinct action.

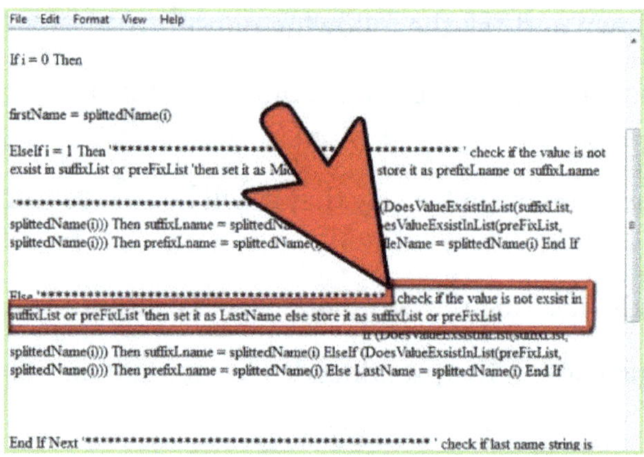

4. Add comments, if necessary. In actual computer code, comments serve the role of identifying tasks and parts of the code to the reader. Pseudocode should clearly explain these steps in nearly-plain English, so you will probably not need to use comments until you translate your pseudocode into a programming language.

- Many programmers choose to work their pseudocode into the final code in the form of comments. This helps other programmers—who might be collaborating, reviewing, or learning from the code—understand the intention behind each line.

- Begin comments with / / so that the computer does not read them. Make sure that the double slashes are indented. For instance:

  - //IF robot has no obstacle in front THEN

    - ◊ // Call Move robot

- ◊ // Add the move command to the command history
- ◊ // RETURN true

o //ELSE

- ◊ // RETURN false without moving the robot

o //END IF

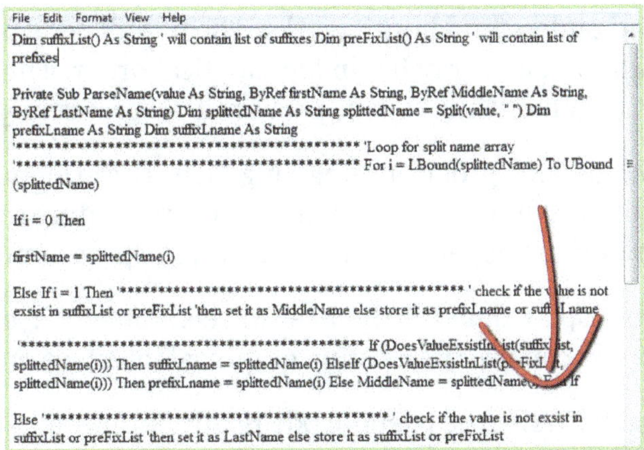

```
File Edit Format View Help
Dim suffixList() As String ' will contain list of suffixes Dim preFixList() As String ' will contain list of prefixes

Private Sub ParseName(value As String, ByRef firstName As String, ByRef MiddleName As String, ByRef LastName As String) Dim splittedName As String splittedName = Split(value, " ") Dim prefixLname As String Dim suffixLname As String
'********************************************* 'Loop for split name array
'********************************************* For i = LBound(splittedName) To UBound (splittedName)

If i = 0 Then

firstName = splittedName(i)

Else If i = 1 Then '********************************************* ' check if the value is not exsist in suffixList or preFixList 'then set it as MiddleName else store it as prefixLname or suffixLname

'********************************************* If (DoesValueExsistInList(suffixList, splittedName(i))) Then suffixLname = splittedName(i) ElseIf (DoesValueExsistInList(preFixList, splittedName(i))) Then prefixLname = splittedName(i) Else MiddleName = splittedName(i) End If

Else '********************************************* ' check if the value is not exsist in suffixList or preFixList 'then set it as LastName else store it as suffixList or preFixList
```

5. Read over the finished project for logic and syntax errors. Again, syntax does not have to be exact, but your pseudocode should still make sense. Try to put yourself into the shoes of another person reading this code, and consider whether your directions are as clear as they can be.

- Assess your code modules according to the various elements that they comprise. For example: core operations for the computer include reading or getting information from a file, writing to a file or display on the screen, doing mathematical calculations, valuing data variables, and comparing one or more elements. Each of these has its own place in a computer code project, as well as in the pseudocode that you write to support that project.
- Work specific tasks into the pseudocode. When you have identified each task, represent it with readable pseudocode that, while mimicking the actual code language that you will use, need not exactly follow the computer programming language.
- Make sure all of the applicable elements are in the pseudocode. Even though you may not need some of the more technical items, like variable declarations, you will still need to represent every task and element clearly in the text.

6. Review the pseudocode. Once the pseudocode describes the process reasonably well, without gross errors, review it with any other stakeholders in the project. Ask your team members to give you feedback on which parts of the pseudocode need improvement. Descriptions of processes are often incomplete, so this will help fill in the details of the process. If you are working on the code all by yourself, read through what you have written and consider asking someone else to proofread it.

- If your team does not approve the pseudocode, rewrite it for clarity. Ask your team what went wrong: are your steps just unclear, or did you forget to include an important piece of the process?

7. Save your pseudocode. Once you and your team have approved the pseudocode, save it in an archive. When you write the actual computer-readable code, be sure to include the pseudocode as a comment in the computer code file. Again, begin comments with / / so that the computer does not read them.

Part 5

Translating Pseudocode to a Programming Language

1. Trace the pseudocode and understand how it works. The pseudocode presents you an algorithm. For instance, the code might sort an array list in alphabetical order. The basic, "genetic" code will guide you as you build out the algorithm in your preferred programming language.

2. Use coding elements that fit your programming language. These elements might include declaration of variables, if statements, and loop statements. Each procedure line can be implemented in many different ways. Your options depend on the level of your programming language.

- For example, try to display data for the user to see. You can use a notification window to display the data, or you can use the existing graphical interface on which you are designing.

3. Implement the pseudocode. Write the pseudocode neatly, simply and efficiently. A well-written pseudocode could make the entire algorithm more efficient and error-free when you launch the program.

4. Re-trace and compare the actual code to the pseudocode. Make sure that your actual, implemented code follows the instructions laid out by the pseudocode. For example: if the Pseudocode accepts input and output, try all possible inputs, and compare the output of your implemented code to the output computed from the pseudocode. You can ask a fellow programmer to do the tracing or recommend a better method to your code.

Chapter 4

Object Oriented Approach to Programming

Object oriented programing is the programing where each object has a set of variables that can store relevant data. The programs designed by this programming paradigm consists of objects which can interact with each other. The topics discussed in the chapter are of great importance to broaden the existing knowledge on programming languages.

Assembly Language

An assembly (or assembler) language, often abbreviated asm, is a low-level programming language for a computer, or other programmable device, in which there is a very strong (but often not one-to-one) correspondence between the language and the architecture's machine code instructions. Each assembly language is specific to a particular computer architecture. In contrast, most high-level programming languages are generally portable across multiple architectures but require interpreting or compiling. Assembly language may also be called *symbolic machine code*.

Assembly language is converted into executable machine code by a utility program referred to as an *assembler*. The conversion process is referred to as *assembly*, or *assembling* the source code. *Assembly time* is the computational step where an assembler is run.

Assembly language uses a mnemonic to represent each low-level machine instruction or opcode, typically also each architectural register, flag, etc. Many operations require one or more operands in order to form a complete instruction and most assemblers can take expressions of numbers and named constants as well as registers and labels as operands, freeing the programmer from tedious repetitive calculations. Depending on the architecture, these elements may also be combined for specific instructions or addressing modes using offsets or other data as well as fixed addresses. Many assemblers offer additional mechanisms to facilitate program development, to control the assembly process, and to aid debugging.

How to start Programming in Assembly

Assembly programming is often a crucial starting point when computer programmers are learning their craft. Assembly language (also known as ASM) is a programming language for computers and other devices, and it's generally considered a low-level variant when compared to more advanced languages that offer additional functionality. Once you've written the code, an assembler converts it into machine code (1s and 0s). While the applications for assembly programming have grown more limited given the growing complexity of processors, Assembly remains useful for a number of purposes including writing code for stand-alone executables or device drivers.

Part 1

Familiarizing yourself with Assembly Language

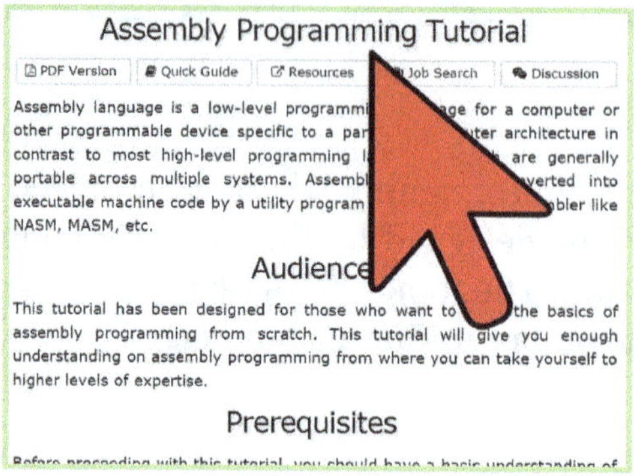

1. Read up on Assembly Language. Before embarking upon any attempt to write code, it's always a good idea to first understand the language itself. There are a number of available resources ranging from textbooks to online guides.

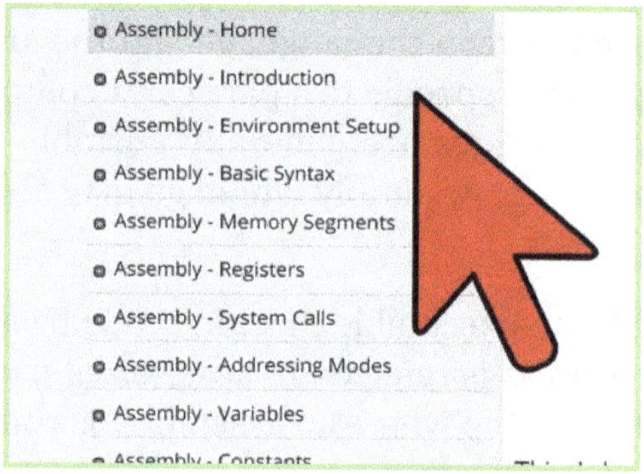

2. Learn basic terms. For example, you'll want to know that an IDE (integrated development environment) provides a coding interface that handles things like text editing, debugging and compiling. You may also wish to better understand the way assembly actually works, like the fact that "registers" are what store the numbers associated with program code. Better understanding terminology will make it easier to learn the code-writing process itself.

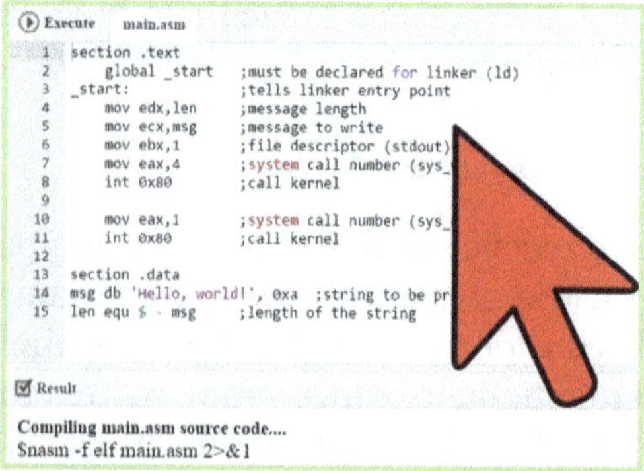

3. Decide whether assemblers are right for you. Remember that there are a number of programming languages, including some that provide far more functionality than assembly. There are,

however, still a range of applications for which assembly is useful—from creating standalone executables for telephone firmware and air-conditioning control systems to developing certain processor-specific instructions.

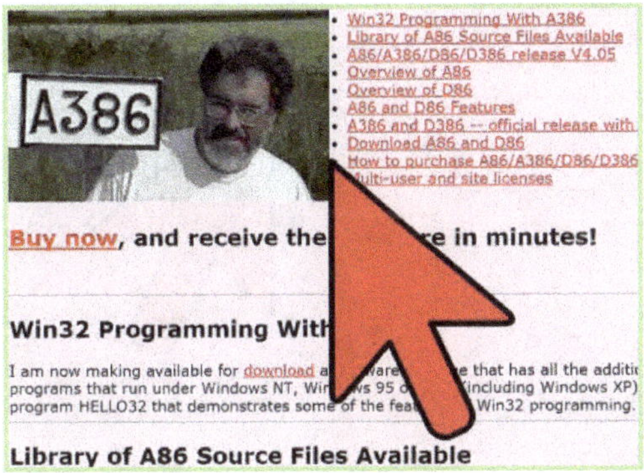

4. Determine which assembler you wish to use. Assemblers like A86, NASM or GNU generally perform less complex functions and may be appropriate starting points for beginners. Every assembler works a bit differently, so subsequent instruction will work under the assumption that you're using MASM (Microsoft Macro Assembler)—a basic assembler that works with Windows operating systems. It uses x86 assembly language and Intel syntax.

Part 2

Downloading and Installing the Assembler and IDE

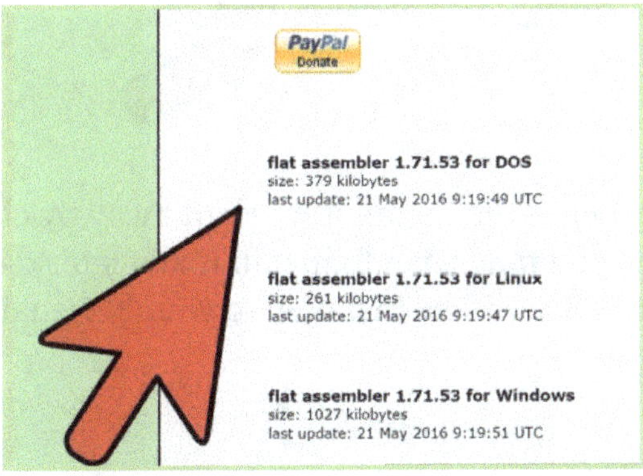

1. Download the assembler itself. You can find the latest version of MASM contained in Visual Studio Enterprise 2015 (a comprehensive IDE including a number of tools), but the more basic original version (MASM 8.0). MASM 8.0 is free to download. Note that some assemblers—like Flat Assembler—can be used on multiple operating systems including Windows, DOS and Linux. Other assemblers—including Netwide Assembler (NASM) or GNU Assembler (GAS)—will work with Mac operating systems.

- To download MASM 8.0, simply click on the Download button near the top of the page referenced in this step.
- System requirements will vary depending on the assembler you select, but MASM 8.0 requires Windows 2000 Service Pack 3, Windows Server 2003 or Windows XP Service Pack 2.

- Installing MASM 8.0 will also require that you have previously downloaded and installed Visual C++ 2005 Express Edition.

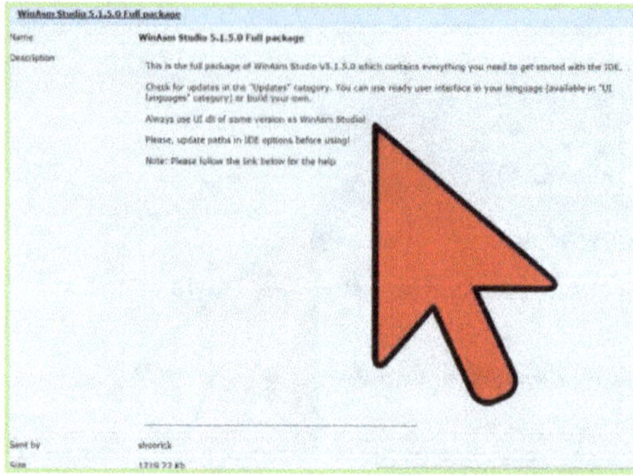

2. Download an IDE. Simply perform a search for "WinAsm download" to find and install the WinAsm IDE, which generally works well with MASM. Other IDEs may be more appropriate depending on which programming language you're using. One popular alternative is RadAsm.

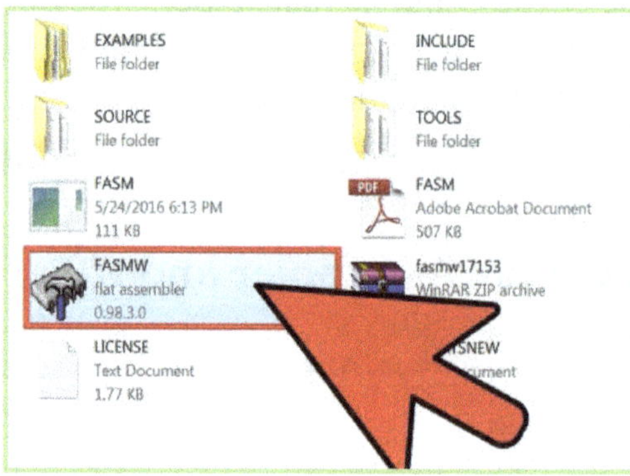

3. Install MASM 8.0. You may begin the installation right away by clicking Run once the program has downloaded. Alternatively, you may wish to install it at a later date, in which case simply click Save. Upon clicking Run, MASM 8.0 will be installed to your "[Visual C++ Express]\bin" directory and labeled ml.exe.

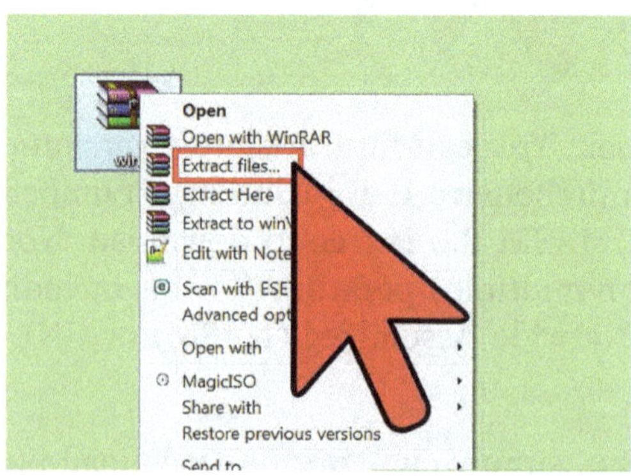

4. Install your IDE. After WinAsm has been downloaded, you simply extract the files and copy them to your "c:\program files\" folder. You may also wish to place a shortcut on your desktop in order for easier access.

5. Configure Your IDE. First, launch the WinAsm program. If you've placed a shortcut on your desktop, simply double-click it. Note that this process will differ if you're using another assembler or IDE.

6. Integrate WinAsm with MASM 8.0. Begin by clicking on WinAsm's Tools tab, selecting Options from said tab and finally selecting the Files and Paths tab. Then change the first three entries (referencing paths) to your MASM installation folder. When finished, click OK.

- Upon adjusting information under the Files and Paths tab, the first three entries should read as follows. The Binary Path should be C:\Masm32\Bin; the Include Path should be C:\Masm32\Include; and the Library Path should be C:\Masm32\Bin.

Part 3

Writing Code

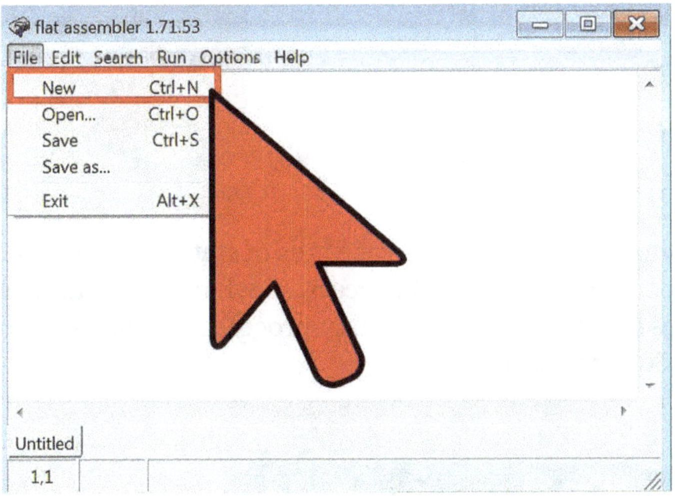

1. Start writing code. Begin by launching WinAsm and clicking on the File tab. Then select New Projects, and you'll see several options. Those options include Console Application and Standard EXE. If you're attempting created a GUI (graphical user interface) based application, for example, you'd select the latter.

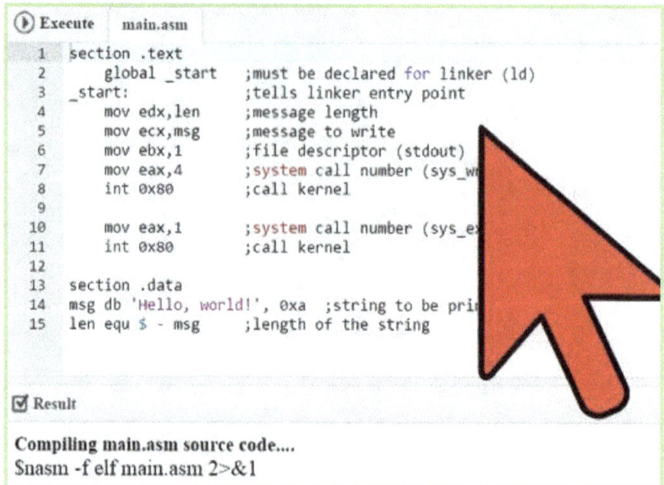

2. Use assembly program structure. A typical structure might include a line defining architecture, a data section (section.data) including initialized data or constants, a bss section (section.bss) that declares variables and a text section (section.text) in which you place your actual program code. That final section always begins with a global _start declaration. Each sequence is known as a block of code.

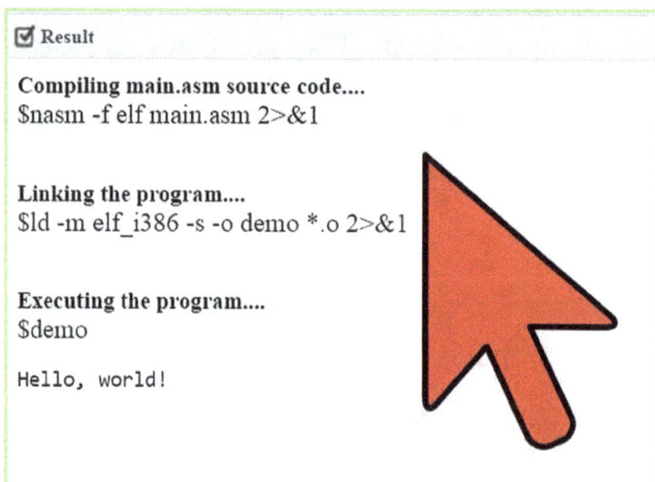

3. Understand basic commands. There are three kinds of statements in assembly language: executable instructions or instructions (these tell processors what to do via operation code), assembler directives or pseudo-ops (these describe assembly processes to the assembler) and macros (these serve as a text-substitution mechanism).

Object-oriented Programming

Object-oriented programming (OOP) is a programming paradigm based on the concept of "objects", which may contain data, in the form of fields, often known as *attributes;* and code, in the form of procedures, often known as *methods.* A feature of objects is that an object's procedures can access and often modify the data fields of the object with which they are associated (objects have a notion of "this" or "self"). In OOP, computer programs are designed by making them out of objects that interact with one another. There is significant diversity of OOP languages, but the most popular ones are class-based, meaning that objects are instances of classes, which typically also determine their type.

Many of the most widely used programming languages (such as C++, Object Pascal, Java, Python etc.) are multi-paradigm programming languages that support object-oriented programming to a greater or lesser degree, typically in combination with imperative, procedural programming. Significant object-oriented languages include Java, C++, C#, Python, PHP, Ruby, Perl, Object Pascal, Objective-C, Dart, Swift, Scala, Common Lisp, and Smalltalk.

Features

Object-oriented programming uses objects, but not all of the associated techniques and structures are supported directly in languages that claim to support OOP. The features listed below are, however, common among languages considered strongly class- and object-oriented (or multi-paradigm with OOP support), with notable exceptions mentioned.

Shared with Non-OOP Predecessor Languages

Object-oriented programming languages typically share low-level features with high-level procedural programming languages (which were invented first). The fundamental tools that can be used to construct a program include:

- Variables that can store information formatted in a small number of built-in data types like integers and alphanumeric characters. This may include data structures like strings, lists, and hash tables that are either built-in or result from combining variables using memory pointers
- Procedures – also known as functions, methods, routines, or subroutines – that take input, generate output, and manipulate data. Modern languages include structured programming constructs like loops and conditionals.

Modular programming support provides the ability to group procedures into files and modules for organizational purposes. Modules are namespaced so code in one module will not be accidentally confused with the same procedure or variable name in another file or module.

Objects and Classes

Languages that support object-oriented programming typically use inheritance for code reuse and extensibility in the form of either classes or prototypes. Those that use classes support two main concepts:

- Classes – the definitions for the data format and available procedures for a given type or class of object; may also contain data and procedures (known as class methods) themselves, i.e. classes contains the data members and member functions
- Objects – instances of classes

Objects sometimes correspond to things found in the real world. For example, a graphics program may have objects such as "circle", "square", "menu". An online shopping system might have objects such as "shopping cart", "customer", and "product". Sometimes objects represent more abstract entities, like an object that represents an open file, or an object that provides the service of translating measurements from U.S. customary to metric.

Each object is said to be an instance of a particular class (for example, an object with its name field set to "Mary" might be an instance of class Employee). Procedures in object-oriented programming are known as methods; variables are also known as fields, members, attributes, or properties. This leads to the following terms:

- Class variables – belong to the *class as a whole*; there is only one copy of each one
- Instance variables or attributes – data that belongs to individual *objects*; every object has its own copy of each one
- Member variables – refers to both the class and instance variables that are defined by a particular class
- Class methods – belong to the *class as a whole* and have access only to class variables and inputs from the procedure call
- Instance methods – belong to *individual objects*, and have access to instance variables for the specific object they are called on, inputs, and class variables

Objects are accessed somewhat like variables with complex internal structure, and in many languages are effectively pointers, serving as actual references to a single instance of said object in memory within a heap or stack. They provide a layer of abstraction which can be used to separate internal from external code. External code can use an object by calling a specific instance method with a certain set of input parameters, read an instance variable, or write to an instance variable. Objects are created by calling a special type of method in the class known as a constructor. A program may create many instances of the same class as it runs, which operate independently. This is an easy way for the same procedures to be used on different sets of data.

Object-oriented programming that uses classes is sometimes called class-based programming, while prototype-based programming does not typically use classes. As a result, a significantly different yet analogous terminology is used to define the concepts of *object* and *instance*.

In some languages classes and objects can be composed using other concepts like traits and mixins.

Dynamic Dispatch/Message Passing

It is the responsibility of the object, not any external code, to select the procedural code to execute in response to a method call, typically by looking up the method at run time in a table associated with the object. This feature is known as dynamic dispatch, and distinguishes an object from an abstract data type (or module), which has a fixed (static) implementation of the operations for all instances. If there are multiple methods that might be run for a given name, it is known as multiple dispatch.

A method call is also known as *message passing*. It is conceptualized as a message (the name of the method and its input parameters) being passed to the object for dispatch.

Encapsulation

Encapsulation is an object-oriented programming concept that binds together the data and functions that manipulate the data, and that keeps both safe from outside interference and misuse. Data encapsulation led to the important OOP concept of data hiding.

If a class does not allow calling code to access internal object data and permits access through methods only, this is a strong form of abstraction or information hiding known as encapsulation. Some languages (Java, for example) let classes enforce access restrictions explicitly, for example denoting internal data with the private keyword and designating methods intended for use by code outside the class with the public keyword. Methods may also be designed public, private, or intermediate levels such as protected (which allows access from the same class and its subclasses, but not objects of a different class). In other languages (like Python) this is enforced only by convention (for example, private methods may have names that start with an underscore). Encapsulation prevents external code from being concerned with the internal workings of an object. This facilitates code refactoring, for example allowing the author of the class to change how objects of that class represent their data internally without changing any external code (as long as "public" method calls work the same way). It also encourages programmers to put all the code that is concerned with a certain set of data in the same class, which organizes it for easy comprehension by other programmers. Encapsulation is a technique that encourages decoupling.

Composition, Inheritance and Delegation

Objects can contain other objects in their instance variables; this is known as object composition. For example, an object in the Employee class might contain (point to) an object in the Address class, in addition to its own instance variables like "first_name" and "position". Object composition is used to represent "has-a" relationships: every employee has an address, so every Employee object has a place to store an Address object.

Languages that support classes almost always support inheritance. This allows classes to be arranged in a hierarchy that represents "is-a-type-of" relationships. For example, class Employee might inherit from class Person. All the data and methods available to the parent class also appear in the child class with the same names. For example, class Person might define variables "first_name" and "last_name" with method "make_full_name()". These will also be available in class Employee, which might add the variables "position" and "salary". This technique allows easy re-use of the same procedures and data definitions, in addition to potentially mirroring real-world relationships in an intuitive way. Rather than utilizing database tables and programming subroutines, the developer utilizes objects the user may be more familiar with: objects from their application domain.

Subclasses can override the methods defined by superclasses. Multiple inheritance is allowed in some languages, though this can make resolving overrides complicated. Some languages have special support for mixins, though in any language with multiple inheritance, a mixin is simply a class that does not represent an is-a-type-of relationship. Mixins are typically used to add the same methods to multiple classes. For example, class UnicodeConversionMixin might provide a method unicode_to_ascii() when included in class FileReader and class WebPageScraper, which don't share a common parent.

Abstract classes cannot be instantiated into objects; they exist only for the purpose of inheritance into other "concrete" classes which can be instantiated. In Java, the final keyword can be used to prevent a class from being subclassed.

The doctrine of composition over inheritance advocates implementing has-a relationships using composition instead of inheritance. For example, instead of inheriting from class Person, class Employee could give each Employee object an internal Person object, which it then has the opportunity to hide from external code even if class Person has many public attributes or methods. Some languages, like Go do not support inheritance at all.

The "open/closed principle" advocates that classes and functions "should be open for extension, but closed for modification".

Delegation is another language feature that can be used as an alternative to inheritance.

Polymorphism

Subtyping, a form of polymorphism, is when calling code can be agnostic as to whether an object belongs to a parent class or one of its descendants. For example, a function might call "make_full_name()" on an object, which will work whether the object is of class Person or class Employee. This is another type of abstraction which simplifies code external to the class hierarchy and enables strong separation of concerns.

Open Recursion

In languages that support open recursion, object methods can call other methods on the same object (including themselves), typically using a special variable or keyword called this or self. This variable is *late-bound*; it allows a method defined in one class to invoke another method that is defined later, in some subclass thereof.

OOP Languages

Simula (1967) is generally accepted as being the first language with the primary features of an object-oriented language. It was created for making simulation programs, in which what came to be called objects were the most important information representation. Smalltalk (1972 to 1980) is another early example, and the one with which much of the theory of OOP was developed. Concerning the degree of object orientation, the following distinctions can be made:

- Languages called "pure" OO languages, because everything in them is treated consistently as an object, from primitives such as characters and punctuation, all the way up to whole classes, prototypes, blocks, modules, etc. They were designed specifically to facilitate, even enforce, OO methods. Examples: Python, Ruby, Scala, Smalltalk, Eiffel, Emerald, JADE, Self.
- Languages designed mainly for OO programming, but with some procedural elements. Examples: Java, C++, C#, Delphi/Object Pascal, VB.NET.

- Languages that are historically procedural languages, but have been extended with some OO features. Examples: PHP, Perl, Visual Basic (derived from BASIC), MATLAB, COBOL 2002, Fortran 2003, ABAP, Ada 95, Pascal.
- Languages with most of the features of objects (classes, methods, inheritance), but in a distinctly original form. Examples: Oberon (Oberon-1 or Oberon-2).
- Languages with abstract data type support which may be used to resemble OO programming, but without all features of object-orientation. This includes object-*based* and prototype-based languages. Examples: JavaScript, Lua, Modula-2, CLU.
- Chameleon languages that support multiple paradigms, including OO. Tcl stands out among these for TclOO, a hybrid object system that supports both prototype-based programming and class-based OO.

OOP in Dynamic Languages

In recent years, object-oriented programming has become especially popular in dynamic programming languages. Python, PowerShell, Ruby and Groovy are dynamic languages built on OOP principles, while Perl and PHP have been adding object-oriented features since Perl 5 and PHP 4, and ColdFusion since version 6.

The Document Object Model of HTML, XHTML, and XML documents on the Internet has bindings to the popular JavaScript/ECMAScript language. JavaScript is perhaps the best known prototype-based programming language, which employs cloning from prototypes rather than inheriting from a class (contrast to class-based programming). Another scripting language that takes this approach is Lua.

OOP in a Network Protocol

The messages that flow between computers to request services in a client-server environment can be designed as the linearizations of objects defined by class objects known to both the client and the server. For example, a simple linearized object would consist of a length field, a code point identifying the class, and a data value. A more complex example would be a command consisting of the length and code point of the command and values consisting of linearized objects representing the command's parameters. Each such command must be directed by the server to an object whose class (or superclass) recognizes the command and is able to provide the requested service. Clients and servers are best modeled as complex object-oriented structures. Distributed Data Management Architecture (DDM) took this approach and used class objects to define objects at four levels of a formal hierarchy:

- Fields defining the data values that form messages, such as their length, codepoint and data values.
- Objects and collections of objects similar to what would be found in a Smalltalk program for messages and parameters.
- Managers similar to AS/400 objects, such as a directory to files and files consisting of metadata and records. Managers conceptually provide memory and processing resources for their contained objects.

- A client or server consisting of all the managers necessary to implement a full processing environment, supporting such aspects as directory services, security and concurrency control.

The initial version of DDM defined distributed file services. It was later extended to be the foundation of Distributed Relational Database Architecture (DRDA).

Design Patterns

Challenges of object-oriented design are addressed by several methodologies. Most common is known as the design patterns codified by Gamma *et al.*. More broadly, the term "design patterns" can be used to refer to any general, repeatable solution to a commonly occurring problem in software design. Some of these commonly occurring problems have implications and solutions particular to object-oriented development.

Inheritance and Behavioral Subtyping

It is intuitive to assume that inheritance creates a semantic "is a" relationship, and thus to infer that objects instantiated from subclasses can always be *safely* used instead of those instantiated from the superclass. This intuition is unfortunately false in most OOP languages, in particular in all those that allow mutable objects. Subtype polymorphism as enforced by the type checker in OOP languages (with mutable objects) cannot guarantee behavioral subtyping in any context. Behavioral subtyping is undecidable in general, so it cannot be implemented by a program (compiler). Class or object hierarchies must be carefully designed, considering possible incorrect uses that cannot be detected syntactically. This issue is known as the Liskov substitution principle.

Gang of Four Design Patterns

Design Patterns: Elements of Reusable Object-Oriented Software is an influential book published in 1995 by Erich Gamma, Richard Helm, Ralph Johnson, and John Vlissides, often referred to humorously as the "Gang of Four". Along with exploring the capabilities and pitfalls of object-oriented programming, it describes 23 common programming problems and patterns for solving them. As of April 2007, the book was in its 36th printing.

The book describes the following patterns:

- *Creational patterns* (5): Factory method pattern, Abstract factory pattern, Singleton pattern, Builder pattern, Prototype pattern
- *Structural patterns* (7): Adapter pattern, Bridge pattern, Composite pattern, Decorator pattern, Facade pattern, Flyweight pattern, Proxy pattern
- *Behavioral patterns* (11): Chain-of-responsibility pattern, Command pattern, Interpreter pattern, Iterator pattern, Mediator pattern, Memento pattern, Observer pattern, State pattern, Strategy pattern, Template method pattern, Visitor pattern

Object-orientation and Databases

Both object-oriented programming and relational database management systems (RDBMSs) are extremely common in software today. Since relational databases don't store objects directly, there is a general need to bridge the two worlds. The problem of bridging object-oriented programming accesses and data patterns with relational databases is known as object-relational impedance mismatch. There are a number of approaches to cope with this problem, but no general solution without downsides. One of the most common approaches is object-relational mapping, as found in IDE languages such as Visual FoxPro and libraries such as Java Data Objects and Ruby on Rails' ActiveRecord.

There are also object databases that can be used to replace RDBMSs, but these have not been as technically and commercially successful as RDBMSs.

Real-world Modeling and Relationships

OOP can be used to associate real-world objects and processes with digital counterparts. However, not everyone agrees that OOP facilitates direct real-world mapping (see Criticism section) or that real-world mapping is even a worthy goal; Bertrand Meyer argues in *Object-Oriented Software Construction* that a program is not a model of the world but a model of some part of the world; "Reality is a cousin twice removed". At the same time, some principal limitations of OOP have been noted. For example, the circle-ellipse problem is difficult to handle using OOP's concept of inheritance.

However, Niklaus Wirth (who popularized the adage now known as Wirth's law: "Software is getting slower more rapidly than hardware becomes faster") said of OOP in his paper, "Good Ideas through the Looking Glass", "This paradigm closely reflects the structure of systems 'in the real world', and it is therefore well suited to model complex systems with complex behaviours" (contrast KISS principle).

Steve Yegge and others noted that natural languages lack the OOP approach of strictly prioritizing *things* (objects/nouns) before *actions* (methods/verbs). This problem may cause OOP to suffer more convoluted solutions than procedural programming.

OOP and Control Flow

OOP was developed to increase the reusability and maintainability of source code. Transparent representation of the control flow had no priority and was meant to be handled by a compiler. With the increasing relevance of parallel hardware and multithreaded coding, developing transparent control flow becomes more important, something hard to achieve with OOP.

Responsibility- vs. Data-driven Design

Responsibility-driven design defines classes in terms of a contract, that is, a class should be defined around a responsibility and the information that it shares. This is contrasted by Wirfs-Brock and Wilkerson with data-driven design, where classes are defined around the data-structures that must be held. The authors hold that responsibility-driven design is preferable.

SOLID and GRASP Guidelines

SOLID is a mnemonic invented by Michael Feathers that stands for and advocates five programming practices:

- Single responsibility principle

- Open/closed principle
- Liskov substitution principle
- Interface segregation principle
- Dependency inversion principle

GRASP (General Responsibility Assignment Software Patterns) is another set of guidelines advocated by Craig Larman.

Formal Semantics

Objects are the run-time entities in an object-oriented system. They may represent a person, a place, a bank account, a table of data, or any item that the program has to handle.

There have been several attempts at formalizing the concepts used in object-oriented programming. The following concepts and constructs have been used as interpretations of OOP concepts:

- co algebraic data types
- abstract data types (which have existential types) allow the definition of modules but these do not support dynamic dispatch
- recursive types
- encapsulated state
- inheritance
- records are basis for understanding objects if function literals can be stored in fields (like in functional-programming languages), but the actual calculi need be considerably more complex to incorporate essential features of OOP. Several extensions of System $F_{<:}$ that deal with mutable objects have been studied; these allow both subtype polymorphism and parametric polymorphism (generics)

Attempts to find a consensus definition or theory behind objects have not proven very successful and often diverge widely. For example, some definitions focus on mental activities, and some on program structuring. One of the simpler definitions is that OOP is the act of using "map" data structures or arrays that can contain functions and pointers to other maps, all with some syntactic and scoping sugar on top. Inheritance can be performed by cloning the maps (sometimes called "prototyping").

How to Understand Object Oriented Programming

Understanding object-oriented programming can be a difficult task no matter what language you are using. However, understanding the underlying concept can make programmatic understanding and usage much easier.

Steps

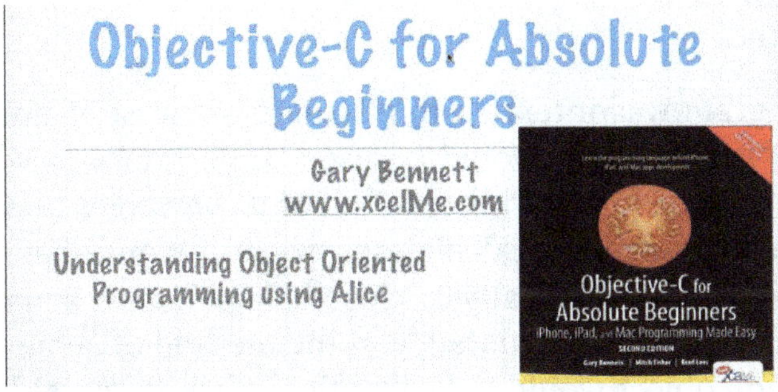

1. Understand that there are generally three main parts to object oriented programming. These are Abstraction, Inheritance and Encapsulation.

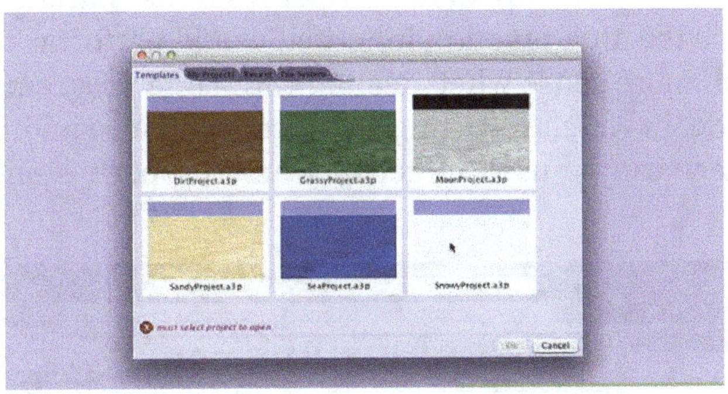

2. In Object-Oriented Programming Languages, programs are designed with the concept of objects, where each object contains its own set of variables to store data about or relevant to that object, and functions to perform action (like outputting text or making an API call to the operating system), perform calculations, add data to variables inside the object, etc. This contrasts with Structured Programming Languages, in which programs are designed with collections of functions that are called in different parts of the program, more like a script or job list.

3. Objects represent various things in a program, like a Square. This is called Abstraction. An object for a square in a math program would have a set of variables, length and width, that can only be accessed by functions inside the object. This is called Encapsulation. This concept reduces the chance of 'breaking' something when programming, as when done properly only the object itself can directly manipulate its variables, so debugging problems is easier. The next part of an object, functions, represent things that the object can do or ways to interact with it. In the case of the square object, a function called "area" would calculate the area of the square the object represents, using the contents of the length and width variables inside the object. Those variables may already

contain the length and width of the square, in the case they did not, the area function might also take user input for the length and width of the square the object represents and then calculate the area based on the user input.

4. In the case a math program was intended to calculate the area of not only squares, but other shapes, such as a circle, "Inheritance" would be used. Inheritance is when an object is created based on another object, so therefore, it "inherits" all of its variables and functions. For example, an extension to the earlier square area calculation program would have a main object, called a polygon. In geometry, a polygon is basically a "closed shape", i.e a square, triangle, circle, cube, etc. All polygons can have their area calculated, just the method of achieving such is different. So, in our program, the polygon object would have length and width variables, and an area function. Since a polygon is not actually a shape, but a class of shapes, the area function would not do anything. When you want to create an object for a particular kind of polygon (i.e a triangle), you would use inheritance to create the object with all the properties of its "parent", the polygon object. You would then cite the actions the area function inherited would perform. This concept is called "Inheritance". It makes much more sense when dealing with large programs, where objects typically contain lots of lines of code, in which rewriting an object similar to another would be tedious and pointless, when Inheritance can be used to get the same properties and methods of the parent object.

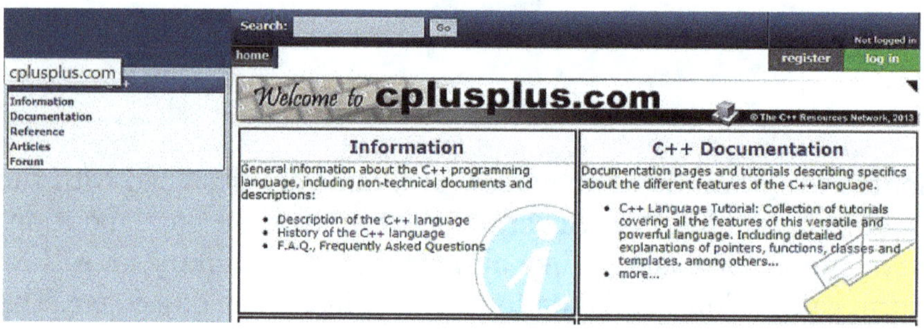

5. Many programmers have a hard time deciding which programming language to use. In Object-Oriented Programming, the two big languages are Java and C++. Both are good languages for various things. Many people will try to tell you that one is good and the other is bad, though you should try both and decide for yourself which one you like more.

Chapter 5 Programming in C and C++

C and C++ are complex computer languages that are very popular. They are also compiled languages which require compilers to run them. C and C++ programming languages are best understood in confluence with the major topics listed in the following chapter.

C (Programming Language)

C is a general-purpose, imperative computer programming language, supporting structured programming, lexical variable scope and recursion, while a static type system prevents many unintended operations. By design, C provides constructs that map efficiently to typical machine instructions, and therefore it has found lasting use in applications that had formerly been coded in assembly language, including operating systems, as well as various application software for computers ranging from supercomputers to embedded systems.

C was originally developed by Dennis Ritchie between 1969 and 1973 at Bell Labs, and used to re-implement the Unix operating system. It has since become one of the most widely used programming languages of all time, with C compilers from various vendors available for the majority of existing computer architectures and operating systems. C has been standardized by the American National Standards Institute (ANSI) since 1989 and subsequently by the International Organization for Standardization (ISO).

C is an imperative procedural language. It was designed to be compiled using a relatively straightforward compiler, to provide low-level access to memory, to provide language constructs that map efficiently to machine instructions, and to require minimal run-time support. Despite its low-level capabilities, the language was designed to encourage cross-platform programming. A standards-compliant and portably written C program can be compiled for a very wide variety of computer platforms and operating systems with few changes to its source code. The language has become available on a very wide range of platforms, from embedded microcontrollers to supercomputers.

Overview

Like most imperative languages in the ALGOL tradition, C has facilities for structured programming and allows lexical variable scope and recursion, while a static type system prevents many unintended operations. In C, all executable code is contained within subroutines, which are called "functions" (although not in the strict sense of functional programming). Function parameters are always passed by value. Pass-by-reference is simulated in C by explicitly passing pointer values. C program source text is free-format, using the semicolon as a statement terminator and curly braces for grouping blocks of statements.

The C language also exhibits the following characteristics:

- There is a small, fixed number of keywords, including a full set of flow of control primitives: `for`, `if/else`, `while`, `switch`, and `do/while`. User-defined names are not distinguished from keywords by any kind of sigil.
- There are a large number of arithmetical and logical operators, such as +, +=, `++`, `&`, `~`, etc.
- More than one assignment may be performed in a single statement.
- Function return values can be ignored when not needed.
- Typing is static, but weakly enforced: all data has a type, but implicit conversions may be performed.
- Declaration syntax mimics usage context. C has no "define" keyword; instead, a statement beginning with the name of a type is taken as a declaration. There is no "function" keyword; instead, a function is indicated by the parentheses of an argument list.
- User-defined (`typedef`) and compound types are possible.
    - Heterogeneous aggregate data types (`struct`) allow related data elements to be accessed and assigned as a unit.
    - Array indexing is a secondary notation, defined in terms of pointer arithmetic. Unlike structs, arrays are not first-class objects; they cannot be assigned or compared using single built-in operators. There is no "array" keyword, in use or definition; instead, square brackets indicate arrays syntactically, for example `month`.
    - Enumerated types are possible with the `enum` keyword. They are not tagged, and are freely interconvertible with integers.
    - Strings are not a separate data type, but are conventionally implemented as null-terminated arrays of characters.
- Low-level access to computer memory is possible by converting machine addresses to typed pointers.
- Procedures (subroutines not returning values) are a special case of function, with an untyped return type `void`.
- Functions may not be defined within the lexical scope of other functions.
- Function and data pointers permit *ad hoc* run-time polymorphism.
- A preprocessor performs macro definition, source code file inclusion, and conditional compilation.
- There is a basic form of modularity: files can be compiled separately and linked together, with control over which functions and data objects are visible to other files via `static` and `extern` attributes.
- Complex functionality such as I/O, string manipulation, and mathematical functions are consistently delegated to library routines.

While C does not include some features found in some other languages, such as object orientation or garbage collection, such features can be implemented or emulated in C, often by way of external libraries (e.g., the Boehm garbage collector or the GLib Object System).

Relations to other Languages

Many later languages have borrowed directly or indirectly from C, including C++, D, Go, Rust, Java, JavaScript, Limbo, LPC, C#, Objective-C, Perl, PHP, Python, Swift, Verilog (hardware description language), and Unix's C shell. These languages have drawn many of their control structures and other basic features from C. Most of them (with Python being the most dramatic exception) are also very syntactically similar to C in general, and they tend to combine the recognizable expression and statement syntax of C with underlying type systems, data models, and semantics that can be radically different.

Syntax

C has a formal grammar specified by the C standard. Line endings are generally not significant in C; however, line boundaries do have significance during the preprocessing phase. Comments may appear either between the delimiters `/*` and `*/`, or (since C99) following `//` until the end of the line. Comments delimited by `/*` and `*/` do not nest, and these sequences of characters are not interpreted as comment delimiters if they appear inside string or character literals.

C source files contain declarations and function definitions. Function definitions, in turn, contain declarations and statements. Declarations either define new types using keywords such as `struct`, `union`, and `enum`, or assign types to and perhaps reserve storage for new variables, usually by writing the type followed by the variable name. Keywords such as `char` and `int` specify built-in types. Sections of code are enclosed in braces (`{` and `}`, sometimes called "curly brackets") to limit the scope of declarations and to act as a single statement for control structures.

As an imperative language, C uses *statements* to specify actions. The most common statement is an *expression statement*, consisting of an expression to be evaluated, followed by a semicolon; as a side effect of the evaluation, functions may be called and variables may be assigned new values. To modify the normal sequential execution of statements, C provides several control-flow statements identified by reserved keywords. Structured programming is supported by `if(-else)` conditional execution and by `do-while`, `while`, and `for` iterative execution (looping). The `for` statement has separate initialization, testing, and reinitialization expressions, any or all of which can be omitted. `break` and `continue` can be used to leave the innermost enclosing loop statement or skip to its reinitialization. There is also a non-structured `goto` statement which branches directly to the designated label within the function. `switch` selects a `case` to be executed based on the value of an integer expression.

Expressions can use a variety of built-in operators and may contain function calls. The order in which arguments to functions and operands to most operators are evaluated is unspecified. The evaluations may even be interleaved. However, all side effects (including storage to variables) will occur before the next "sequence point"; sequence points include the end of each expression statement, and the entry to and return from each function call. Sequence points also occur during evaluation of expressions containing certain operators (`&&`, `||`, `?:` and the comma operator). This permits a high degree of object code optimization by the compiler, but requires C programmers to take more care to obtain reliable results than is needed for other programming languages.

Kernighan and Ritchie say in the Introduction of *The C Programming Language*: "C, like any other language, has its blemishes. Some of the operators have the wrong precedence; some parts of the syntax could be better." The C standard did not attempt to correct many of these blemishes, because of the impact of such changes on already existing software.

Character Set

The basic C source character set includes the following characters:

- Lowercase and uppercase letters of ISO Basic Latin Alphabet: a–z A–Z
- Decimal digits: 0–9
- Graphic characters: `! " # % & ' ( ) * + , - . / : ; < = > ? [ \ ] ^ _ { | } ~`
- Whitespace characters: *space, horizontal tab, vertical tab, form feed, newline*

Newline indicates the end of a text line; it need not correspond to an actual single character, although for convenience C treats it as one.

Additional multi-byte encoded characters may be used in string literals, but they are not entirely portable. The latest C standard (C11) allows multi-national Unicode characters to be embedded portably within C source text by using `\uXXXX` or `\UXXXXXXXX` encoding (where the X denotes a hexadecimal character), although this feature is not yet widely implemented.

The basic C execution character set contains the same characters, along with representations for alert, backspace, and carriage return. Run-time support for extended character sets has increased with each revision of the C standard.

Reserved Words

C89 has 32 reserved words, also known as keywords, which are the words that cannot be used for any purposes other than those for which they are predefined:

auto	double	int	struct
break	else	long	switch
case	enum	register	typedef
char	extern	return	union
const	float	short	unsigned
continue	for	signed	void
default	goto	sizeof	volatile
do	if	static	while

C99 reserved five more words:

_Bool	_Imaginary	restrict
_Complex	inline	

C11 reserved seven more words:

_Alignas	_Atomic	_Noreturn	_Thread_local
_Alignof	_Generic	_Static_assert	

Most of the recently reserved words begin with an underscore followed by a capital letter, because identifiers of that form were previously reserved by the C standard for use only by implementations. Since existing program source code should not have been using these identifiers, it would not be affected when C implementations started supporting these extensions to the programming language. Some standard headers do define more convenient synonyms for underscored identifiers. The language previously included a reserved word called `entry`, but this was seldom implemented, and has now been removed as a reserved word.

Operators

C supports a rich set of operators, which are symbols used within an expression to specify the manipulations to be performed while evaluating that expression. C has operators for:

- arithmetic: +, -, *, /, %
- assignment: =
- augmented assignment: +=, -=, *=, /=, %=, &=, |=, ^=, <<=, >>=
- bitwise logic: ~, &, |, ^
- bitwise shifts: <<, >>
- boolean logic: !, &&, ||
- conditional evaluation: ? :
- equality testing: ==, !=
- calling functions: ( )
- increment and decrement: ++, --
- member selection: ., ->
- object size: sizeof
- order relations: <, <=, >, >=
- reference and dereference: &, *, [ ]
- sequencing: ,

- subexpression grouping: `( )`
- type conversion: `(typename)`

C uses the operator = (used in mathematics to express equality) to indicate assignment, following the precedent of Fortran and PL/I, but unlike ALGOL and its derivatives. C uses the operator == to test for equality. The similarity between these two operators (assignment and equality) may result in the accidental use of one in place of the other, and in many cases, the mistake does not produce an error message (although some compilers produce warnings). For example, the conditional expression `if(a==b+1)` might mistakenly be written as `if(a=b+1)`, which will be evaluated as true if a is not zero after the assignment.

The C operator precedence is not always intuitive. For example, the operator == binds more tightly than (is executed prior to) the operators & (bitwise AND) and | (bitwise OR) in expressions such as `x & 1 == 0`, which must be written as `(x & 1) == 0` if that is the coder's intent.

Data Types

The type system in C is static and weakly typed, which makes it similar to the type system of ALGOL descendants such as Pascal. There are built-in types for integers of various sizes, both signed and unsigned, floating-point numbers, and enumerated types (`enum`). Integer type char is often used for single-byte characters. C99 added a boolean datatype. There are also derived types including arrays, pointers, records (`struct`), and untagged unions (`union`).

C is often used in low-level systems programming where escapes from the type system may be necessary. The compiler attempts to ensure type correctness of most expressions, but the programmer can override the checks in various ways, either by using a *type cast* to explicitly convert a value from one type to another, or by using pointers or unions to reinterpret the underlying bits of a data object in some other way.

Some find C's declaration syntax unintuitive, particularly for function pointers. (Ritchie's idea was to declare identifiers in contexts resembling their use: "declaration reflects use".)

C's *usual arithmetic conversions* allow for efficient code to be generated, but can sometimes produce unexpected results. For example, a comparison of signed and unsigned integers of equal width requires a conversion of the signed value to unsigned. This can generate unexpected results if the signed value is negative.

Pointers

C supports the use of pointers, a type of reference that records the address or location of an object or function in memory. Pointers can be *dereferenced* to access data stored at the address pointed to, or to invoke a pointed-to function. Pointers can be manipulated using assignment or pointer arithmetic. The run-time representation of a pointer value is typically a raw memory address (perhaps augmented by an offset-within-word field), but since a pointer's type includes the type of the thing pointed to, expressions including pointers can be type-checked at compile time. Pointer arithmetic is automatically scaled by the size of the pointed-to data type. Pointers are used for many purposes in C. Text strings are commonly manipulated using pointers into arrays of characters. Dynamic memory allocation is performed using pointers. Many data types, such as trees, are commonly implemented as dynamically allocated `struct` objects linked together using pointers. Pointers to functions are useful for passing functions as arguments to higher-order functions (such as qsort or bsearch) or as callbacks to be invoked by event handlers.

A *null pointer value* explicitly points to no valid location. Dereferencing a null pointer value is undefined, often resulting in a segmentation fault. Null pointer values are useful for indicating special cases such as no "next" pointer in the final node of a linked list, or as an error indication from functions returning pointers. In appropriate contexts in source code, such as for assigning to a pointer variable, a *null pointer constant* can be written as 0, with or without explicit casting to a pointer type, or as the `NULL` macro defined by several standard headers. In conditional contexts, null pointer values evaluate to false, while all other pointer values evaluate to true.

Void pointers (`void *`) point to objects of unspecified type, and can therefore be used as "generic" data pointers. Since the size and type of the pointed-to object is not known, void pointers cannot be dereferenced, nor is pointer arithmetic on them allowed, although they can easily be (and in many contexts implicitly are) converted to and from any other object pointer type.

Careless use of pointers is potentially dangerous. Because they are typically unchecked, a pointer variable can be made to point to any arbitrary location, which can cause undesirable effects. Although properly used pointers point to safe places, they can be made to point to unsafe places by using invalid pointer arithmetic; the objects they point to may continue to be used after deallocation (dangling pointers); they may be used without having been initialized (wild pointers); or they may be directly assigned an unsafe value using a cast, union, or through another corrupt pointer. In general, C is permissive in allowing manipulation of and conversion between pointer types, although compilers typically provide options for various levels of checking. Some other programming languages address these problems by using more restrictive reference types.

Arrays

Array types in C are traditionally of a fixed, static size specified at compile timc. (The more recent C99 standard also allows a form of variable-length arrays.) However, it is also possible to allocate a block of memory (of arbitrary size) at run-time, using the standard library's `malloc` function, and treat it as an array. C's unification of arrays and pointers means that declared arrays and these dynamically allocated simulated arrays are virtually interchangeable.

Since arrays are always accessed (in effect) via pointers, array accesses are typically *not* checked against the underlying array size, although some compilers may provide bounds checking as an option. Array bounds violations are therefore possible and rather common in carelessly written code, and can lead to various repercussions, including illegal memory accesses, corruption of data, buffer overruns, and run-time exceptions. If bounds checking is desired, it must be done manually.

C does not have a special provision for declaring multi-dimensional arrays, but rather relies on recursion within the type system to declare arrays of arrays, which effectively accomplishes the same thing. The index values of the resulting "multi-dimensional array" can be thought of as increasing in row-major order.

Multi-dimensional arrays are commonly used in numerical algorithms (mainly from applied linear algebra) to store matrices. The structure of the C array is well suited to this particular task. However, since arrays are passed merely as pointers, the bounds of the array must be known fixed values or else explicitly passed to any subroutine that requires them, and dynamically sized arrays of arrays cannot be accessed using double indexing. (A workaround for this is to allocate the array with an additional "row vector" of pointers to the columns.)

C99 introduced "variable-length arrays" which address some, but not all, of the issues with ordinary C arrays.

Array–pointer Interchangeability

The subscript notation `x[i]` (where x designates a pointer) is syntactic sugar for `*(x+i)`. Taking advantage of the compiler's knowledge of the pointer type, the address that `x + i` points to is not the base address (pointed to by `x`) incremented by i bytes, but rather is defined to be the base address incremented by `i` multiplied by the size of an element that `x` points to. Thus, `x[i]` designates the `i+1th` element of the array.

Furthermore, in most expression contexts (a notable exception is as operand of `sizeof`), the name of an array is automatically converted to a pointer to the array's first element. This implies that an array is never copied as a whole when named as an argument to a function, but rather only the address of its first element is passed. Therefore, although function calls in C use pass-by-value semantics, arrays are in effect passed by reference.

The size of an element can be determined by applying the operator `sizeof` to any dereferenced element of x, as in `n = sizeof *x` or `n = sizeof x`, and the number of elements in a declared array A can be determined as `sizeof A / sizeof A`. The latter only applies to array names: variables declared with subscripts `(int A)`. Due to the semantics of C, it is not possible to determine the entire size of arrays through pointers to arrays or those created by dynamic allocation (`malloc`); code such as `sizeof arr / sizeof arr` (where `arr` designates a pointer) will not work since the compiler assumes the size of the pointer itself is being requested. Since array name arguments to `sizeof` are not converted to pointers, they do not exhibit such ambiguity. However, arrays created by dynamic allocation are accessed by pointers rather than true array variables, so they suffer from the same `sizeof` issues as array pointers.

Thus, despite this apparent equivalence between array and pointer variables, there is still a distinction to be made between them. Even though the name of an array is, in most expression contexts, converted into a pointer (to its first element), this pointer does not itself occupy any storage; the array name is not an l-value, and its address is a constant, unlike a pointer variable. Consequently, what an array "points to" cannot be changed, and it is impossible to assign a new address to an array name. Array contents may be copied, however, by using the `memcpy` function, or by accessing the individual elements.

Memory Management

One of the most important functions of a programming language is to provide facilities for managing memory and the objects that are stored in memory. C provides three distinct ways to allocate memory for objects:

- Static memory allocation: space for the object is provided in the binary at compile-time; these objects have an extent (or lifetime) as long as the binary which contains them is loaded into memory.
- Automatic memory allocation: temporary objects can be stored on the stack, and this space is automatically freed and reusable after the block in which they are declared is exited.
- Dynamic memory allocation: blocks of memory of arbitrary size can be requested at run-time using library functions such as `malloc` from a region of memory called the `heap`; these blocks persist until subsequently freed for reuse by calling the library function `realloc` or `free`

These three approaches are appropriate in different situations and have various trade-offs. For example, static memory allocation has little allocation overhead, automatic allocation may involve slightly more overhead, and dynamic memory allocation can potentially have a great deal of overhead for both allocation and deallocation. The persistent nature of static objects is useful for maintaining state information across function calls, automatic allocation is easy to use but stack space is typically much more limited and transient than either static memory or heap space, and dynamic memory allocation allows convenient allocation of objects whose size is known only at run-time. Most C programs make extensive use of all three.

Where possible, automatic or static allocation is usually simplest because the storage is managed by the compiler, freeing the programmer of the potentially error-prone chore of manually allocating and releasing storage. However, many data structures can change in size at runtime, and since static allocations (and automatic allocations before C99) must have a fixed size at compile-time, there are many situations in which dynamic allocation is necessary. Prior to the C99 standard, variable-sized arrays were a common example of this. Unlike automatic allocation, which can fail at run time with uncontrolled consequences, the dynamic allocation functions return an indication (in the form of a null pointer value) when the required storage cannot be allocated. (Static allocation that is too large is usually detected by the linker or loader, before the program can even begin execution.)

Unless otherwise specified, static objects contain zero or null pointer values upon program startup. Automatically and dynamically allocated objects are initialized only if an initial value is explicitly specified; otherwise they initially have indeterminate values (typically, whatever bit pattern happens to be present in the storage, which might not even represent a valid value for that type). If the program attempts to access an uninitialized value, the results are undefined. Many modern compilers try to detect and warn about this problem, but both false positives and false negatives can occur.

Another issue is that heap memory allocation has to be synchronized with its actual usage in any program in order for it to be reused as much as possible. For example, if the only pointer to a heap memory allocation goes out of scope or has its value overwritten before `free()` is called, then that memory cannot be recovered for later reuse and is essentially lost to the program, a phenomenon known as a *memory leak*. Conversely, it is possible for memory to be freed but continue to be referenced, leading to unpredictable results. Typically, the symptoms will appear in a portion of the program far removed from the actual error, making it difficult to track down the problem. (Such issues are ameliorated in languages with automatic garbage collection.)

Libraries

The C programming language uses libraries as its primary method of extension. In C, a library is a set of functions contained within a single "archive" file. Each library typically has a header file, which contains the prototypes of the functions contained within the library that may be used by a program, and declarations of special data types and macro symbols used with these functions. In order for a program to use a library, it must include the library's header file, and the library must be linked with the program, which in many cases requires compiler flags (e.g., `-lm`, shorthand for "link the math library").

The most common C library is the C standard library, which is specified by the ISO and ANSI C standards and comes with every C implementation (implementations which target limited environments such as embedded systems may provide only a subset of the standard library). This library supports stream input and output, memory allocation, mathematics, character strings, and time values. Several separate standard headers (for example, `stdio.h`) specify the interfaces for these and other standard library facilities.

Another common set of C library functions are those used by applications specifically targeted for Unix and Unix-like systems, especially functions which provide an interface to the kernel. These functions are detailed in various standards such as POSIX and the Single UNIX Specification.

Since many programs have been written in C, there are a wide variety of other libraries available. Libraries are often written in C because C compilers generate efficient object code; programmers then create interfaces to the library so that the routines can be used from higher-level languages like Java, Perl, and Python.

Language Tools

A number of tools have been developed to help C programmers find and fix statements with undefined behavior or possibly erroneous expressions, with greater rigor than that provided by the compiler. The tool lint was the first such, leading to many others.

Automated source code checking and auditing are beneficial in any language, and for C many such tools exist, such as Lint. A common practice is to use Lint to detect questionable code when a program is first written. Once a program passes Lint, it is then compiled using the C compiler. Also, many compilers can optionally warn about syntactically valid constructs that are likely to actually be errors. MISRA C is a proprietary set of guidelines to avoid such questionable code, developed for embedded systems.

There are also compilers, libraries, and operating system level mechanisms for performing actions that are not a standard part of C, such as bounds checking for arrays, detection of buffer overflow, serialization, dynamic memory tracking, and automatic garbage collection.

Tools such as Purify or Valgrind and linking with libraries containing special versions of the memory allocation functions can help uncover runtime errors in memory usage.

Uses

C is widely used for system programming in implementing operating systems and embedded system applications, because C code, when written for portability, can be used for most purposes, yet when needed, system-specific code can be used to access specific hardware addresses and to perform type punning to match externally imposed interface requirements, with a low run-time demand on system resources.

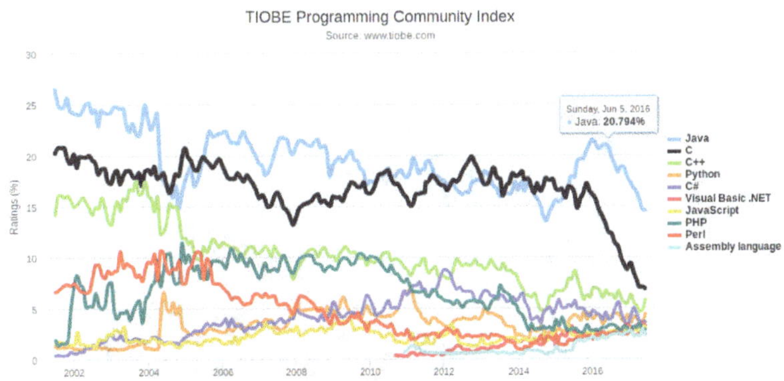

The TIOBE index graph from 2002 to 2015, showing a comparison of the popularity of various programming languages

C can also be used for website programming using CGI as a "gateway" for information between the Web application, the server, and the browser. C is often chosen over interpreted languages because of its speed, stability, and near-universal availability.

One consequence of C wide availability and efficiency is that compilers, libraries and interpreters of other programming languages are often implemented in C. The reference implementations of Python, Perl and PHP, for example, are all written in C.

Because the layer of abstraction is thin and the overhead is low, C enables programmers to create efficient implementations of algorithms and data structures, useful for computationally intense programs. For example, the GNU Multiple Precision Arithmetic Library, the GNU Scientific Library, Mathematica, and MATLAB are completely or partially written in C.

C is sometimes used as an intermediate language by implementations of other languages. This approach may be used for portability or convenience; by using C as an intermediate language, additional machine-specific code generators are not necessary. C has some features, such as line-number preprocessor directives and optional superfluous commas at the end of initializer lists, that support compilation of generated code. However, some of C shortcomings have prompted the development of other C-based languages specifically designed for use as intermediate languages, such as C--.

C has also been widely used to implement end-user applications. However, such applications can also be written in newer, higher-level languages.

How to Learn to Program in C

C is one of the older programming languages. It was developed in the 70s, but it is still very powerful thanks to how low-level it is. Learning C is a great way to introduce yourself to more complex languages as well, and the knowledge you gain will be useful in almost every programming language and can help you get into app development. To learn how to start programming in C.

Part 1

Getting Ready

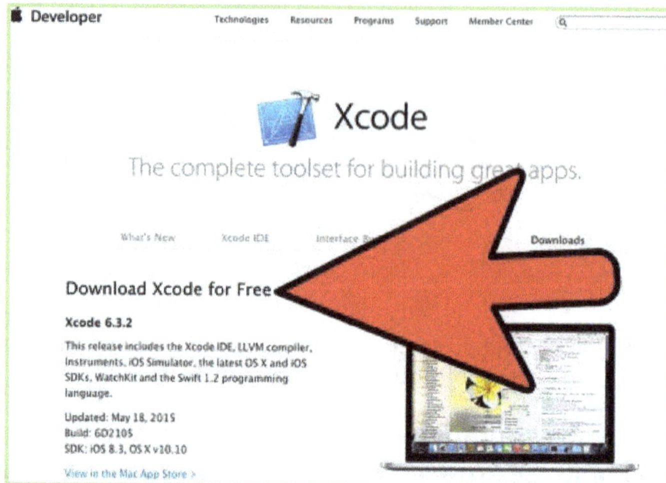

1. Download and install a compiler. C code needs to be compiled by a program that interprets the code into signals that the machine can understand. Compilers are usually free, and different compilers are available for different operating systems.

- For Windows, try Microsoft Visual Studio Express or MinGW.
- For Mac, XCode is one of the best C compilers.
- For Linux, gcc is one of the most popular options.

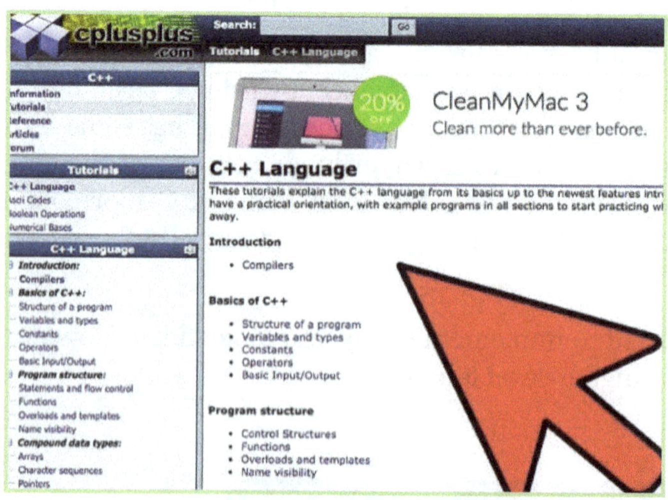

2. Understand the basics. C is one of the older programming languages, and can be very powerful. It was designed for Unix operating systems, but has been ported and expanded for nearly all operating systems. The modern version of C is C++.

- C is essentially comprised of functions, and in these functions you can use variables, conditional statements, loops to store and manipulate data.

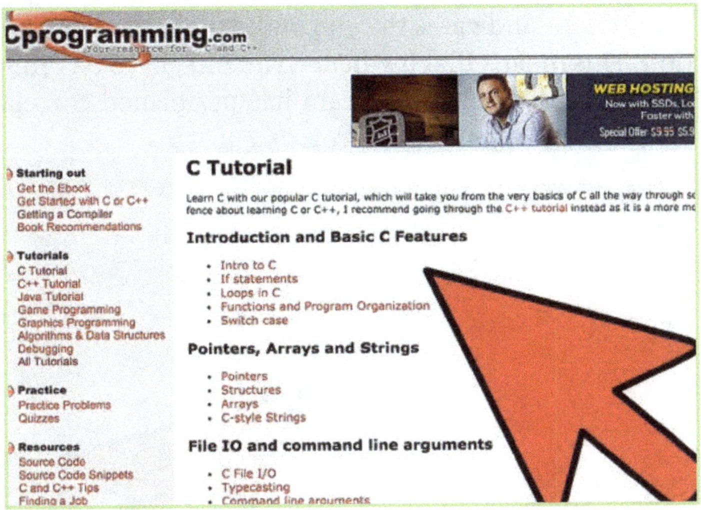

3. Examine some basic code. Take a look at the (very) basic program below to get a good idea about how some of the various aspects of the language work together, and to get an idea of how programs function.

```
#include <stdio.h>
 int main()
{
    printf("Hello, World!\n");
    getchar();
    return 0;
}
```

- The `#include` command occurs before the program starts, and loads libraries that contain the functions you need. In this example, `stdio.h` lets us use the `printf()` and `getchar()` functions.
- The `int main()` command tells the compiler that the program is running the function called "main" and that it will return an integer when it is finished. All C programs run a "main" funct ion.
- The `{}` indicate that everything inside them is part of the function. In this case, they denote that everything inside is a part of the "main" function.
- The `printf()` function displays the contents of the parentheses on the user's screen. The quotes ensure that the string inside is printed literally. The `\n` sequence tells the compiler to move the cursor to the next line.
- The `;` denotes the end of a line. Most lines of C code need to end with a semicolon.
- The `getchar()` command tells the compiler to wait for a keystroke input before moving

on. This is useful because many compilers will run the program and immediately close the window. This keeps the program from finishing until a key is pressed.

- The `return 0` command indicates the end of the function. Note how the "main" function is an `int` function. This means that it will need an integer to be returned once the program is finished. A "0" indicates that the program has performed correctly; any other number will mean that the program ran into an error.

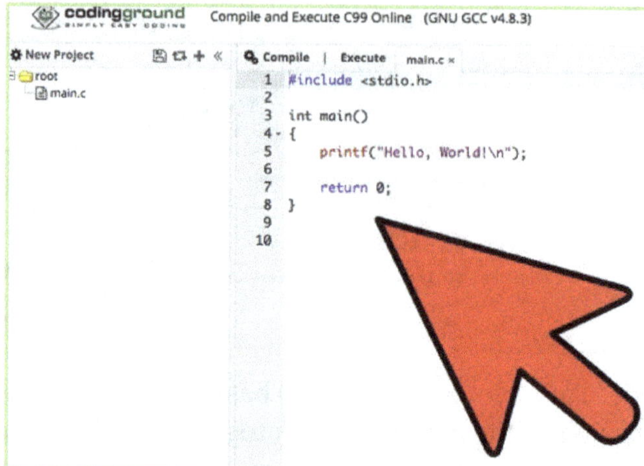

4. Try compiling the program. Enter the code into your code editor and save it as a "*.c" file. Compile it in your compiler, typically by clicking the Build or Run button.

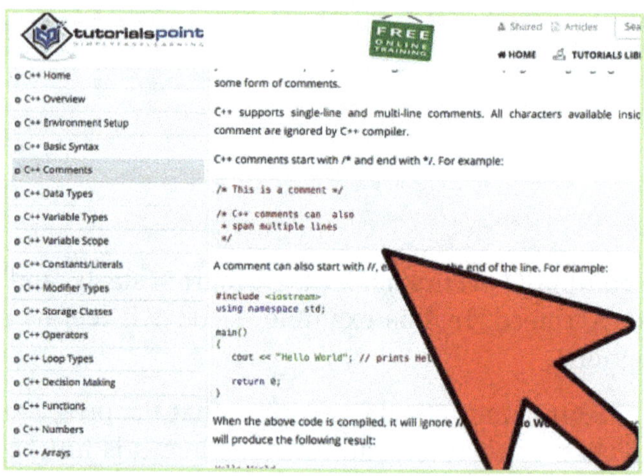

5. Always comment on your code. Comments are part of the code that is not compiled, but allows you to explain what is happening. This is useful for reminding yourself what your code is for, and for helping other developers who might be looking at your code.

- To comment in C place `/*` at the start of the comment and `*/` at the end.
- Comment on all but the most basic parts of your code.
- Comments can be used to quickly remove parts of your code without deleting them. Simply enclose the code you want to exclude with comment tags and then compile. If you want to add the code back, remove the tags.

Part 2

Using Variables

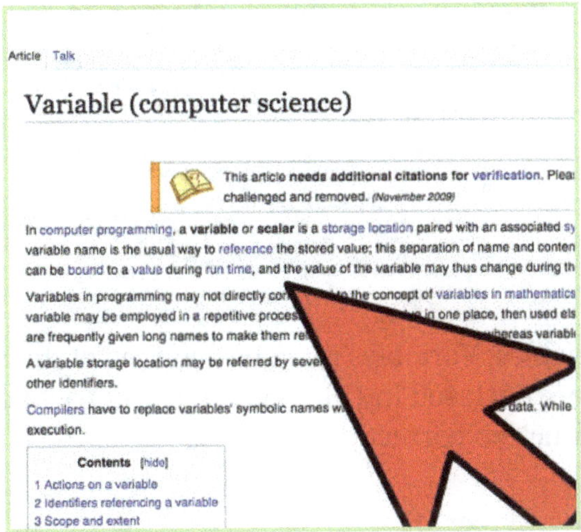

1. Understand the function of variables. Variables allow you to store data, either from computations in the program or from user input. Variables need to be defined before you can use them, and there are several types to choose from.

- Some of the more common variables include `int`, `char`, and `float`. Each one stores a different type of data.

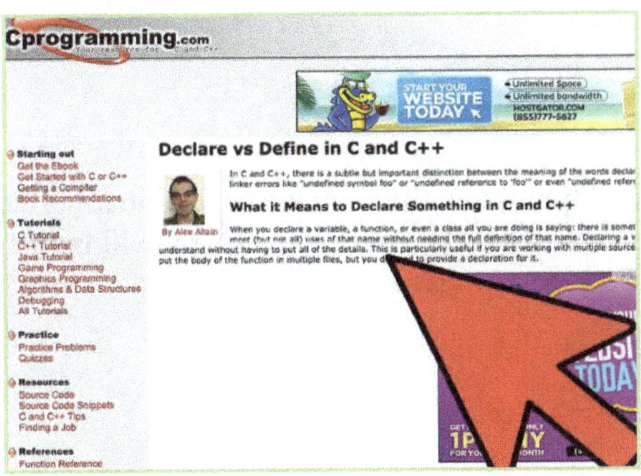

2. Learn how variables are declared. Variables need to be established, or "declared", before they can be used by the program. You declare a variable by entering the data type followed by the variable's name. For example, the following are all valid variable declarations:

```
float x;

char name;

int a, b, c, d;
```

- Note that you can declare multiple variables on the same line, as long as they are the same type. Simply separate the variable names with commas.

- Like many lines in C, each variable declaration line needs to end with a semicolon.

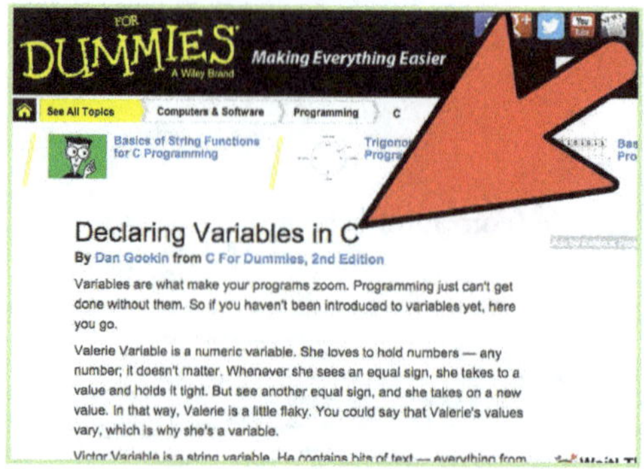

3. Know where to declare variables. Variables must be declared at the beginning of each code block (The parts of your code that are enclosed in {} brackets). If you try to declare a variable later in the block, the program will not function correctly.

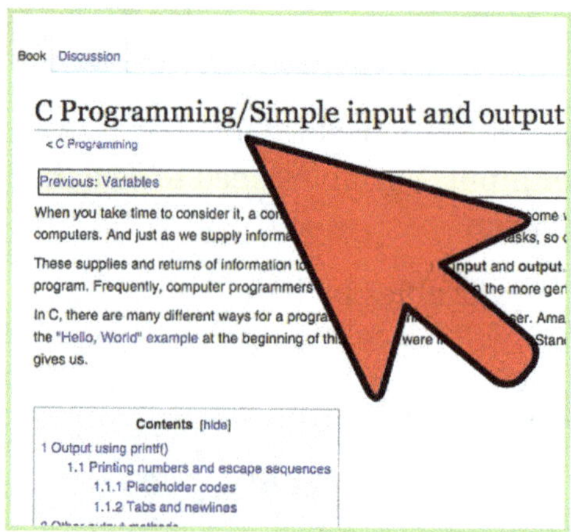

4. Use variables to store user input. Now that you know the basics of how variables work, you can write a simple program that will store the user's input. You will be using another function in the program, called `scanf`. This function searches the input that is provided for specific values.

```
#include <stdio.h>
 int main()
{
  int x;
   printf( "Enter a number: " );
  scanf( "%d", &x );
  printf( "You entered %d", x );
  getchar();
  return 0;
}
```

- The `"%d"` string tells `scanf` to look for integers in the user input.

- The `&` before the variable *x* tells `scanf` where to find the variable in order to change it, and stores the integer in the variable.
- The final `printf` command reads back the input integer to the user.

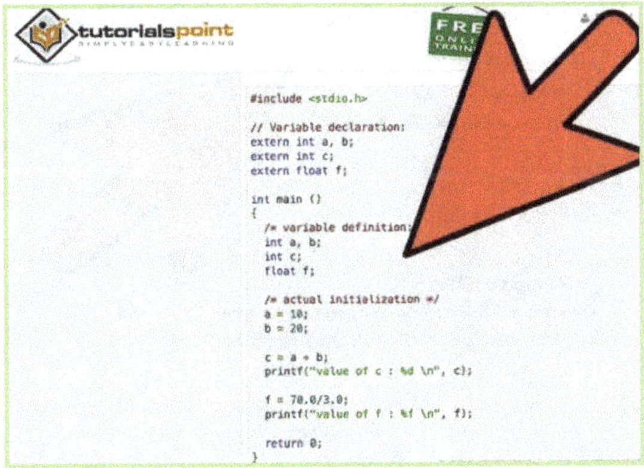

5. Manipulate your variables. You can use mathematical expressions to manipulate the data that you have stored in your variables. The most important distinction to remember for mathematical expressions is that a single = sets the value of the variable, while == compares the values on either side to see if they are equal.

```
x = 3 * 4; /* sets "x" to 3 * 4, or 12 */

x = x + 3; /* adds 3 to the original value of "x", and sets the new value as the variable */

x == 15; /* checks to see if "x" equals 15 */

x < 10; /* checks if the value of "x" is less than 10 */
```

Part 3

Using Conditional Statements

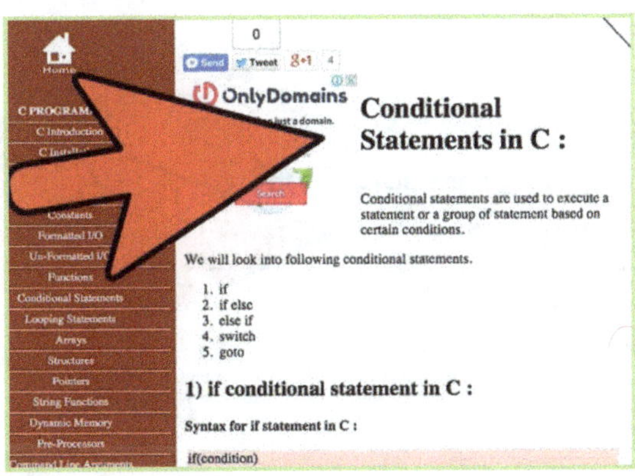

1. Understand the basics of conditional statements. Conditional statements are what drive most programs. They are statements that are determined to be either TRUE or FALSE, and then acted upon based on the result. The most basic of the statements is the `if` statement.

- TRUE and FALSE work differently in C than what you might be used to. TRUE statements always end up equaling a nonzero number. When you perform comparisons, if the result is TRUE then a "1" is returned. If the result is FALSE, then a "0" is returned. Understanding this will help you see how IF statements are processed.

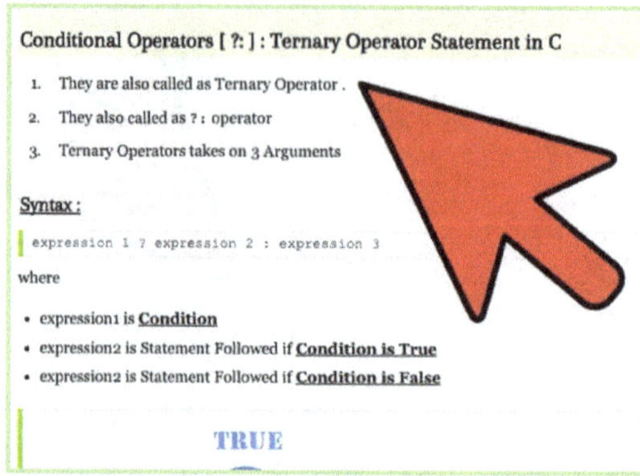

2. Learn the basic conditional operators. Conditional statements revolve around the use of mathematical operators that compare values. The following list contains the most commonly used conditional operators.

```
>   /* greater than */
<   /* less than */
>=  /* greater than or equal to */
<=  /* less than or equal to */
==  /* equal to */
!=  /* not equal to */
10 > 5 TRUE
6 < 15 TRUE
8 >= 8 TRUE
4 <= 8 TRUE
3 == 3 TRUE
4 != 5 TRUE
```

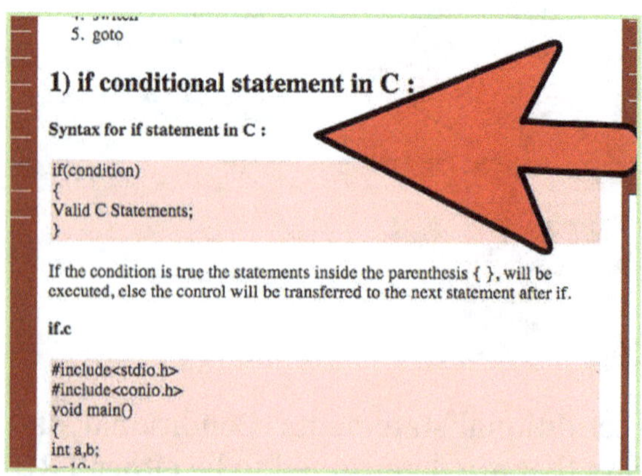

3. Write a basic IF statement. You can use IF statements to determine what the program should do next after the statement is evaluated. You can combine it with other conditional statements later to

create powerful multiple options, but for now write a simple one to get used to them.

```
#include <stdio.h>
 int main()
{
  if ( 3 < 5 )
    printf( “3 is less than 5”);
    getchar();
}
```

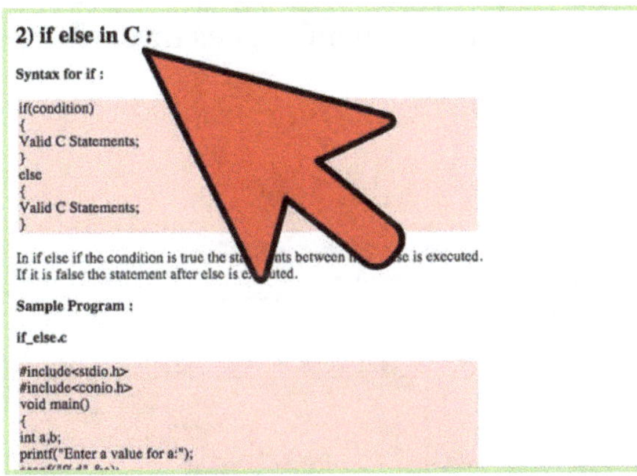

4. Use ELSE/ELSE IF statements to expand your conditions. You can build upon IF statements by using ELSE and ELSE IF statements to handle different results. ELSE statements run if the IF statement is FALSE. ELSE IF statements allow you to include multiple IF statements into one code block to handle various cases. See the example program below to see how they interact.

```
#include <stdio.h>
 int main()
{
  int age;
   printf( “Please enter your current age: ” );
  scanf( “%d”, &age );
  if ( age <= 12 ) {
    printf( “You’re just a kid!\n” );
  }
  else if ( age < 20 ) {
    printf( “Being a teenager is pretty great!\n” );
  }
  else if ( age < 40 ) {
    printf( “You’re still young at heart!\n” );
```

```
    }
    else {
      printf( "With age comes wisdom.\n" );
    }
    return 0;
}
```

- The program takes the input from the user and takes it through the IF statements. If the number satisfies the first statement, then the first `printf` statement is returned. If it does not satisfy the first statement, it is taken through each ELSE IF statement until it finds one that works. If it doesn't match any of them, it goes through the ELSE statement at the end.

Part 4

Learning Loops

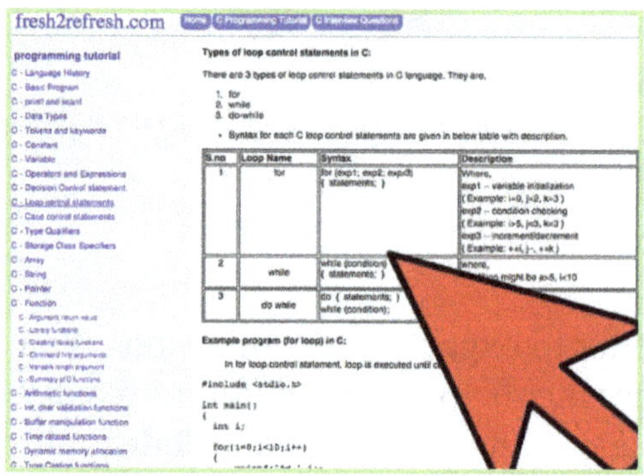

1. Understand how loops work. Loops are one of the most important aspects of programming, as they allow you to repeat blocks of code until specific conditions are met. This can make repeating actions very easy to implement, and keeps you from having to write new conditional statements each time you want something to happen.

- There are three main types of loops: FOR, WHILE, and DO...WHILE.

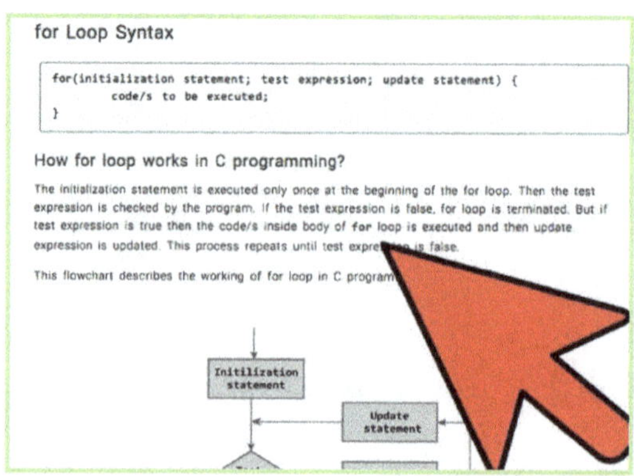

2. Use a FOR loop. This is the most common and useful loop type. It will continue running the function until the conditions set in the FOR loop are met. FOR loops require three conditions:

initializing the variable, the condition to be met, and the way the variable is updated. If you don't need all of these conditions, you will still need to leave a blank space with a semicolon, otherwise the loop will run forever.

```
#include <stdio.h>
int main()
{
  int y;
  for ( y = 0; y < 15; y++;){
    printf( "%d\n", y );
  }
  getchar();
}
```

- In the above program, *y* is set to 0, and the loop continues as long as the value of *y* is less than 15. Each time the value of *y* is printed, 1 is added to the value of *y* and the loop is repeated. Once *y* = 15, the loop will break.

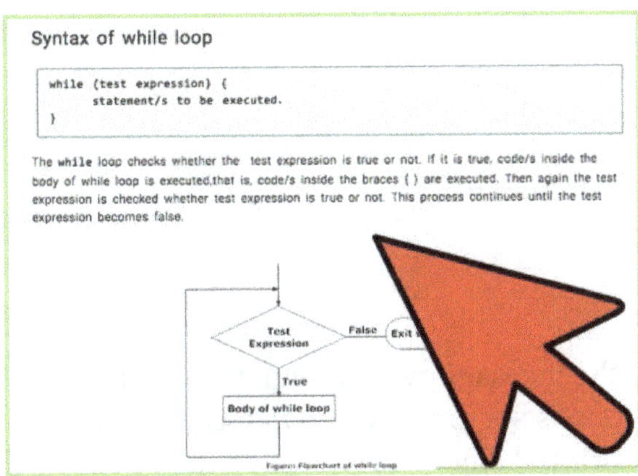

3. Use a WHILE loop. WHILE loops are more simple than FOR loops. They only have one condition, and the loop acts as long as that condition is true. You do not need to initialize or update the variable, though you can do that in the main body of the loop.

```
#include <stdio.h>
int main()
{
  int y;
  while ( y <= 15 ){
    printf( "%d\n", y );
    y++;
  }
  getchar();
}
```

- The `y++` command adds 1 to the *y* variable each time the loop is executed. Once *y* hits 16 (remember, this loop goes as long as *y* is less than *or equal to* 15), the loop breaks.

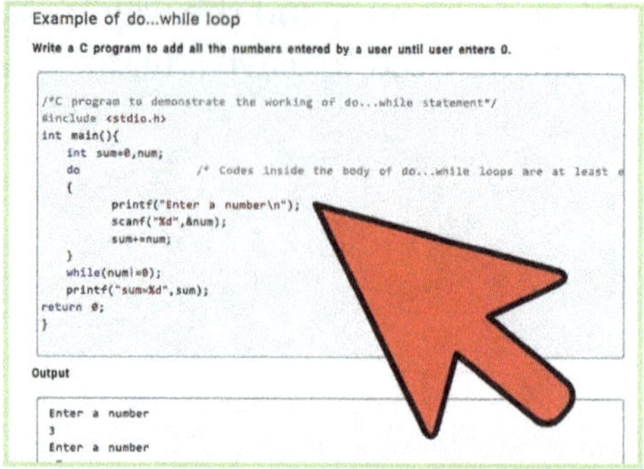

4. Use a DO...WHILE loop. This loop is very useful for loops that you want to ensure run at least once. In FOR and WHILE loops, the condition is checked at the beginning of the loop, meaning it could not pass and fail immediately. DO...WHILE loops check conditions at the end of the loop, ensuring that the loop executes at least once.

```
#include <stdio.h>
int main()
{
  int y;
  y = 5;
  do {
    printf("This loop is running!\n");
  } while ( y != 5 );
  getchar();
}
```

- This loop will display the message even though the condition is FALSE. The variable *y* is set to 5 and the WHILE loop is set to run when *y* does not equal 5, so the loop terminates. The message was already printed since the condition is not checked until the end.
- The WHILE loop in a DO...WHILE set must be ended with a semicolon. This is the only time a loop is ended with a semicolon.

Part 5

Using Functions

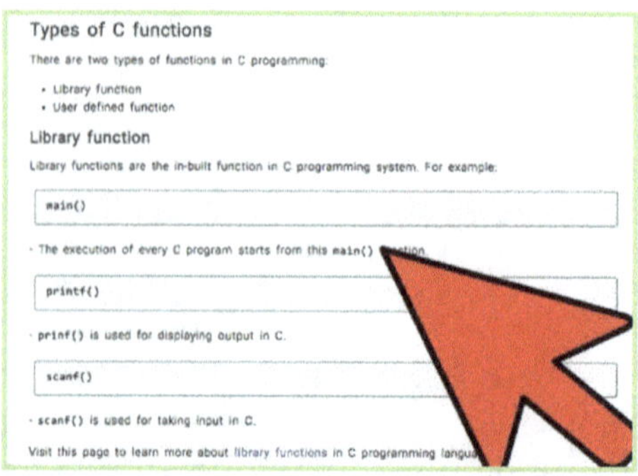

1. Understand the basics of functions. Functions are self-contained blocks of code that can be

called upon by other parts of the program. They make it very easy to repeat code, and they help make the program simpler to read and change. Functions can include all of the previously-covered techniques learned in this article, and even other functions.

- The `main()` line at the beginning of all of the above examples is a function, as is `getchar()`
- Functions are essential to efficient and easy-to-read code. Make good use of functions to streamline your program.

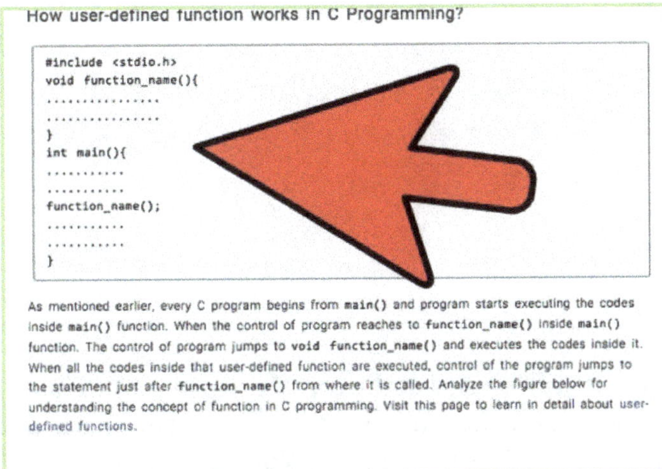

2. Start with an outline. Functions are best created when you outline what you want it to accomplish before you begin the actual coding. The basic syntax for functions is "return_type name (argument1, argument2, etc.);". For example, to create a function that adds two numbers:

```
int add ( int x, int y );
```

- This will create a function that adds two integers (*x* and *y*) and then returns the sum as an integer.

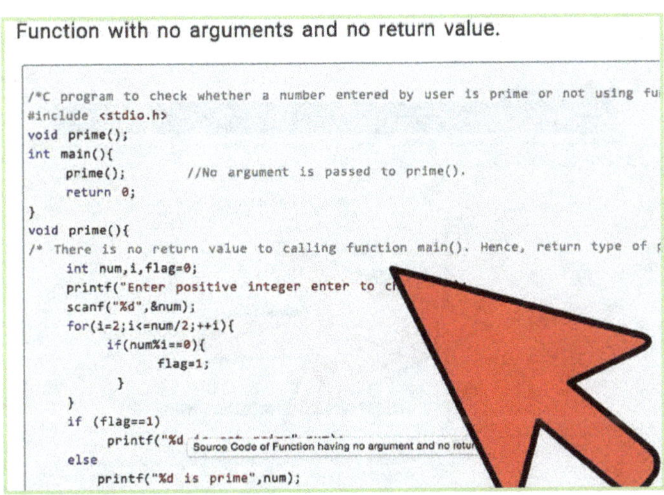

3. Add the function to a program. You can use the outline to create a program that takes two integers that the user enters and then adds them together. The program will define how the "add" function works and use it to manipulate the input numbers.

```
#include <stdio.h>
int add ( int x, int y );
int main()
{
  int x;
  int y;
  printf( "Enter two numbers to add together: " );
  scanf( "%d", &x );
  scanf( "%d", &y );
  printf( "The sum of your numbers is %d\n" , add( x, y ) );
  getchar();
}
int add ( int x , int y )
{
  return x + y;
}
```

- Note that the outline is still located at the top of the program. This tells the compiler what to expect when the function is called and what it will return. This is only necessary if you want to define the function later in the program. You could define `add()` before the `main()` function and the result would be the same without the outline.
- The actual functionality of the function is defined at the bottom of the program. The `main()` function collects the integers from the user and then sends them to the `add()` function to be processed. The `add()` function then returns the results to `main()`
- Now the `add()` has been defined, it can be called anywhere in the program.

Part 6

Continuing to Learn

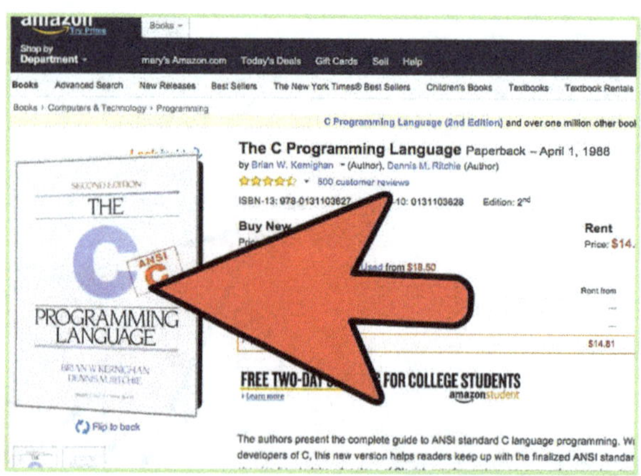

1. Find a few C programming books. This article covers the basics, but it only scratches the surface of C programming and all the associated knowledge. A good reference book will help you solve problems and save you from a lot of headaches down the road.

2. Join some communities. There are lots of communities, both online and in the real world, dedicated to programming and all of the languages that entails. Find some like-minded C programmers to swap code and ideas with, and you will soon find yourself learning a lot.

- Attend some hack-a-thons if possible. These are events where teams and individuals have time limits to come up with programs and solutions, and often foster a lot of creativity. You can meet a lot of good programmers this way, and hack-a-thons happen regularly across the globe.

3. Take some classes. You don't have to go back to school for a Computer Science degree, but taking a few classes can do wonders for your learning. Nothing beats hands-on help from people who are well-versed in the language. You can often find classes at local community centers and junior colleges, and some universities will allow you to audit their computer science programs without having to enroll.

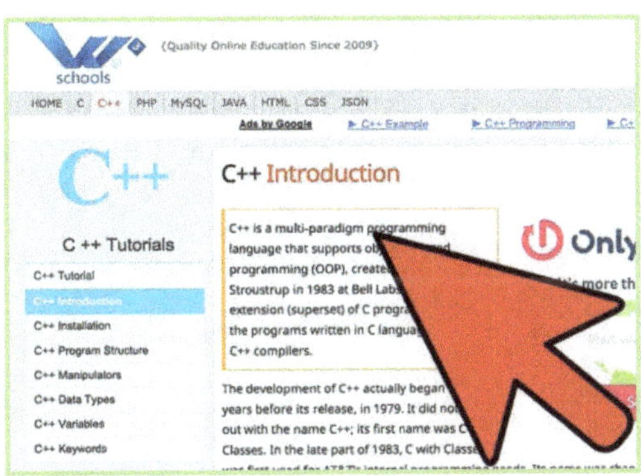

4. Consider learning C++. Once you have a grasp of C, it wouldn't hurt to start taking a look at

C++. This is the more modern version of C, and allows for a lot more flexibility. C++ is designed with object handling in mind, and knowing C++ can enable you to create powerful programs for virtually any operating system.

How to create a Simple Program in C

This tutorial will serve as an introduction to creating a simple C and C++ program on Windows and Linux operating systems. It will cover the following topics: (1) Creating a working directory in order to store your C and C++ programs, (2) Changing into the directory and create and saving your main.c or main.cpp using a text editor, and (3) Compiling and running your program.

Steps

1. Install a compiler. In order to create C and C++ programs you must have a C/C++ compiler installed on your operating system. If you don't have a compiler installed on your system, please consult the appropriate method for installing the GNU C/C++ compiler on your Linux system. If you are on a Windows operating system, check out How to Install MinGW (Minimalist Gnu C/C++ Compiler) on Microsoft Windows.

2. Write these line of codes in your Turbo C IDE. .

```
#include<stdio.h>[[Image:Create a Simple Program in C Step 1 Version 2.jpg|center]]
#include<stdlib.h>
int main()
{
        printf("Hello world");
        return 0;
}
```

C++

C++ is a general-purpose programming language. It has imperative, object-oriented and generic programming features, while also providing facilities for low-level memory manipulation.

It was designed with a bias toward system programming and embedded, resource-constrained and large systems, with performance, efficiency and flexibility of use as its design highlights. C++ has also been found useful in many other contexts, with key strengths being software infrastructure and resource-constrained applications, including desktop applications, servers (e.g. e-commerce, web search or SQL servers), and performance-critical applications (e.g. telephone switches or space probes). C++ is a compiled language, with implementations of it available on many platforms. Many vendors provide C++ compilers, including the Free Software Foundation, Microsoft, Intel, and IBM.

C++ is standardized by the International Organization for Standardization (ISO), with the latest standard version ratified and published by ISO in December 2014 as *ISO/IEC 14882:2014* (informally known as C++14). The C++ programming language was initially standardized in 1998 as *ISO/IEC 14882:1998*, which was then amended by the C++03, *ISO/IEC 14882:2003*, standard. The current C++14 standard supersedes these and C++11, with new features and an enlarged standard library. Before the initial standardization in 1998, C++ was developed by Bjarne Stroustrup at Bell Labs since 1979, as an extension of the C language as he wanted an efficient and flexible language similar to C, which also provided high-level features for program organization. The C++17 standard is due in July 2017, with the draft largely implemented by some compilers already, and C++20 is the next planned standard thereafter.

Many other programming languages have been influenced by C++, including C#, D, Java, and newer versions of C.

Language

The C++ language has two main components: a direct mapping of hardware features provided primarily by the C subset, and zero-overhead abstractions based on those mappings. Stroustrup describes C++ as "a light-weight abstraction programming language [designed] for building and using efficient and elegant abstractions"; and "offering both hardware access and abstraction is the basis of C++. Doing it efficiently is what distinguishes it from other languages".

C++ inherits most of C's syntax. The following is Bjarne Stroustrup's version of the Hello world program that uses the C++ Standard Library stream facility to write a message to standard output:

```
#include <iostream>
int main()
{
    std::cout << "Hello, world!\n";
    return 0;
}
```

Within functions that define a non-void return type, failure to return a value before control reaches the end of the function results in undefined behaviour (compilers typically provide the means to issue a diagnostic in such a case). The sole exception to this rule is the main function, which implicitly returns a value of zero.

Object Storage

As in C, C++ supports four types of memory management: static storage duration objects, thread storage duration objects, automatic storage duration objects, and dynamic storage duration objects.

Static Storage Duration Objects

Static storage duration objects are created before `main()` is entered and destroyed in reverse order of creation after `main()` exits. The exact order of creation is not specified by the standard to allow implementations some freedom in how to organize their implementation. More formally, objects of this type have a lifespan that "shall last for the duration of the program".

Static storage duration objects are initialized in two phases. First, "static initialization" is performed, and only *after* all static initialization is performed, "dynamic initialization" is performed. In static initialization, all objects are first initialized with zeros; after that, all objects that have a constant initialization phase are initialized with the constant expression (i.e. variables initialized with a literal or `constexpr`). Though it is not specified in the standard, the static initialization phase can be completed at compile time and saved in the data partition of the executable. Dynamic initialization involves all object initialization done via a constructor or function call (unless the function is marked with `constexpr`, in C++11). The dynamic initialization order is defined as the order of declaration within the compilation unit (i.e. the same file). No guarantees are provided about the order of initialization between compilation units.

Thread Storage Duration Objects

Variables of this type are very similar to static storage duration objects. The main difference is the creation time is just prior to thread creation and destruction is done after the thread has been joined.

Automatic Storage Duration Objects

The most common variable types in C++ are local variables inside a function or block, and temporary variables. The common feature about automatic variables is that they have a lifetime that is limited to the scope of the variable. They are created and potentially initialized at the point of declaration and destroyed in the *reverse* order of creation when the scope is left.

Local variables are created as the point of execution passes the declaration point. If the variable has a constructor or initializer this is used to define the initial state of the object. Local variables are destroyed when the local block or function that they are declared in is closed. C++ destructors for local variables are called at the end of the object lifetime, allowing a discipline for automatic resource management termed RAII, which is widely used in C++.

Member variables are created when the parent object is created. Array members are initialized from 0 to the last member of the array in order. Member variables are destroyed when the parent object is destroyed in the reverse order of creation. i.e. If the parent is an "automatic object" then it will be destroyed when it goes out of scope which triggers the destruction of all its members.

Temporary variables are created as the result of expression evaluation and are destroyed when the statement containing the expression has been fully evaluated (usually at the `;` at the end of a statement).

Dynamic Storage Duration Objects

These objects have a dynamic lifespan and are created with a call to new and destroyed explicitly with a call to `delete`.

Templates

C++ templates enable generic programming. C++ supports function, class, alias and variable templates. Templates may be parameterized by types, compile-time constants, and other templates. Templates are implemented by *instantiation* at compile-time. To instantiate a template, compilers substitute specific arguments for a template's parameters to generate a concrete function or class instance. Some substitutions are not possible; these are eliminated by an overload resolution policy described by the phrase "Substitution failure is not an error" (SFINAE). Templates are a powerful tool that can be used for generic programming, template metaprogramming, and code optimization, but this power implies a cost. Template use may increase code size, because each template instantiation produces a copy of the template code: one for each set of template arguments, however, this is the same or smaller amount of code that would be generated if the code was written by hand. This is in contrast to run-time generics seen in other languages (e.g., Java) where at compile-time the type is erased and a single template body is preserved.

Templates are different from macros: while both of these compile-time language features enable conditional compilation, templates are not restricted to lexical substitution. Templates are aware of the semantics and type system of their companion language, as well as all compile-time type definitions, and can perform high-level operations including programmatic flow control based on evaluation of strictly type-checked parameters. Macros are capable of conditional control over compilation based on predetermined criteria, but cannot instantiate new types, recurse, or perform type evaluation and in effect are limited to pre-compilation text-substitution and text-inclusion/exclusion. In other words, macros can control compilation flow based on pre-defined symbols but cannot, unlike templates, independently instantiate new symbols. Templates are a tool for static polymorphism and generic programming.

In addition, templates are a compile time mechanism in C++ that is Turing-complete, meaning that any computation expressible by a computer program can be computed, in some form, by a template metaprogram prior to runtime.

In summary, a template is a compile-time parameterized function or class written without knowledge of the specific arguments used to instantiate it. After instantiation, the resulting code is equivalent to code written specifically for the passed arguments. In this manner, templates provide a way to decouple generic, broadly applicable aspects of functions and classes (encoded in templates) from specific aspects (encoded in template parameters) without sacrificing performance due to abstraction.

Objects

C++ introduces object-oriented programming (OOP) features to C. It offers classes, which provide the four features commonly present in OOP (and some non-OOP) languages: abstraction, encapsulation, inheritance, and polymorphism. One distinguishing feature of C++ classes compared to classes in other programming languages is support for deterministic destructors, which in turn provide support for the Resource Acquisition is Initialization (RAII) concept.

Encapsulation

Encapsulation is the hiding of information to ensure that data structures and operators are used as intended and to make the usage model more obvious to the developer. C++ provides the ability to define classes and functions as its primary encapsulation mechanisms. Within a class, members can be declared as either public, protected, or private to explicitly enforce encapsulation. A public member of the class is accessible to any function. A private member is accessible only to functions that are members of that class and to functions and classes explicitly granted access permission by the class ("friends"). A protected member is accessible to members of classes that inherit from the class in addition to the class itself and any friends.

The OO principle is that all of the functions (and only the functions) that access the internal representation of a type should be encapsulated within the type definition. C++ supports this (via member functions and friend functions), but does not enforce it: the programmer can declare parts or all of the representation of a type to be public, and is allowed to make public entities that are not part of the representation of the type. Therefore, C++ supports not just OO programming, but other decomposition paradigms, like modular programming.

It is generally considered good practice to make all data private or protected, and to make public only those functions that are part of a minimal interface for users of the class. This can hide the details of data implementation, allowing the designer to later fundamentally change the implementation without changing the interface in any way.

Inheritance

Inheritance allows one data type to acquire properties of other data types. Inheritance from a base class may be declared as public, protected, or private. This access specifier determines whether unrelated and derived classes can access the inherited public and protected members of the base class. Only public inheritance corresponds to what is usually meant by "inheritance". The other two forms are much less frequently used. If the access specifier is omitted, a "class" inherits privately, while a "struct" inherits publicly. Base classes may be declared as virtual; this is called virtual inheritance. Virtual inheritance ensures that only one instance of a base class exists in the inheritance graph, avoiding some of the ambiguity problems of multiple inheritance.

Multiple inheritance is a C++ feature not found in most other languages, allowing a class to be derived from more than one base class; this allows for more elaborate inheritance relationships. For example, a "Flying Cat" class can inherit from both "Cat" and "Flying Mammal". Some other languages, such as C# or Java, accomplish something similar (although more limited) by allowing inheritance of multiple interfaces while restricting the number of base classes to one (interfaces, unlike classes, provide only declarations of member functions, no implementation or member data). An interface as in C# and Java can be defined in C++ as a class containing only pure virtual functions, often known as an abstract base class or "ABC". The member functions of such an abstract base class are normally explicitly defined in the derived class, not inherited implicitly. C++ virtual inheritance exhibits an ambiguity resolution feature called dominance.

Operators and Operator Overloading

Operators that cannot be overloaded	
Operator	**Symbol**
Scope resolution operator	::
Conditional operator	?:
dot operator	.
Member selection operator	.*
"sizeof" operator	sizeof
"typeid" operator	typeid

C++ provides more than 35 operators, covering basic arithmetic, bit manipulation, indirection, comparisons, logical operations and others. Almost all operators can be overloaded for user-defined types, with a few notable exceptions such as member access (. and .*) as well as the conditional operator. The rich set of overloadable operators is central to making user-defined types in C++ seem like built-in types.

Overloadable operators are also an essential part of many advanced C++ programming techniques, such as smart pointers. Overloading an operator does not change the precedence of calculations involving the operator, nor does it change the number of operands that the operator uses (any operand may however be ignored by the operator, though it will be evaluated prior to execution). Overloaded "&&" and "||" operators lose their short-circuit evaluation property.

Polymorphism

Polymorphism enables one common interface for many implementations, and for objects to act differently under different circumstances.

C++ supports several kinds of *static* (resolved at compile-time) and *dynamic* (resolved at run-time) polymorphisms, supported by the language features described above. Compile-time polymorphism does not allow for certain run-time decisions, while runtime polymorphism typically incurs a performance penalty.

Static Polymorphism

Function overloading allows programs to declare multiple functions having the same name but with different arguments (i.e. *ad hoc* polymorphism). The functions are distinguished by the number or types of their formal parameters. Thus, the same function name can refer to different functions depending on the context in which it is used. The type returned by the function is not used to distinguish overloaded functions and would result in a compile-time error message.

When declaring a function, a programmer can specify for one or more parameters a default value. Doing so allows the parameters with defaults to optionally be omitted when the function is called, in which case the default arguments will be used. When a function is called with fewer arguments than there are declared parameters, explicit arguments are matched to parameters in left-to-right order, with any unmatched parameters at the end of the parameter list being assigned their default arguments. In many cases, specifying default arguments in a single function declaration is preferable to providing overloaded function definitions with different numbers of parameters.

Templates in C++ provide a sophisticated mechanism for writing generic, polymorphic code (i.e. parametric polymorphism). In particular, through the curiously recurring template pattern, it's possible to implement a form of static polymorphism that closely mimics the syntax for overriding virtual functions. Because C++ templates are type-aware and Turing-complete, they can also be used to let the compiler resolve recursive conditionals and generate substantial programs through template metaprogramming. Contrary to some opinion, template code will not generate a bulk code after compilation with the proper compiler settings.

Dynamic Polymorphism

Inheritance

Variable pointers and references to a base class type in C++ can also refer to objects of any derived classes of that type. This allows arrays and other kinds of containers to hold pointers to objects of differing types (references cannot be directly held in containers). This enables dynamic (run-time) polymorphism, where the referred objects can behave differently depending on their (actual, derived) types.

C++ also provides the `dynamic_cast` operator, which allows code to safely attempt conversion of an object, via a base reference/pointer, to a more derived type: *downcasting*. The *attempt* is necessary as often one does not know which derived type is referenced. (*Upcasting*, conversion to a more general type, can always be checked/performed at compile-time via `static_cast`, as ancestral classes are specified in the derived class's interface, visible to all callers.) `dynamic_cast` relies on run-time type information (RTTI), metadata in the program that enables differentiating types and their relationships. If a `dynamic_cast` to a pointer fails, the result is the `nullptr` constant, whereas if the destination is a reference (which cannot be null), the cast throws an exception. Objects *known* to be of a certain derived type can be cast to that with `static_cast`, bypassing RTTI and the safe runtime type-checking of `dynamic_cast`, so this should be used only if the programmer is very confident the cast is, and will always be, valid.

Virtual Member Functions

Ordinarily, when a function in a derived class overrides a function in a base class, the function to call is determined by the type of the object. A given function is overridden when there exists no difference in the number or type of parameters between two or more definitions of that function.

Hence, at compile time, it may not be possible to determine the type of the object and therefore the correct function to call, given only a base class pointer; the decision is therefore put off until runtime. This is called dynamic dispatch. Virtual member functions or *methods* allow the most specific implementation of the function to be called, according to the actual run-time type of the object. In C++ implementations, this is commonly done using virtual function tables. If the object type is known, this may be bypassed by prepending a fully qualified class name before the function call, but in general calls to virtual functions are resolved at run time.

In addition to standard member functions, operator overloads and destructors can be virtual. As a rule of thumb, if any function in the class is virtual, the destructor should be as well. As the type of an object at its creation is known at compile time, constructors, and by extension copy constructors, cannot be virtual. Nonetheless a situation may arise where a copy of an object needs to be created when a pointer to a derived object is passed as a pointer to a base object. In such a case, a common solution is to create a clone() (or similar) virtual function that creates and returns a copy of the derived class when called.

A member function can also be made "pure virtual" by appending it with = 0 after the closing parenthesis and before the semicolon. A class containing a pure virtual function is called an *abstract class*. Objects cannot be created from an abstract class; they can only be derived from. Any derived class inherits the virtual function as pure and must provide a non-pure definition of it (and all other pure virtual functions) before objects of the derived class can be created. A program that attempts to create an object of a class with a pure virtual member function or inherited pure virtual member function is ill-formed.

Lambda Expressions

C++ provides support for anonymous functions, which are also known as lambda expressions and have the following form:

```
[capture](parameters) -> return_type { function_body }
```

The `[capture]` list supports the definition of closures. Such lambda expressions are defined in the standard as syntactic sugar for an unnamed function object. An example lambda function may be defined as follows:

```
[](int x, int y) -> int { return x + y; }
```

Exception Handling

Exception handling is used to communicate the existence of a runtime problem or error from where it was detected to where the issue can be handled. It permits this to be done in a uniform manner and separately from the main code, while detecting all errors. Should an error occur, an exception is thrown (raised), which is then caught by the nearest suitable exception handler. The exception causes the current scope to be exited, and also each outer scope (propagation) until a suitable handler is found, calling in turn the destructors of any objects in these exited scopes. At the same time, an exception is presented as an object carrying the data about the detected problem.

The exception-causing code is placed inside a `try` block. The exceptions are handled in separate catch blocks (the handlers); each try block can have multiple exception handlers, as it is visible in the example below.

```
#include <iostream>
#include <vector>
#include <stdexcept>
int main() {
    try {
        std::vector<int> vec{3,4,3,1};
        int i{vec.at(4)}; // Throws an exception, std::out_of_range (indexing for vec is from 0-3 not 1-4)
    }
    // An exception handler, catches std::out_of_range, which is thrown by vec.at(4)
    catch (std::out_of_range& e) {
        std::cerr << "Accessing a non-existent element: " << e.what() << '\n';
    }
    // To catch any other standard library exceptions (they derive from std::exception)
    catch (std::exception& e) {
        std::cerr << "Exception thrown: " << e.what() << '\n';
    }
    // Catch any unrecognised exceptions (i.e. those which don't derive from std::exception)
    catch (...) {
        std::cerr << "Some fatal error\n";
    }
}
```

It is also possible to raise exceptions purposefully, using the throw keyword; these exceptions are handled in the usual way. In some cases, exceptions cannot be used due to technical reasons. One such example is a critical component of an embedded system, where every operation must be guaranteed to complete within a specified amount of time. This cannot be determined with exceptions as no tools exist to determine the maximum time required for an exception to be handled.

Standard Library

The C++ standard consists of two parts: the core language and the standard library. C++ programmers expect the latter on every major implementation of C++; it includes vectors, lists, maps, algorithms (find, for_each, binary_search, random_shuffle, etc.), sets, queues, stacks, arrays, tuples, input/output facilities (iostream, for reading from and writing to the console and files), smart pointers for automatic memory management, regular expression support, multi-threading library, atomics support (allowing a variable to be read or written to by at most one thread at a time without any external synchronisation), time utilities (measurement, getting current time, etc.), a system for converting error reporting that doesn't use C++ exceptions into C++ exceptions, a random number generator and a slightly modified version of the C standard library (to make it comply with the C++ type system).

A large part of the C++ library is based on the Standard Template Library (STL). Useful tools provided by the STL include containers as the collections of objects (such as vectors and lists), iterators that provide array-like access to containers, and algorithms that perform operations such as searching and sorting.

Furthermore, (multi)maps (associative arrays) and (multi)sets are provided, all of which export compatible interfaces. Therefore, using templates it is possible to write generic algorithms that work with any container or on any sequence defined by iterators. As in C, the features of the library are accessed by using the `#include` directive to include a standard header. C++ provides 105 standard headers, of which 27 are deprecated.

The standard incorporates the STL that was originally designed by Alexander Stepanov, who experimented with generic algorithms and containers for many years. When he started with C++, he finally found a language where it was possible to create generic algorithms (e.g., STL sort) that perform even better than, for example, the C standard library qsort, thanks to C++ features like using inlining and compile-time binding instead of function pointers. The standard does not refer to it as "STL", as it is merely a part of the standard library, but the term is still widely used to distinguish it from the rest of the standard library (input/output streams, internationalization, diagnostics, the C library subset, etc.).

Most C++ compilers, and all major ones, provide a standards conforming implementation of the C++ standard library.

Compatibility

To give compiler vendors greater freedom, the C++ standards committee decided not to dictate the implementation of name mangling, exception handling, and other implementation-specific features. The downside of this decision is that object code produced by different compilers is expected to be incompatible. There were, however, attempts to standardize compilers for particular machines or operating systems (for example C++ ABI), though they seem to be largely abandoned now.

With C

C++ is often considered to be a superset of C, but this is not strictly true. Most C code can easily be made to compile correctly in C++, but there are a few differences that cause some valid C code to be invalid or behave differently in C++. For example, C allows implicit conversion from `void*` to other pointer types, but C++ does not (for type safety reasons). Also, C++ defines many new keywords, such as `new` and `class`, which may be used as identifiers (for example, variable names) in a C program.

Some incompatibilities have been removed by the 1999 revision of the C standard (C99), which now supports C++ features such as line comments (`//`), and declarations mixed with code. On the other hand, C99 introduced a number of new features that C++ did not support, were incompatible or redundant in C++, such as variable-length arrays, native complex-number types (however, the `std::complex` class in the C++ standard library provides similar functionality, although not code-compatible), designated initializers, compound literals, and the `restrict` keyword. Some of the C99-introduced features were included in the subsequent version of the C++ standard, C++11 (out of those which were not redundant). However, the C++11 standard introduces new incompatibilities, such as disallowing assignment of a string literal to a character pointer, which remains valid C.

To intermix C and C++ code, any function declaration or definition that is to be called from/used both in C and C++ must be declared with C linkage by placing it within an `extern "C" {/*...*/}` block. Such a function may not rely on features depending on name mangling (i.e., function overloading).

How to Learn C++ Programming

Learning programming definitely isn't an overnight thing, and takes a large amount of hard work and dedication (especially with C++). This guide will help you through the process.

Steps

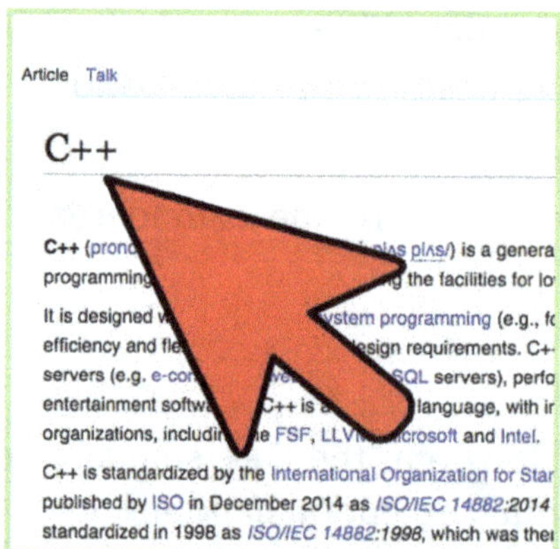

1. Learn about C++'s history. The best way to start programming a language is to learn its roots. Even though you may not understand everything that you read, some of these pages will introduce you to important terms that will come up later (such as "Object-Oriented Programming").

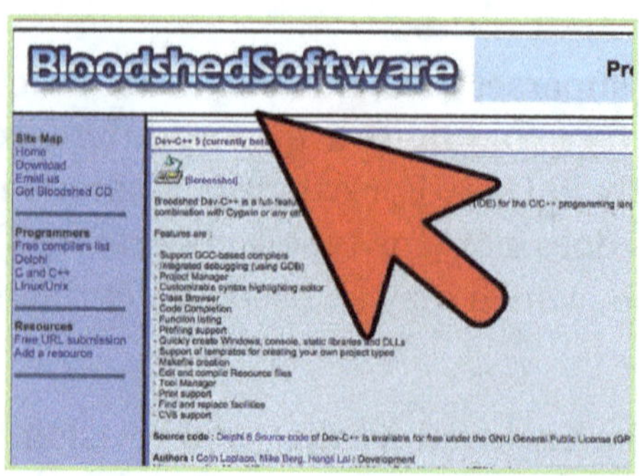

2. Install a C++ compiler (and possible IDE). A compiler is required for programming in C++,

because the actual source code has to be compiled into a file that your computer can run. If you are using Windows a good option would be Visual C++ 2010 Express, or if your using Linux a good one is Geany. Both come with an IDE (independent development environment) built in, which can make the process of writing source code easier. (NOTE: Many people online will recommend that you use the Bloodshed Dev-C++ IDE and compiler. DON'T. It has not been updated in 5 years and has pages and pages of known bugs.

- Learn how to use your IDE efficiently. Some IDEs that are out there have their own individual quirks that could get in the way down the road, so it would be beneficial to read through or keep a reference for the different options and settings of your IDE.

3. Choose a tutorial or two to start learning C++. This step is, along with the compiler, one of the most important steps of all. There are a few things that you have to make sure of during this step. First of all, make sure the guide is written for complete newbies to programming, as those are the most thorough in their descriptions. Next, make sure that the code in the tutorial follows the C++03 standard or even the new C++11 (still not standardized, so beware of compiler issues), because modern compilers will have trouble compiling outdated code, or will just reject it altogether. A few good ones are c programming.com's C++ tutorial and the tutorial at www.cplusplus.com/doc/tutorial/.

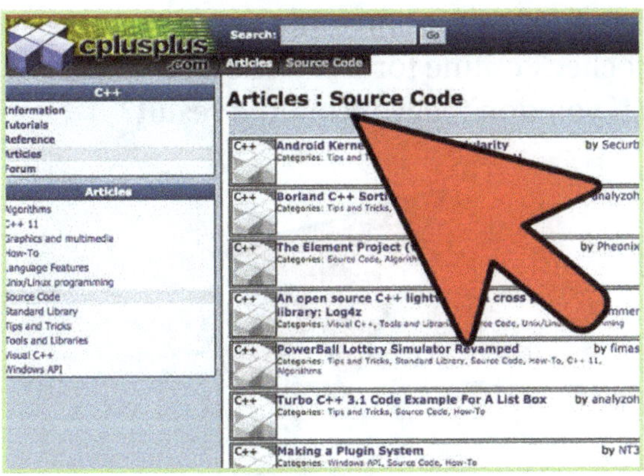

4. Try out each new concept. An important part of programming is not only reading about the different concepts, but using them in your own code. Copy-pasting the code into your IDE will only go so far. It is much more beneficial to type out each example and even try creating your own program ideas that use the concept being taught to maximize the amount of information retained.

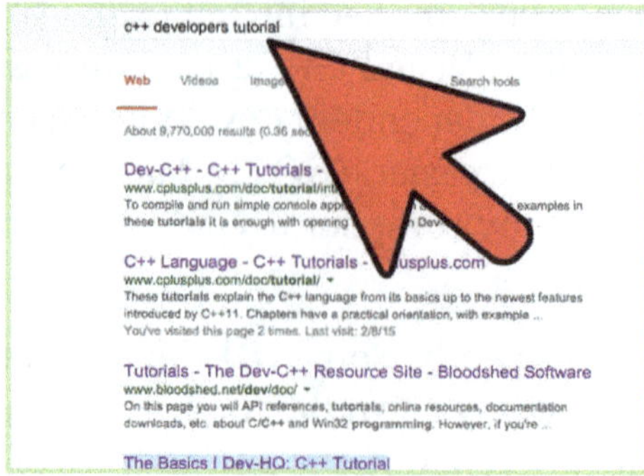

5. Learn from other developers. One of the best things about programming is that no matter what level of skill you have in programming, there will always be source code readily available that is at that same level or one step above you. A good way to learn from more complicated source code is to read through until you reach a point which you don't understand, then try to work it out in your head; if you don't know a certain part of the code, read about it in your tutorial or reference material until you do.

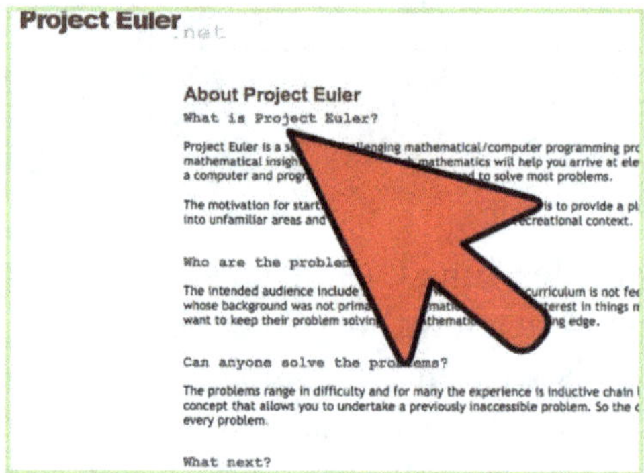

6. Work through problems using the concepts you have learned. The absolute best way to retain what you learn isn't just writing out source code examples, but actually accomplishing a set task with them. Both c programming.com and Project Euler have good problems that you could try solving to apply concepts in real-life situations. If you absolutely can't create an algorithm for a problem, then as a last resort check online for one done by someone else and learn from it. What's the use of solving a problem if you don't learn from the result?

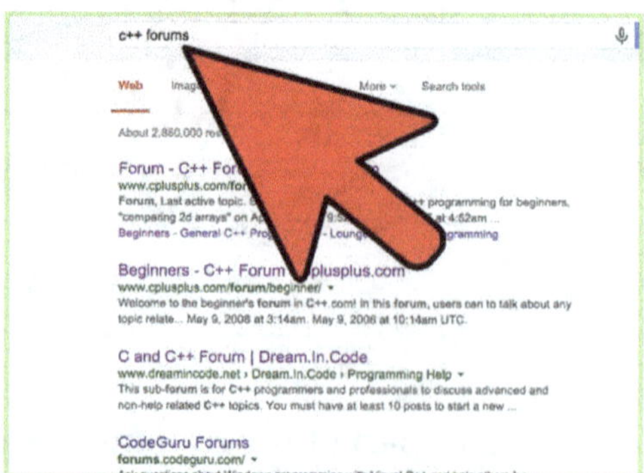

7. Help others who need help. Now that you have learned about C++, you should start helping other newbies online with their problems and get them started on the same journey you had! Don't

get frustrated if the person who asked you for help doesn't want to listen to your advice: someone else could learn from the answer you provide even if the original poster didn't.

How to write Standard Code in C++

There are infinitely many ways to program computers. Ultimately, it is the choice of the programmer how to accomplish what they need. There are, however, many "best practices" for styles and function usage for better compilation and safer programs. Some care should be taken to ensure that future programmers (including yourself) on your project can read and Method 1

Writing Standard Code

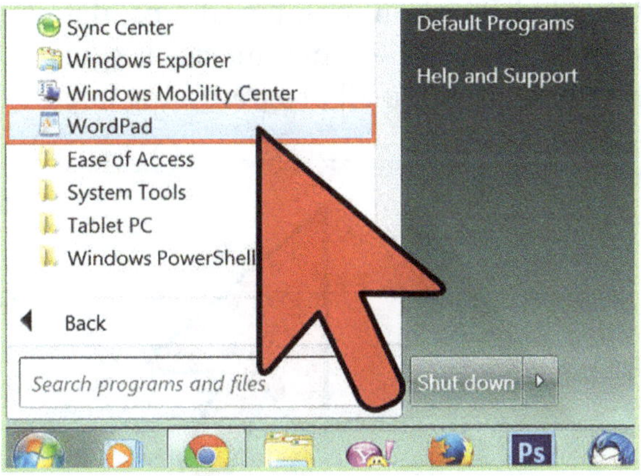

1. Download a C++ IDE (integrated development environment) such as Eclipse, Netbeans, and CodeBlocks, or you can use a plain text editor such as Notepad++ or VIM. You can also run programs from the command line, in that case any text-editor will suffice. It might be handy to choose an editor which supports syntax highlighting and line-numbers. Most programmers find that unix-like systems (linux, OS X, BSD) are the best environments for development.

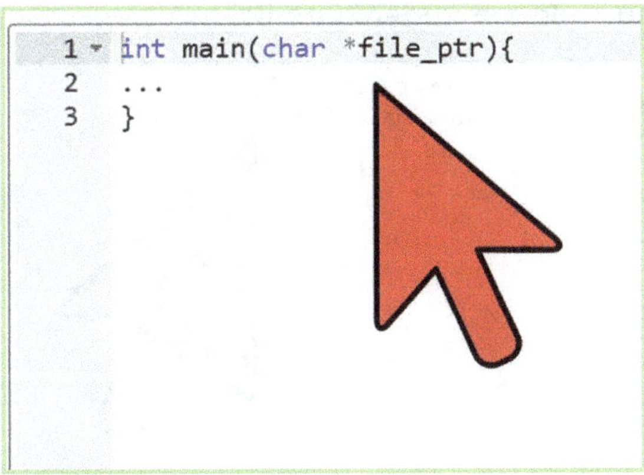

2. Create a main program file. The main file must include a function called main(). This is where execution of the program begins. From here, you should be calling functions, instantiating classes, etc. Other files of your application as well as libraries can be included into this file.

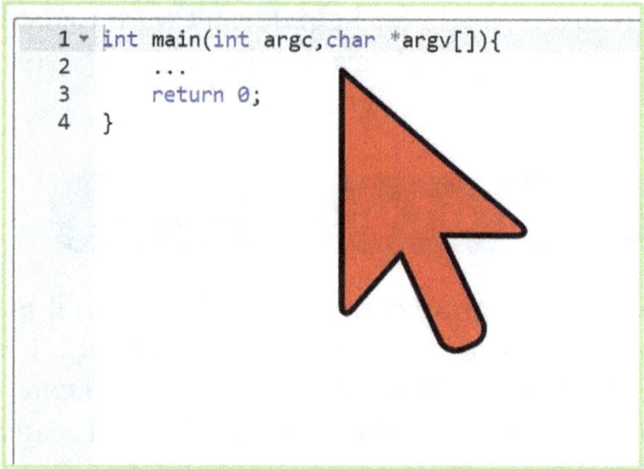

3. Begin writing your program. Insert your code or the program that you need to build. Learn the syntax, semantics, Object-Oriented Programming paradigms, data striations, algorithm designs such as linked lists, priority queues, etc. C++ is not an easy language to program in, but doing so teaches you the fundamentals that extend to all programming languages.

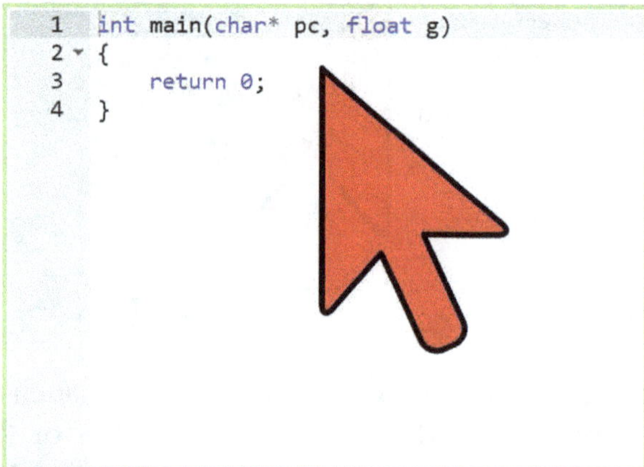

4. Insert comments in your code. Explain what your functions do and what variables are for. Choose clear names for variables and functions. Capitalize the names of global variables. In general: make sure that anyone reading your code can understand it.

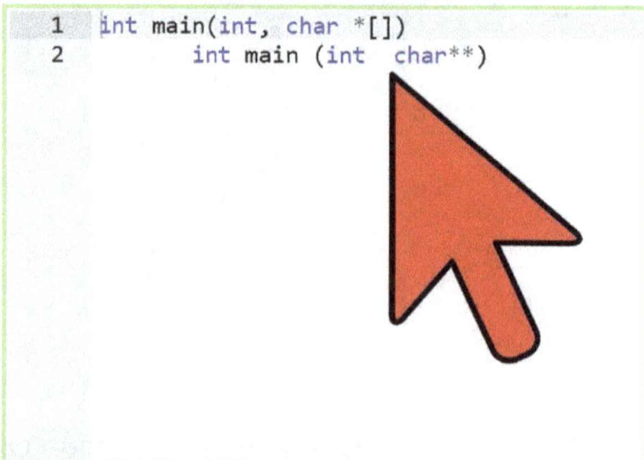

5. Use proper indenting in your code.

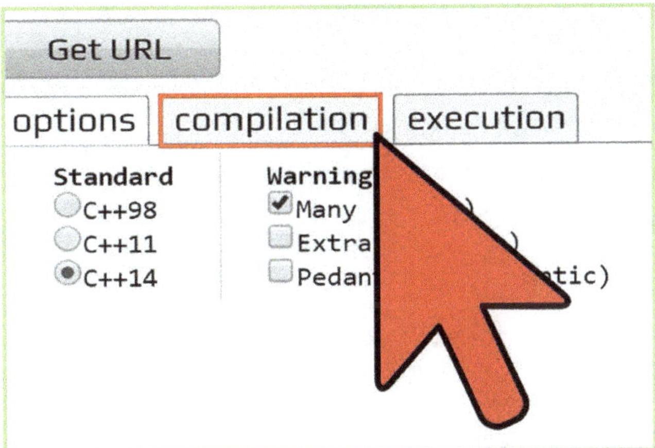

6. Compile your code with

```
g++ main.cpp
```

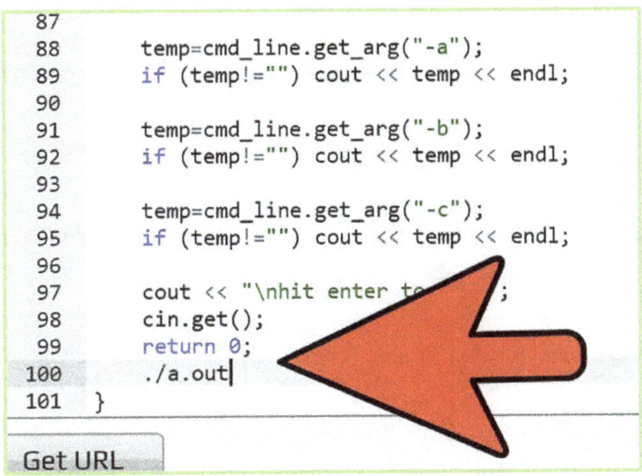

7. Run your program by typing:

```
./a.out
```

Method 2

Following Examples

1. Take a look at Example 1:

```
/* This Is A Simple Program Just To Understand The Basic OF g++ Style.
This Is A Program With g++ Compiler.*/
 #include <iostream> /* include input and output functions */
using namespace std; /* we are using the std (standard) functions */
 int main() /* declare the main function; you can have int main(void) too.
                                     */
```

```
    {
        cout << "\n Hello Daddy" ; /* '\n' is a newline (\t is a tab) */
        cout << "\n Hello Mummy" ;
        cout << "\n This Is My First Program" ;
        cout << "\n Date 11/03/2007" ;
        return 0;
    }
```

2. Consider this Example 2:

```
/* This Program Calculates The Sum Of Two Numbers */
 #include <iostream>
using namespace std;
int main()
    {
        float num1,num2,res; /* declare variables; int, double, long.. work too */
        cout << "\n Enter the first number= " ;
        cin >> num1; /* put user's value into num1 */
        cout << "\n Enter the second number= " ;
        cin >> num2;
        res = num1 + num2;
        cout << "\n The sum of "<< num1 <<" and "<< num2 <<" = "<<res '\n' ;
        return 0;
    }
```

3. Learn from Example 3:

```
/* Product Of Two Numbers */
 #include <iostream>
 using namespace std;
 int main()
    {
        float num1;
        int num2;
        double res;
        cout << "\n Enter the first number= " ;
        cin >> num1;
        cout << "\n Enter the second number= " ;
        cin >> num2;
```

```
        res = num1 * num2;
        cout << "\n The Product of two numbers = " << res '\n' ;
        return 0;
    }
```

4. Take a look at Example 4:

```
// Looping to find a math equation. In this case, it figures out the answer to
// Question #1 on Project Euler.
#include <iostream>
using namespace std;
int main() { // Opening Main.
    int sum1=0; int sum2=0; int sum3=0; int sum4=0; // Creates the integers needed in order to figure out the answer.
    for (int a=0; a < 1000; a=a+3) {sum1 = sum1+a;} // Loops until a is 1000 or over, adding 3 to a every loop. Also adds a to sum1.
    for (int b=0; b < 1000; b=b+5) {sum2 = sum2+b;} // Loops until b is 1000 or over, adding 5 to b every loop. Also adds b to sum2.
    for (int c=0; c < 1000; c=c+15) {sum3 = sum3+c;} // Loops until c is 1000 or over, adding 15 to c every loop. Also adds c to sum3.
    sum4 = sum1 + sum2 - sum3; // sum4 takes the sum of sum1 and sum2, and subtracts sum3.
    cout << sum4; // Outputs sum4, the answer.
    cin.get(); // Waits for user to press enter.
    return 0; // Return statement.
} // Closing Main.
```

5. Take a look at this example of different styles:

```
int main(){
  int i = 0;
  if(1+1==2){
    i = 2;
  }
}
/* This is Whitesmiths style */
int main()
{
   int i;
   if (1+1==2)
```

```
        {
        i = 2;
        }
}
/* This is GNU style */
int main ()
{
   int i;
   if (condition)
      {
        i = 2;
        function ();
      }
}
```

How to Start Learning C Programming in Turbo C++ IDE

C is one of the oldest and most powerful programming language that was first developed in the 1970s by Dennis Ritchie. However, if C programming is mastered, learning other programming languages will be easy. This article will help you to start learning C programming, by using the compiler *Turbo C++ IDE.*

Steps

1. Download Turbo C++ IDE for your operating system.
   - Turbo C++ may not work in Windows Vista and Windows 7. You may have to run it through another program called *DosBox.*

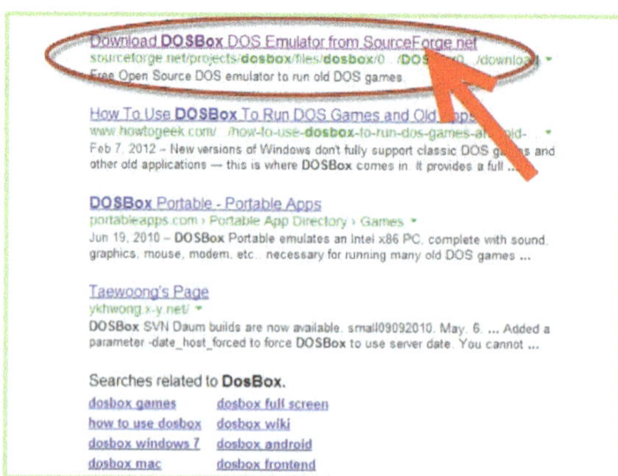

   - Install the software DOSBox version 0.74

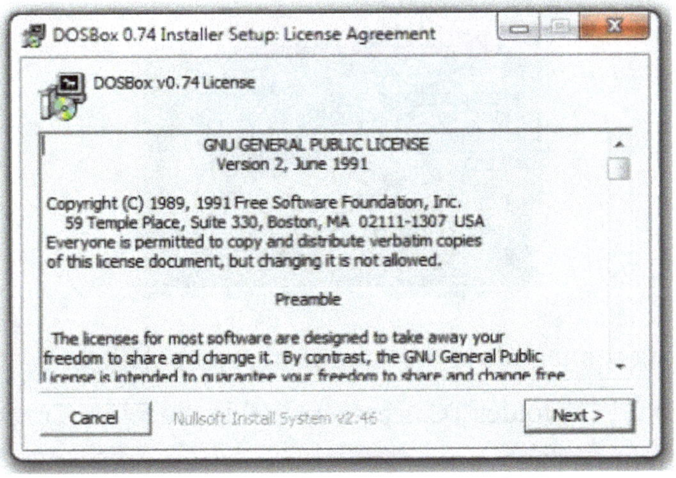

- Create a folder,for example “Turbo” (C:\Turbo\):

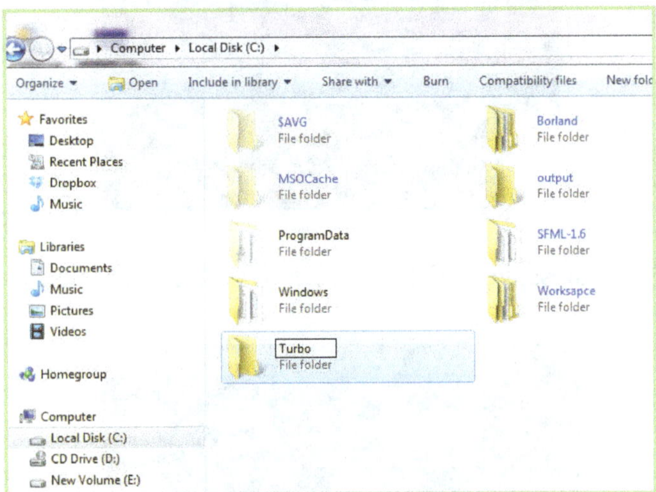

- Download and extract TC into the Turbo folder (c:\Turbo\):

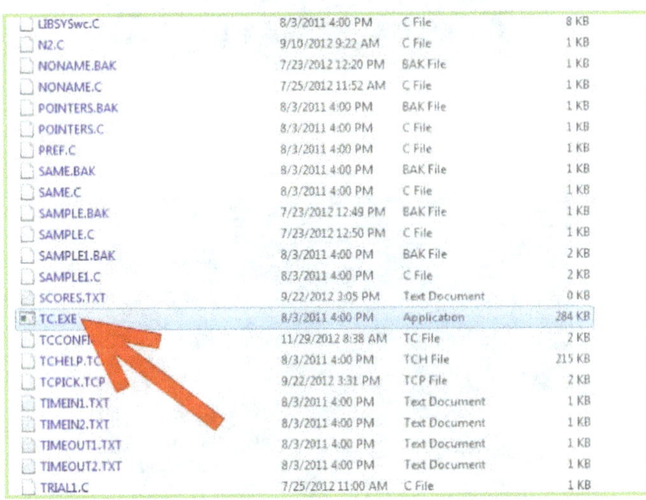

- Run the DOSBox 0.74 from the icon located on the desktop:

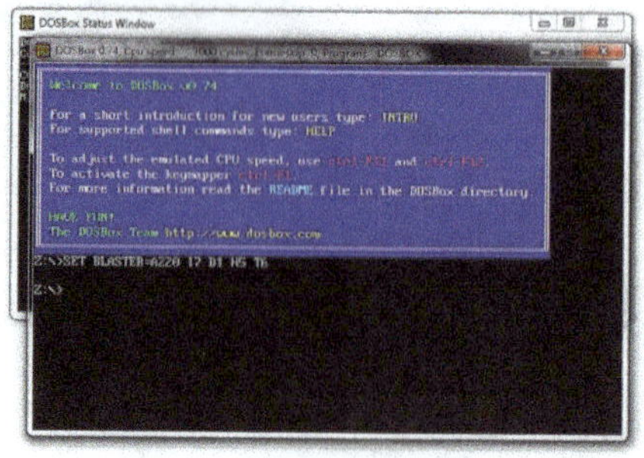

- Type the following commands at the command prompt [Z]:
- mount d c:\Turbo\ [The folder TC is present inside the folder Turbo]

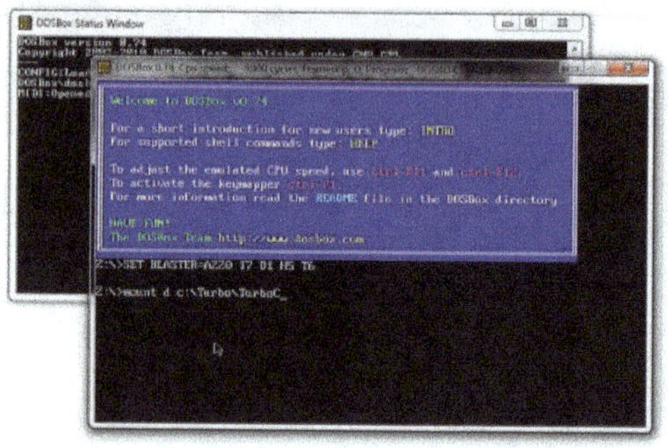

- Now you should get a message which says: Drive D is mounted as a local directory c:\Turbo\

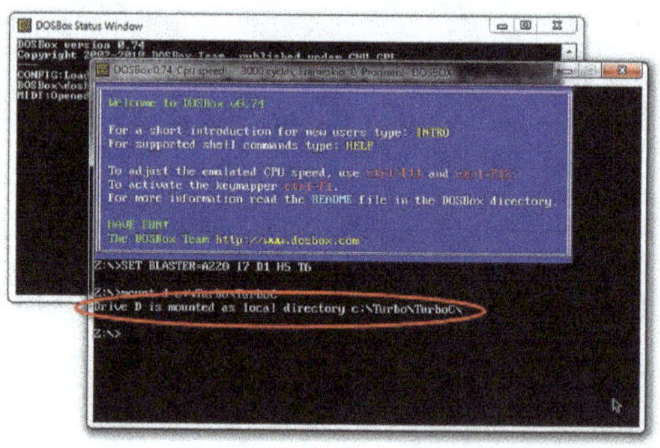

- Type d: to shift to d:

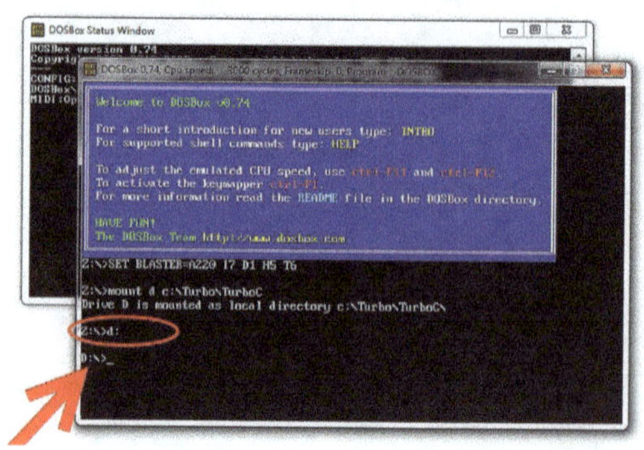

- Next follow the commands below:

- *cd tc*

  cd bin

  tc or tc.exe

  [This starts you the Turbo C++ 3.0]

- In the Turbo C++ go to Options>Directories> Change the source of TC to the source directory [D] (i.e. virtual D: refers to original c:\Turbo\ . So make the path change to something like D:\TC\include and D:\TC\lib respectively)

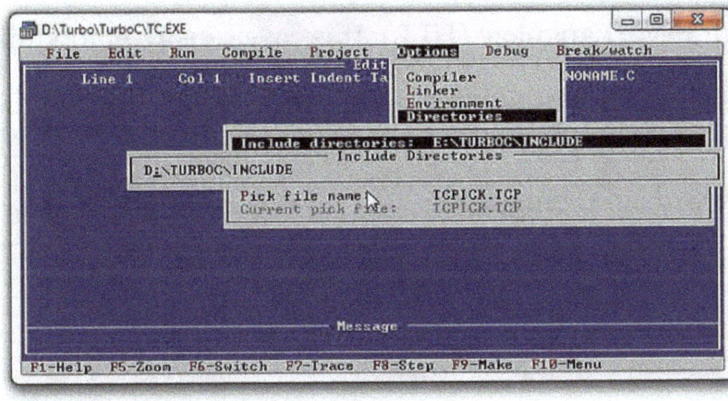

- You can save yourself some time by having DOSBox automatically mount your folders and start TurboC++:

- For DOSBox versions older then 0.74 browse into program installation folder and open the dosbox.conf file in any text editor. For version 0.73 go to Start Menu and click on "Configuration" and then "Edit Configuration". Then scroll down to the very end, and add the lines which you want to automatically execute when DOSBox starts.

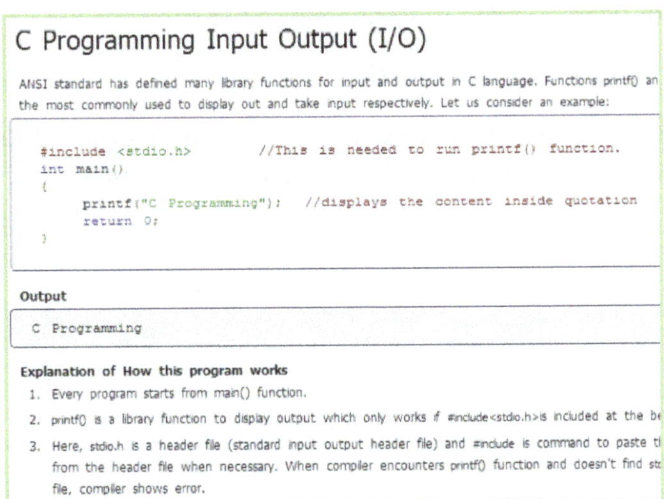

C Programming Input Output (I/O)

ANSI standard has defined many library functions for input and output in C language. Functions printf() an the most commonly used to display out and take input respectively. Let us consider an example:

```
#include <stdio.h>        //This is needed to run printf() function.
int main()
{
    printf("C Programming");   //displays the content inside quotation
    return 0;
}
```

Output

```
C Programming
```

Explanation of How this program works

1. Every program starts from main() function.
2. printf() is a library function to display output which only works if #include<stdio.h>is included at the be
3. Here, stdio.h is a header file (standard input output header file) and #include is command to paste t from the header file when necessary. When compiler encounters printf() function and doesn't find st file, compiler shows error.

2. Once you have got yourself the Turbo C++ compiler, learn about the #include, printf (Printf is used to print a message onto the console) and scanf (Scanf is used to scan a message from the console to the memory) functions.

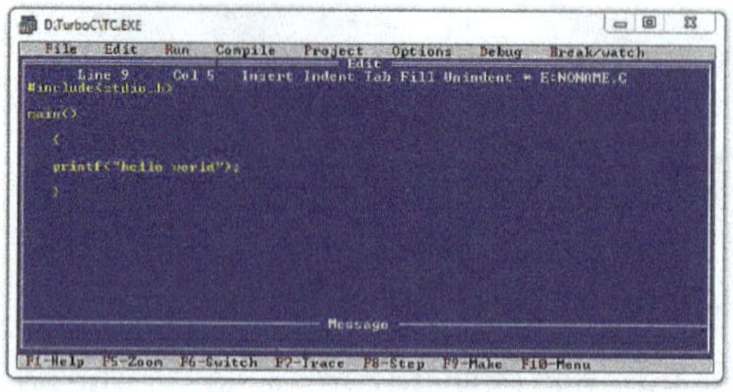

3. Create a basic Hello World program and run it. Congratulate yourself, you're starting to learn C programming in Turbo C++ IDE.

4. Remember, C is a High Level Language (HLL). It is case sensitive, modular and structured.

5. Learn about keywords. These are predefined words reserved by the language. Each keyword has a specific function. We cannot use keywords for any other purpose.

- There are 32 keywords in C language.

Table 2-2 D Keywords

auto*	goto*
break*	if*
case*	import*+
char	inline
const	int
continue*	long
counter*+	offsetof+
default*	probe*+
do*	provider*+
double	register*
else*	restrict*
enum	return+
extern	self+
float	short
for*	signed

- Every keyword is case sensitive.
- A keyword cannot be an identifier, variable or a function.
- Examples of keywords : *void, if, else, do.*

6. Learn about variables. Variables are names given to certain memory blocks where the program will store certain values. To use a variable, the programmer will have to declare it first.

Data Types and Sizes

D provides fundamental data types for integers and floating-point constants. Arithmetic may only be performed on int data structures, but floating-point arithmetic is not permitted in D. D provides a 32-bit and 64-bit data model for use ir is the native data model associated with the active operating system kernel. You can determine the native data mode

The names of the integer types and their sizes in each of the two data models are shown in the following table. Integ encoding order of your system.

Table 2-3 D Integer Data Types

Type name	32-bit Size
char	1 byte
short	2 bytes
int	4 bytes
long	4 bytes
long long	8 bytes

Integer types may be prefixed with the signed or unsigned qualifier. If no sign qualifier is present, the type is assume the following table:

Table 2-4 D Integer Type Aliases

7. Datatype : These indicate the type of value represented by certain variable. Given below are the 4 most common and important data types and on the right hand side is their format-specifier.

- int --> %d
- float --> %f
- char --> %c
- double --> %f (Yes, float & double have the same format specifier)
- Strings are a part of *char* but the format specifier for strings is %s

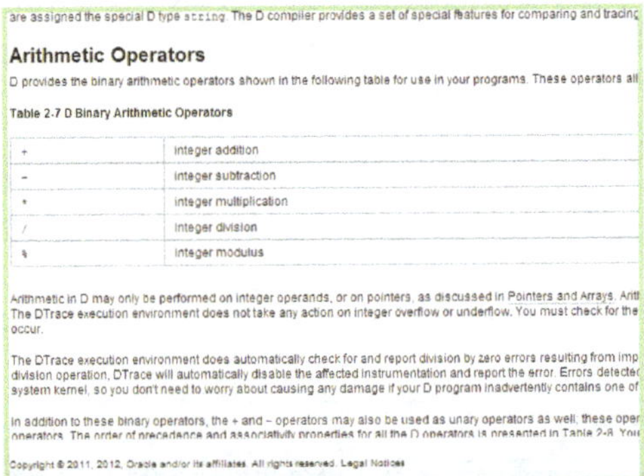

8. Learn about Arithmetic operators, logical operators, increment/ decrement operators, conditional operator, control flow structure (if-else, if statement, nested if) and looping (while, do-while, for).

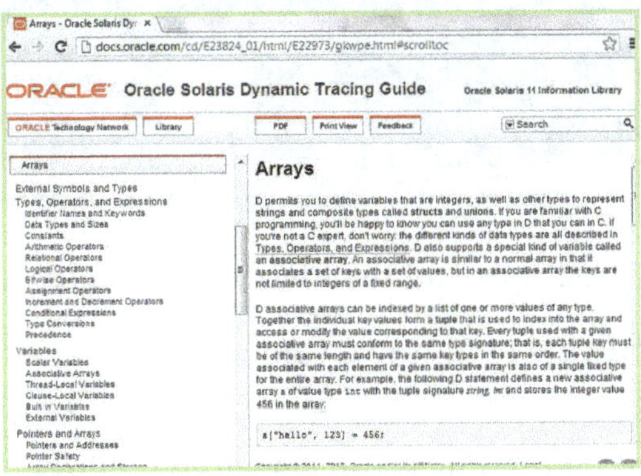

9. Learn about arrays, sorting.

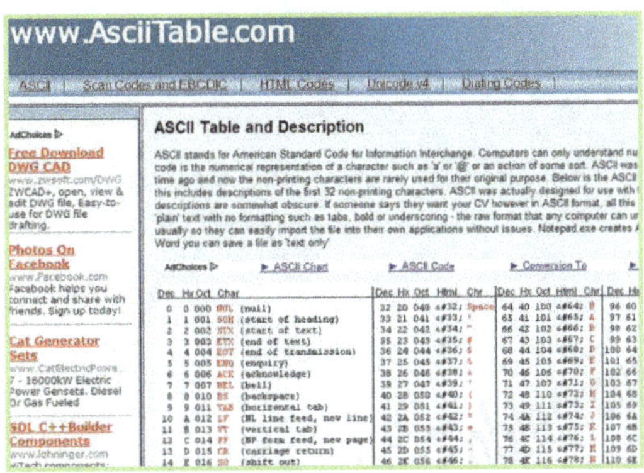

10. Learn about the ASCII (American Standard Code for Information Interchange). ASCII is used occasionally in C programming.

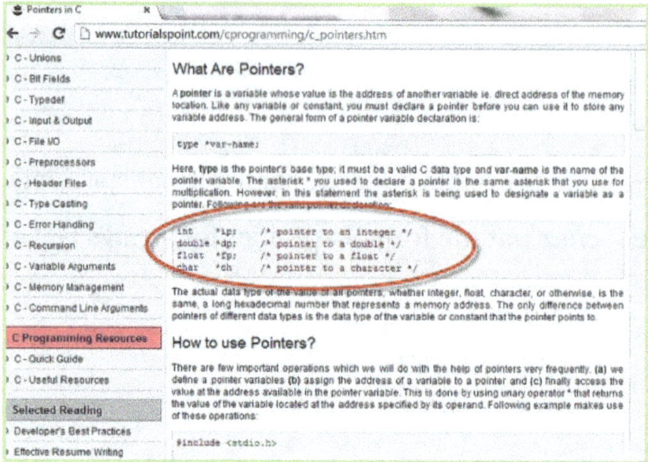

11. Learn about pointers.

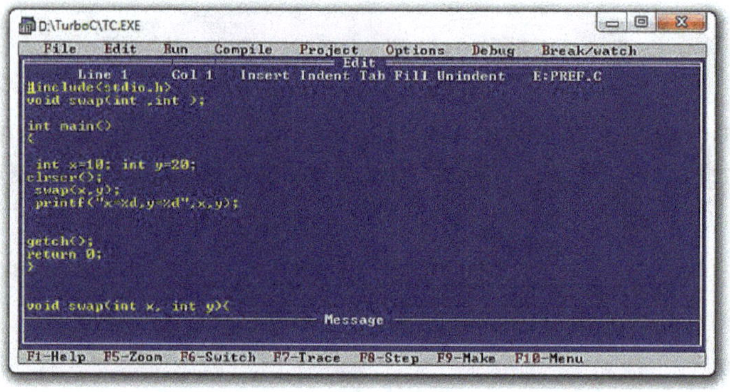

12. Start with basic and small programs and then move on to more complicated ones.

13. Get enrolled with certain courses to improve your command over C programming. Read books related to C programming.

- Remember, you cannot master any language without determination and hard work.

Chapter 6 Web Programming

HTML, Fortran and Java are popular web programming languages. They can be used to make web applications and web pages. Java is a very easy language to use for web programming. This chapter is an overview of the subject matter incorporating all the major aspects of programming languages with respect to web programming.

Java (Programming Language)

Java is a general-purpose computer programming language that is concurrent, class-based, object-oriented, and specifically designed to have as few implementation dependencies as possible. It is intended to let application developers "write once, run anywhere" (WORA), meaning that compiled Java code can run on all platforms that support Java without the need for recompilation. Java applications are typically compiled to bytecode that can run on any Java virtual machine (JVM) regardless of computer architecture. As of 2016, Java is one of the most popular programming languages in use, particularly for client-server web applications, with a reported 9 million developers. Java was originally developed by James Gosling at Sun Microsystems (which has since been acquired by Oracle Corporation) and released in 1995 as a core component of Sun Microsystems' Java platform. The language derives much of its syntax from C and C++, but it has fewer low-level facilities than either of them.

The original and reference implementation Java compilers, virtual machines, and class libraries were originally released by Sun under proprietary licenses. As of May 2007, in compliance with the specifications of the Java Community Process, Sun relicensed most of its Java technologies under the GNU General Public License. Others have also developed alternative implementations of these Sun technologies, such as the GNU Compiler for Java (bytecode compiler), GNU Classpath (standard libraries), and IcedTea-Web (browser plugin for applets).

The latest version is Java 8 which is the only version currently supported for free by Oracle, although earlier versions are supported both by Oracle and other companies on a commercial basis.

Practices

Java Platform

One design goal of Java is portability, which means that programs written for the Java platform must run similarly on any combination of hardware and operating system with adequate runtime support. This is achieved by compiling the Java language code to an intermediate representation called Java bytecode, instead of directly to architecture-specific machine code. Java bytecode instructions are analogous to machine code, but they are intended to be executed by a virtual machine (VM) written specifically for the host hardware. End users commonly use a Java Runtime Environment (JRE) installed on their own machine for standalone Java applications, or in a web browser for Java applets.

Standard libraries provide a generic way to access host-specific features such as graphics, threading, and networking.

The use of universal bytecode makes porting simple. However, the overhead of interpreting bytecode into machine instructions made interpreted programs almost always run more slowly than native executables. Just-in-time (JIT) compilers that compile bytecodes to machine code during runtime were introduced from an early stage. Java itself is platform-independent and is adapted to the particular platform it is to run on by a Java virtual machine for it, which translates the Java bytecode into the platform's machine language.

Implementations

Oracle Corporation is the current owner of the official implementation of the Java SE platform, following their acquisition of Sun Microsystems on January 27, 2010. This implementation is based on the original implementation of Java by Sun. The Oracle implementation is available for Microsoft Windows (still works for XP, while only later versions currently officially supported), macOS, Linux, and Solaris. Because Java lacks any formal standardization recognized by Ecma International, ISO/IEC, ANSI, or other third-party standards organization, the Oracle implementation is the de facto standard.

The Oracle implementation is packaged into two different distributions: The Java Runtime Environment (JRE) which contains the parts of the Java SE platform required to run Java programs and is intended for end users, and the Java Development Kit (JDK), which is intended for software developers and includes development tools such as the Java compiler, Javadoc, Jar, and a debugger.

OpenJDK is another notable Java SE implementation that is licensed under the GNU GPL. The implementation started when Sun began releasing the Java source code under the GPL. As of Java SE 7, OpenJDK is the official Java reference implementation.

The goal of Java is to make all implementations of Java compatible. Historically, Sun's trademark license for usage of the Java brand insists that all implementations be "compatible". This resulted in a legal dispute with Microsoft after Sun claimed that the Microsoft implementation did not support RMI or JNI and had added platform-specific features of their own. Sun sued in 1997, and, in 2001, won a settlement of US$20 million, as well as a court order enforcing the terms of the license from Sun. As a result, Microsoft no longer ships Java with Windows.

Platform-independent Java is essential to Java EE, and an even more rigorous validation is required to certify an implementation. This environment enables portable server-side applications.

Performance

Programs written in Java have a reputation for being slower and requiring more memory than those written in C++. However, Java programs' execution speed improved significantly with the introduction of just-in-time compilation in 1997/1998 for Java 1.1, the addition of language features supporting better code analysis (such as inner classes, the StringBuilder class, optional assertions, etc.), and optimizations in the Java virtual machine, such as HotSpot becoming the default for Sun's JVM in 2000. With Java 1.5, the performance was improved with the addition of the java.util.concurrent package, including Lock free implementations of the ConcurrentMaps and other multi-core collections, and it was improved further Java 1.6.

Some platforms offer direct hardware support for Java; there are microcontrollers that can run Java in hardware instead of a software Java virtual machine, and some ARM based processors could have hardware support for executing Java bytecode through their Jazelle option, though support has mostly been dropped in current implementations of ARM.

Automatic Memory Management

Java uses an automatic garbage collector to manage memory in the object lifecycle. The programmer determines when objects are created, and the Java runtime is responsible for recovering the memory once objects are no longer in use. Once no references to an object remain, the unreachable memory becomes eligible to be freed automatically by the garbage collector. Something similar to a memory leak may still occur if a programmer's code holds a reference to an object that is no longer needed, typically when objects that are no longer needed are stored in containers that are still in use. If methods for a nonexistent object are called, a "null pointer exception" is thrown.

One of the ideas behind Java's automatic memory management model is that programmers can be spared the burden of having to perform manual memory management. In some languages, memory for the creation of objects is implicitly allocated on the stack or explicitly allocated and deallocated from the heap. In the latter case, the responsibility of managing memory resides with the programmer. If the program does not deallocate an object, a memory leak occurs. If the program attempts to access or deallocate memory that has already been deallocated, the result is undefined and difficult to predict, and the program is likely to become unstable or crash. This can be partially remedied by the use of smart pointers, but these add overhead and complexity. Note that garbage collection does not prevent "logical" memory leaks, *i.e.*, those where the memory is still referenced but never used.

Garbage collection may happen at any time. Ideally, it will occur when a program is idle. It is guaranteed to be triggered if there is insufficient free memory on the heap to allocate a new object; this can cause a program to stall momentarily. Explicit memory management is not possible in Java.

Java does not support C/C++ style pointer arithmetic, where object addresses and unsigned integers (usually long integers) can be used interchangeably. This allows the garbage collector to relocate referenced objects and ensures type safety and security.

As in C++ and some other object-oriented languages, variables of Java's primitive data types are either stored directly in fields (for objects) or on the stack (for methods) rather than on the heap, as is commonly true for non-primitive data types (but see escape analysis). This was a conscious decision by Java's designers for performance reasons.

Java contains multiple types of garbage collectors. By default, HotSpot uses the parallel scavenge garbage collector. However, there are also several other garbage collectors that can be used to manage the heap. For 90% of applications in Java, the Concurrent Mark-Sweep (CMS) garbage collector is sufficient. Oracle aims to replace CMS with the Garbage-First collector (G1).

Syntax

The syntax of Java is largely influenced by C++. Unlike C++, which combines the syntax for structured, generic, and object-oriented programming, Java was built almost exclusively as an object-oriented language. All code is written inside classes, and every data item is an object, with the exception of the primitive data types, (*i.e.* integers, floating-point numbers, boolean values, and characters), which are not objects for performance reasons. Java reuses some popular aspects of C++ (such as printf() method).

Unlike C++, Java does not support operator overloading or multiple inheritance for *classes*, though multiple inheritance is supported for interfaces. This simplifies the language and aids in preventing potential errors and anti-pattern design.

Java uses comments similar to those of C++. There are three different styles of comments: a single line style marked with two slashes (//), a multiple line style opened with /* and closed with */, and the Javadoc commenting style opened with /** and closed with */. The Javadoc style of commenting allows the user to run the Javadoc executable to create documentation for the program and can be read by some integrated development environments (IDEs) such as Eclipse to allow developers to access documentation within the IDE.

Example:

```
// This is an example of a single line comment using two slashes

/* This is an example of a multiple line comment using the slash and asterisk.

 This type of comment can be used to hold a lot of information or deactivate

 code, but it is very important to remember to close the comment. */

package fibsandlies;

import java.util.HashMap;

/**

 * This is an example of a Javadoc comment; Javadoc can compile documentation

 * from this text. Javadoc comments must immediately precede the class, method, or field
being documented.

 */

public class FibCalculator extends Fibonacci implements Calculator {

    private static Map<Integer, Integer> memoized = new HashMap<Integer, Integer>();

    /*

     * The main method written as follows is used by the JVM as a starting point for the
program.

     */

    public static void main(String[] args) {
```

```
        memoized.put(1, 1);
        memoized.put(2, 1);
        System.out.println(fibonacci(12)); //Get the 12th Fibonacci number and print to console
    }
    /**
     * An example of a method written in Java, wrapped in a class.
     * Given a non-negative number FIBINDEX, returns
     * the Nth Fibonacci number, where N equals FIBINDEX.
     * @param fibIndex The index of the Fibonacci number
     * @return The Fibonacci number
     */
    public static int fibonacci(int fibIndex) {
        if (memoized.containsKey(fibIndex)) {
            return memoized.get(fibIndex);
        } else {
            int answer = fibonacci(fibIndex - 1) + fibonacci(fibIndex - 2);
            memoized.put(fibIndex, answer);
            return answer;
        }
    }
}
```

Special Classes

Applet

Java applets are programs that are embedded in other applications, typically in a Web page displayed in a web browser.

```
// Hello.java
import javax.swing.JApplet;
import java.awt.Graphics;

public class Hello extends JApplet {
    public void paintComponent(final Graphics g) {
        g.drawString("Hello, world!", 65, 95);
    }
}
```

The import statements direct the Java compiler to include the `javax.swing.JApplet` and `java.awt.Graphics` classes in the compilation. The import statement allows these classes to be referenced in the source code using the *simple class name* (i.e. `JApplet`) instead of the *fully qualified class name* (*FQCN*, i.e. `javax.swing.JApplet`).

The `Hello` class extends (subclasses) the `JApplet` (Java Applet) class; the JApplet class provides the framework for the host application to display and control the lifecycle of the applet. The `JApplet` class is a JComponent (Java Graphical Component) which provides the applet with the capability to display a graphical user interface (GUI) and respond to user events.

The `Hello` class overrides the `paintComponent(Graphics)` method (additionally indicated with the annotation, supported as of JDK 1.5, `Override`) inherited from the `Container` superclass to provide the code to display the applet. The `paintComponent()` method is passed a Graphics object that contains the graphic context used to display the applet. The `paintComponent()` method calls the graphic context `drawString(String, int, int)` method to display the "Hello, world!" string at a pixel offset of (65, 95) from the upper-left corner in the applet's display.

```
<!DOCTYPE HTML PUBLIC "-//W3C//DTD HTML 4.01//EN"
"http://www.w3.org/TR/html4/strict.dtd">
<!-- Hello.html -->
<html>
    <head>
        <title>Hello World Applet</title>
    </head>
    <body>
        <applet code="Hello.class" width="200" height="200">
        </applet>
    </body>
</html>
```

An applet is placed in an HTML document using the `<applet>` HTML element. The `applet` tag has three attributes set: `code="Hello"` specifies the name of the `JApplet` class and `width="200" height="200"` sets the pixel width and height of the applet. Applets may also be embedded in HTML using either the `object` or `embed` element, although support for these elements by web browsers is inconsistent. However, the `applet` tag is deprecated, so the `object` tag is preferred where supported.

The host application, typically a Web browser, instantiates the `Hello` applet and creates an `AppletContext` for the applet. Once the applet has initialized itself, it is added to the AWT display hierarchy. The `paintComponent()` method is called by the AWT event dispatching thread whenever the display needs the applet to draw itself.

Servlet

Java Servlet technology provides Web developers with a simple, consistent mechanism for extending the functionality of a Web server and for accessing existing business systems. Servlets are server-side Java EE components that generate responses (typically HTML pages) to requests (typically HTTP requests) from clients. A servlet can almost be thought of as an applet that runs on the server side—without a face.

```
// Hello.java

import java.io.*;

import javax.servlet.*;


public class Hello extends GenericServlet {

    public void service(final ServletRequest request, final ServletResponse response)

    throws ServletException, IOException {

        response.setContentType("text/html");

        final PrintWriter pw = response.getWriter();

        try {

            pw.println("Hello, world!");

        } finally {

            pw.close();

        }

    }

}
```

The import statements direct the Java compiler to include all the public classes and interfaces from the `java.io` and `javax.servlet` packages in the compilation. Packages make Java well suited for large scale applications.

The `Hello` class `extends` the `GenericServlet` class; the `GenericServlet` class provides the interface for the server to forward requests to the servlet and control the servlet's lifecycle.

The `Hello` class overrides the `service(ServletRequest, ServletResponse)` method defined by the `Servlet` interface to provide the code for the service request handler. The `service()` method is passed: a `ServletRequest` object that contains the request from the client and a ServletResponse object used to create the response returned to the client. The `service()` method declares that it throws the exceptions `ServletException` and `IOException` if a problem prevents it from responding to the request.

The `setContentType(String)` method in the response object is called to set the MIME content type of the returned data to "text/html". The `getWriter()` method in the response returns a `PrintWriter` object that is used to write the data that is sent to the client. The `println(String)` method is called to write the "Hello, world!" string to the response and then the `close()` method is called to close the print writer, which causes the data that has been written to the stream to be returned to the client.

JavaServer Pages

JavaServer Pages (JSP) are server-side Java EE components that generate responses, typically HTML pages, to HTTP requests from clients. JSPs embed Java code in an HTML page by using the special delimiters `<%` and `%>`. A JSP is compiled to a Java *servlet*, a Java application in its own right, the first time it is accessed. After that, the generated servlet creates the response.

Swing Application

Swing is a graphical user interface library for the Java SE platform. It is possible to specify a different look and feel through the pluggable look and feel system of Swing. Clones of Windows, GTK+, and Motif are supplied by Sun. Apple also provides an Aqua look and feel for macOS. Where prior implementations of these looks and feels may have been considered lacking, Swing in Java SE 6 addresses this problem by using more native GUI widget drawing routines of the underlying platforms.

This example Swing application creates a single window with "Hello, world!" inside:

```
// Hello.java (Java SE 5)
import javax.swing.*;
public class Hello extends JFrame {
    public Hello() {
        super("hello");
        super.setDefaultCloseOperation(WindowConstants.EXIT_ON_CLOSE);
        super.add(new JLabel("Hello, world!"));
        super.pack();
        super.setVisible(true);
    }
    public static void main(final String[] args) {
        new Hello();
    }
}
```

The first import includes all the public classes and interfaces from the `javax.swing` package.

The `Hello` class `extends` the `JFrame` class; the `JFrame` class implements a window with a title bar and a close control.

The `Hello()` constructor initializes the frame by first calling the superclass constructor, passing the parameter `"hello"`, which is used as the window's title. It then calls the `setDefaultCloseOperation(int)` method inherited from `JFrame` to set the default operation when the close control on the title bar is selected to `WindowConstants.EXIT_ON_CLOSE` – this causes the `JFrame` to be disposed of when the frame is closed (as opposed to merely hidden), which allows the Java virtual machine to exit and the program to terminate. Next, a `JLabel` is created for the string "Hello, world!" and the `add(Component)` method inherited from the `Container` superclass is called to add the label to the frame. The `pack()` method inherited from the Window superclass is called to size the `window` and lay out its contents.

The `main()` method is called by the Java virtual machine when the program starts. It instantiates a new Hello frame and causes it to be displayed by calling the `setVisible(boolean)` method inherited from the `Component` superclass with the boolean parameter `true`. Once the frame is displayed, exiting the `main` method does not cause the program to terminate because the AWT event dispatching thread remains active until all of the Swing top-level windows have been disposed.

Generics

In 2004, generics were added to the Java language, as part of J2SE 5.0. Prior to the introduction of generics, each variable declaration had to be of a specific type. For container classes, for example, this is a problem because there is no easy way to create a container that accepts only specific types of objects. Either the container operates on all subtypes of a class or interface, usually `Object`, or a different container class has to be created for each contained class. Generics allow compile-time type checking without having to create many container classes, each containing almost identical code. In addition to enabling more efficient code, certain runtime exceptions are prevented from occurring, by issuing compile-time errors. If Java prevented all runtime type errors (ClassCast`Exception's`) from occurring, it would be type safe.

In 2016, the type system was shown not to be safe at all, it was proven unsound.

Use Outside the Java Platform

The Java programming language requires the presence of a software platform in order for compiled programs to be executed. Oracle supplies the Java platform for use with Java. The Android SDK is an alternative software platform, used primarily for developing Android applications.

Android

The Android operating system makes extensive use of Java-related technology.

The Java language is a key pillar in Android, an open source mobile operating system. Although Android, built on the Linux kernel, is written largely in C, the Android SDK uses the Java language as the basis for Android applications. The bytecode language supported by the Android SDK is incompatible with Java bytecode and runs on its own virtual machine, optimized for low-memory devices such as smartphones and tablet computers. Depending on the Android version, the bytecode is either interpreted by the Dalvik virtual machine or compiled into native code by the Android Runtime.

Android does not provide the full Java SE standard library, although the Android SDK does include an independent implementation of a large subset of it. It supports Java 6 and some Java 7 features, offering an implementation compatible with the standard library (Apache Harmony).

Controversy

The use of Java-related technology in Android led to a legal dispute between Oracle and Google. On May 7, 2012, a San Francisco jury found that if APIs could be copyrighted, then Google had infringed Oracle's copyrights by the use of Java in Android devices. District Judge William Haskell Alsup ruled on May 31, 2012, that APIs cannot be copyrighted, but this was reversed by the United States Court of Appeals for the Federal Circuit in May 2014. On May 26, 2016, the district court decided in favor of Google, ruling the copyright infringement of the Java API in Android constitutes fair use.

Class Libraries

The Java Class Library is the standard library, developed to support application development in Java. It is controlled by Sun Microsystems in cooperation with others through the Java Community Process program. Companies or individuals participating in this process can influence the design and development of the APIs. This process has been a subject of controversy. The class library contains features such as:

- The core libraries, which include:
  - IO/NIO
  - Networking
  - Reflection
  - Concurrency
  - Generics
  - Scripting/Compiler
  - Functional programming (Lambda, Streaming)
  - Collection libraries that implement data structures such as lists, dictionaries, trees, sets, queues and double-ended queue, or stacks
  - XML Processing (Parsing, Transforming, Validating) libraries
  - Security
  - Internationalization and localization libraries

- The integration libraries, which allow the application writer to communicate with external systems. These libraries include:
    - The Java Database Connectivity (JDBC) API for database access
    - Java Naming and Directory Interface (JNDI) for lookup and discovery
    - RMI and CORBA for distributed application development
    - JMX for managing and monitoring applications
- User interface libraries, which include:
    - The (heavyweight, or native) Abstract Window Toolkit (AWT), which provides GUI components, the means for laying out those components and the means for handling events from those components
    - The (lightweight) Swing libraries, which are built on AWT but provide (non-native) implementations of the AWT widgetry
    - APIs for audio capture, processing, and playback
    - JavaFX
- A platform dependent implementation of the Java virtual machine that is the means by which the bytecodes of the Java libraries and third party applications are executed
- Plugins, which enable applets to be run in web browsers
- Java Web Start, which allows Java applications to be efficiently distributed to end users across the Internet
- Licensing and documentation

Documentation

Javadoc is a comprehensive documentation system, created by Sun Microsystems, used by many Java developers. It provides developers with an organized system for documenting their code. Javadoc comments have an extra asterisk at the beginning, i.e. the delimiters are `/**` and `*/`, whereas the normal multi-line comments in Java are set off with the delimiters `/*` and `*/`.

Editions

Sun has defined and supports four editions of Java targeting different application environments and segmented many of its APIs so that they belong to one of the platforms. The platforms are:

- Java Card for smartcards.
- Java Platform, Micro Edition (Java ME) – targeting environments with limited resources.
- Java Platform, Standard Edition (Java SE) – targeting workstation environments.
- Java Platform, Enterprise Edition (Java EE) – targeting large distributed enterprise or Internet environments.

The classes in the Java APIs are organized into separate groups called packages. Each package contains a set of related interfaces, classes, and exceptions. Refer to the separate platforms for a description of the packages available.

Sun also provided an edition called PersonalJava that has been superseded by later, standards-based Java ME configuration-profile pairings.

How to write your First Program in Java

Java is an object-oriented programming language founded in 1991 by James Gosling, which means that it represents concepts as "objects" with "fields" (which are attributes that describe the object) and "methods" (actions that the object can make). Java is a "write once, run anywhere" language, which means that it is designed to run on one platform and will run on any Java Virtual Machine (JVM). Since Java is a very verbose programming language, it is easy for beginners to learn and understand. This tutorial is an introduction to writing programs in Java.

Method 1

Writing your first Java Program

1. In order to start writing programs in Java, set up your work environment. Many programmers use Integrated Development Environments (IDEs) such as Eclipse and Netbeans for their Java programming, but one can write a Java program and compile it without bloated IDEs.

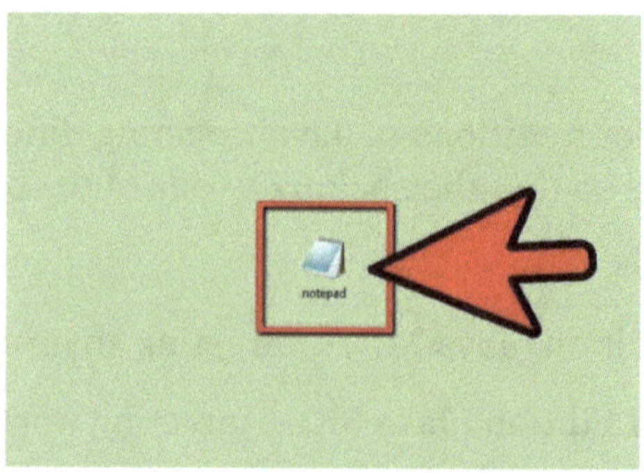

2. Any sort of Notepad-like program will suffice for programming in Java. Hardcore programmers sometimes prefer to use text editors that are within the terminal such as vim and emacs. A very

good text editor that can be installed on both a Windows machine and on a linux-based machine (Mac, Ubuntu, etc.) is Sublime Text, which is what we will be using in this tutorial.

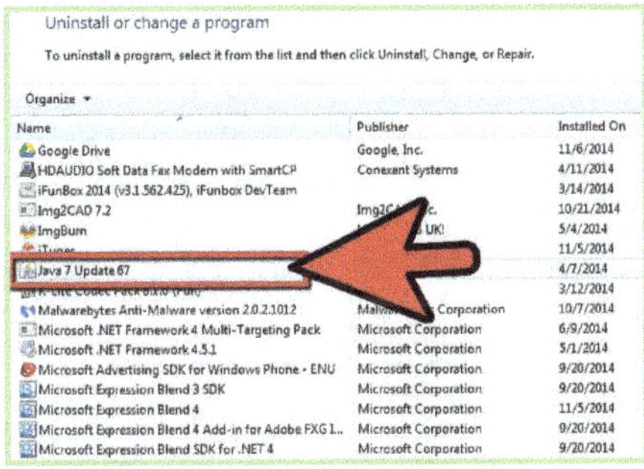

3. Make sure that you have the Java Software Development Kit installed. You will need this for compiling your program.

- In a Windows-based operating system, if the environment variables are not correct, you might get an error when running `javac`. Refer the installation article How to Install the Java Software Development Kit for more details about JDK installation to avoid this error.

Method 2

Hello World Program

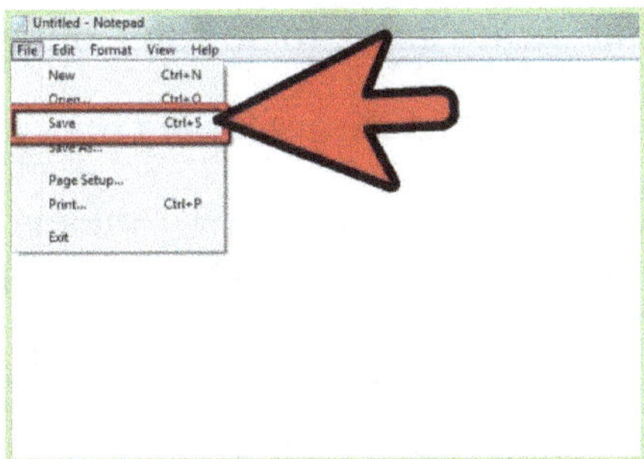

1. We will first create a program that prints "Hello World." In your text editor, create a new file and save it as "HelloWorld.java". HelloWorld is your class name and you will need your class name to be the same name as your file.

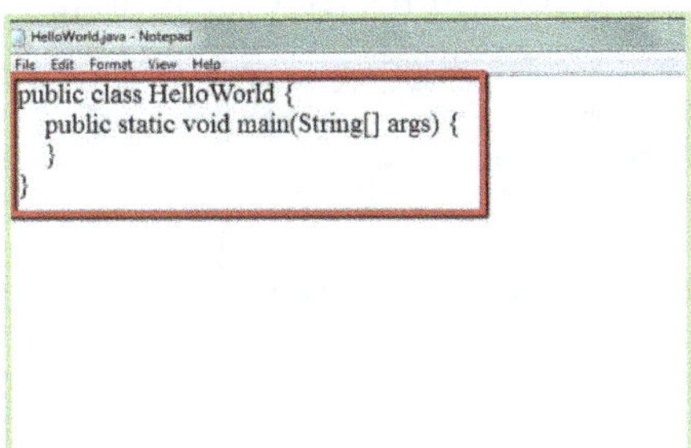

2. Declare your class and your main method. The main method `public static void main(String[] args)` is the method that will be executed when the programming is running. This main method will have the same method declaration in every Java program.

```
public class HelloWorld {
    public static void main(String[] args) {
    }
}
```

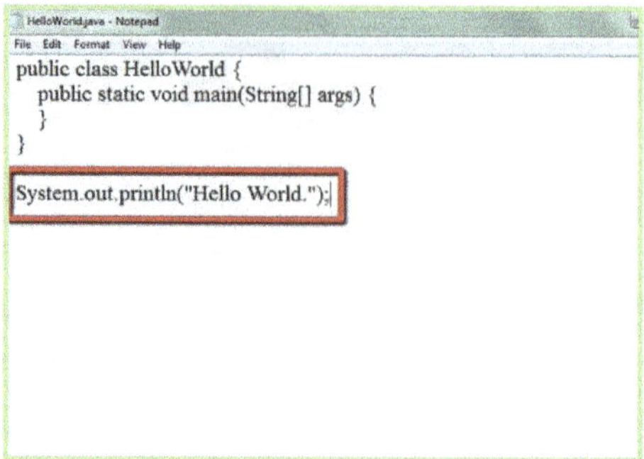

3. Write the line of code that will print out "Hello World."

```
System.out.println("Hello World.");
```

- Let's look at the components of this line:
    - `System` tells the system to do something.
    - `out` tells the system that we are going to do some output stuff.
    - `println` stands for "print line," so we are telling the system to print a line in the output.
    - The parentheses around (`"Hello World."`) means that the method `System.out.println()` takes in a parameter, which, in this case, is the String `"Hello World."`
- Note that there are some rules in Java that we have to adhere to:
    - You must always add a semicolon at the end of every line.
    - Java is case sensitive, so you must write method names, variable names, and class names in the correct case or you will get an error.
    - Blocks of code specific to a certain method or loop are encased between curly brackets.

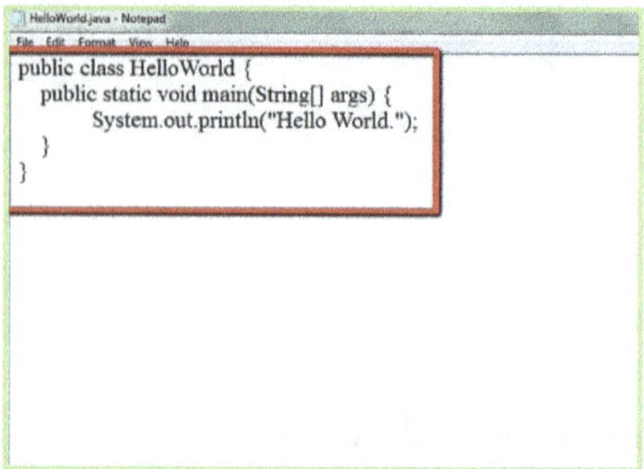

4. Put it all together. Your final Hello World program should look like the following:

```
public class HelloWorld {

    public static void main(String[] args) {

        System.out.println("Hello World.");

    }

}
```

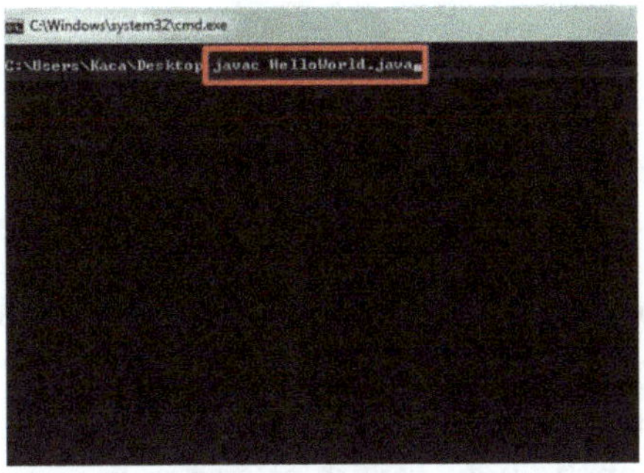

5. Save your file and open up command prompt or terminal to compile the program. Navigate to the folder where you saved HelloWorld.java and type in `javac HelloWorld.java`. This tells the Java compiler that you want to compile HelloWorld.java. If there are errors, the compiler will tell you what you did wrong. Otherwise, you shouldn't see any messages from the compiler. If you look at the directory where you have HelloWorld.java now, you should see HelloWorld.class. This the the file that Java will use to run your program.

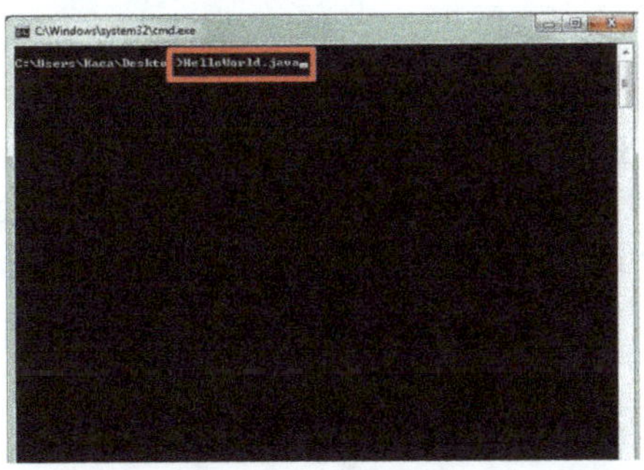

6. Run the program. Finally, we get to run our program! In command prompt or terminal, type in `java HelloWorld`. This tells Java that you want to run the class HelloWorld. You should see “Hello World.” show up in your console.

7. Congratulations, you have made your first Java program.

Method 3

Input and output

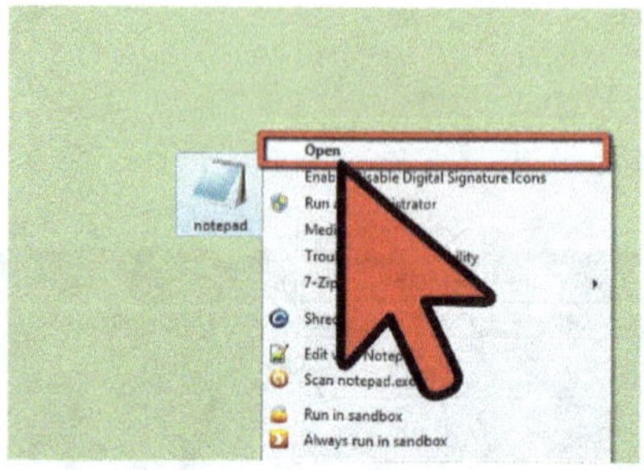

1. We will now extend our Hello World program to take input from the user. In our Hello World program, we printed out a string for the user to see, but the interactive part of programs is when the user gets to enter input into the program. We will now extend our program to prompt the user for his or her name and then greet the user by his or her name.

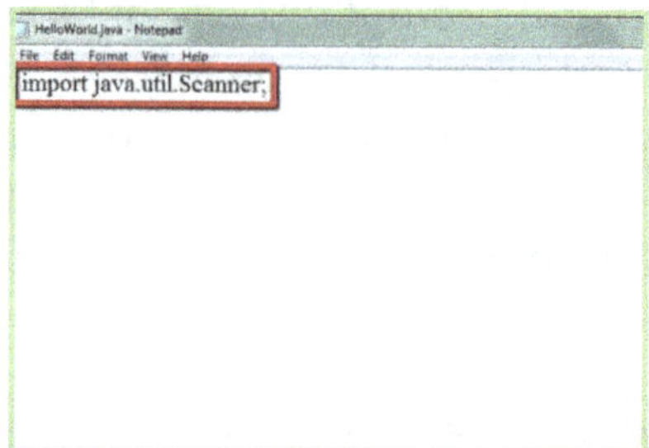

2. Import the Scanner class. In Java, we have some built in libraries that we have access to, but we have to import them. One of these libraries is java.util, which contains the Scanner object that we need to get user input. In order to import the Scanner class, we add the following line to the beginning of our code.

```
import java.util.Scanner;
```

- This tells our program that we want to use the Scanner object which exists in the package java.util.
- If we wanted to have access to every object in the java.util package, we simply write `import java.util.*;` at the beginning of our code.

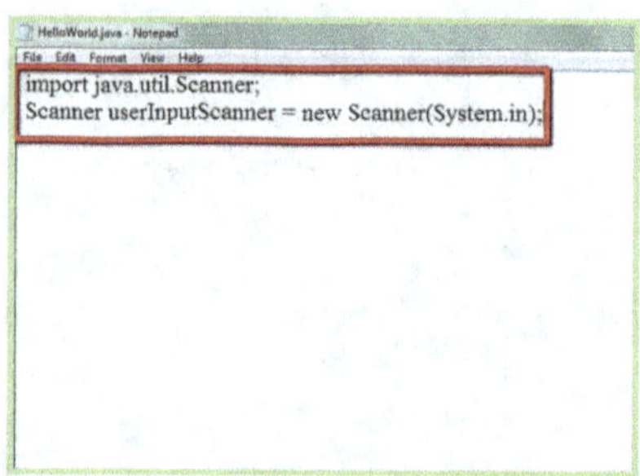

3. Inside our main method, instantiate a new instance of the Scanner object. Java is an object-ori-

ented programming language, so it represents concepts using objects. The Scanner object is an example of an object that has fields and methods. In order to use the Scanner class, we have to create a new Scanner object that we can populate the fields of and use the methods of. To do this, we write:

```
Scanner userInputScanner = new Scanner(System.in);
```

- `userInputScanner` is the name of the Scanner object that we just instantiated. Note that the name is written in camel case; this is the convention for naming variables in Java.
- We use the new operator to create a new instance of an object. So, in this instance, we created a new instance of the Scanner object by writing `new Scanner(System.in)`.
- The Scanner object takes in a parameter that tells the object what to scan. In this case, we put in `System.in` as a parameter. `System.in` tells the program to scan the input from the system, which is the input that the user will type into the program.

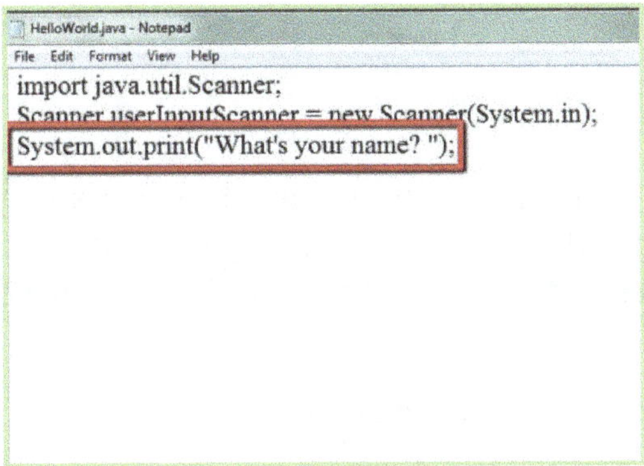

4. Prompt the user for an input. We have to prompt the user for an input so that the user knows when to type something into the console. This can be accomplished with a `System.out.print` or a `System.out.println`.

```
System.out.print("What's your name? ");
```

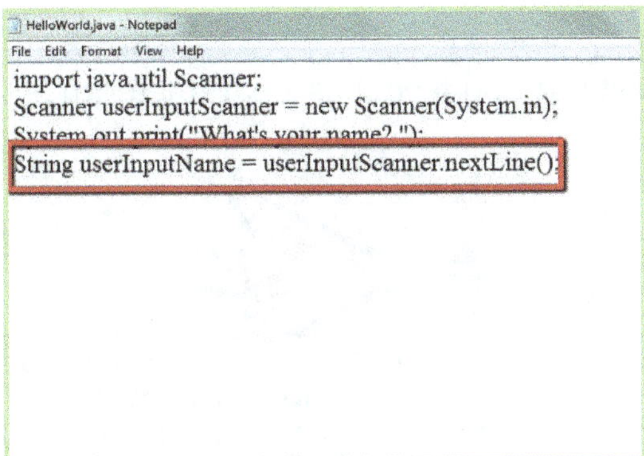

5. Ask the Scanner object to take in the next line that the user types in and store that in a variable. The Scanner will always be taking in data on what the user is typing in. The following line will ask the Scanner to take what the user has typed in for his or her name and store it in a variable:

```
String userInputName = userInputScanner.nextLine();
```

- In Java, the convention for using an object's method is `objectName.methodName`(parameters). In `userInputScanner.nextLine()`, we are calling our Scanner object by the name we just gave it and then we are calling its method `nextLine()` which does not take in any parameters.
- Note that we are storing the next line in another object: the String object. We have named our String object `userInputName`

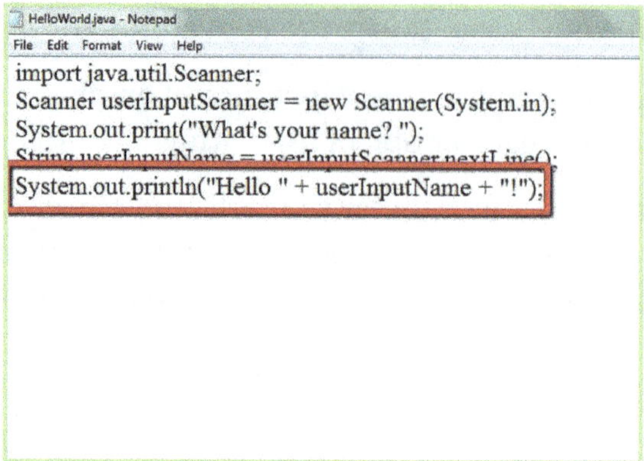

6. Print out a greeting to the user. Now that we have the user's name stored, we can print out a greeting to the user. Remember the `System.out.println("Hello World.");` that we wrote in the main class? All of the code that we just wrote should go above that line. Now we can modify that line to say:

```
System.out.println("Hello " + userInputName + "!");
```

- The way we chained up "Hello ", the user's name, and "!" by writing `"Hello " + userInputName + "!"` is called String concatenation.
- What's happening here is that we have three strings: "Hello ", userInputName, and "!". Strings in Java are immutable, which means that they cannot be changed. So when we are concatenating these three strings, we are essentially created a new string that contains the greeting.
- Then we take this new string and feed it as a parameter to `System.out.println`.

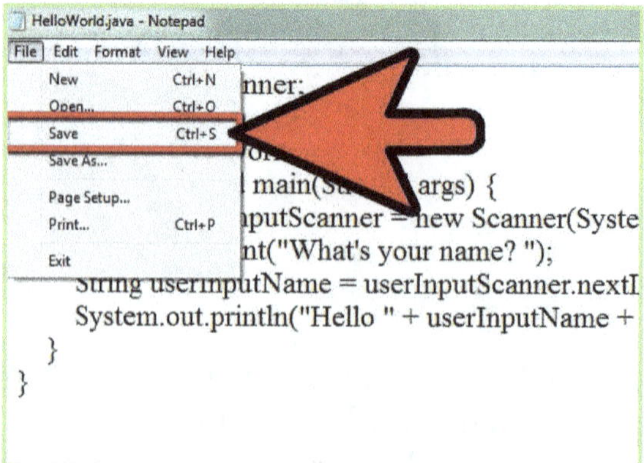

7. Put it all together and save. Our code should now look like this:

```
import java.util.Scanner;
public class HelloWorld {
    public static void main(String[] args) {
        Scanner userInputScanner = new Scanner(System.in);
        System.out.print("What's your name? ");
        String userInputName = userInputScanner.nextLine();
        System.out.println("Hello " + userInputName + "!");
    }
}
```

8. Compile and run. Go into command prompt or terminal and run the same commands as we ran for our first iteration of HelloWorld.java. We have to first compile the program: `javac HelloWorld.java`. Then we can run it: `java HelloWorld`.

How to Compile & Run Java Program using Command Prompt

While many programming environments will allow you to compile and run a program within the environment, you can also compile and run using Command Prompt. Both Windows and Mac have their own versions of Command Prompt, although it is technically called Terminal on the Mac OS. The process is essentially identical for Windows and Mac.

Method 1

Compiling and Running

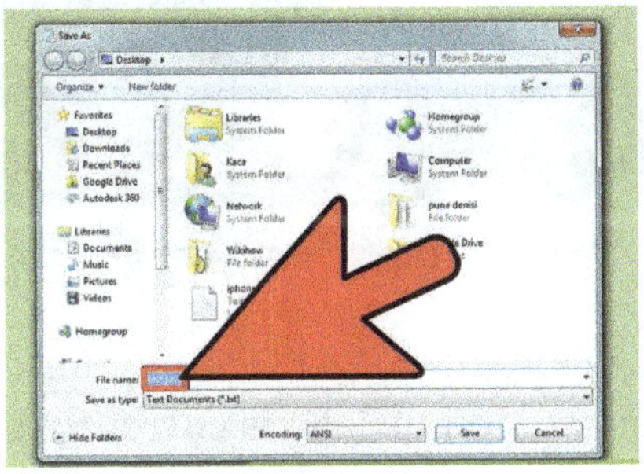

1. Save the program. After using a text editor, such as NotePad, to create your Java program, save

the program with a .java extension. Of course, the file name can be anything. For the purposes of this tutorial, "filename" will be used as a placeholder for your file name.

- To ensure that your file is saved as a .java file, be sure to write .java after the file name, and select All Files from the dropdown extension menu.
- Make note of where you saved the file on your system.
- If you are unsure of how to write a program in Java, check out our tutorial on how to program in Java. For the purposes of learning how to compile and run a program, though, you can use any sort of Java program.

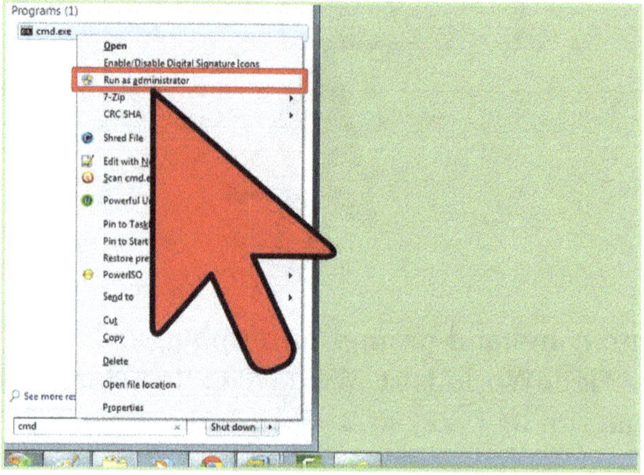

2. Open Command Prompt/Terminal. Accessing the command line differs slightly for Mac and Windows.

- Windows: Press ⇱ Home, then type cmd. Press ↵ Enter to open the Command Prompt.
- Mac: In Finder, press the Go tab, select Applications, select Utilities, then select Terminal.

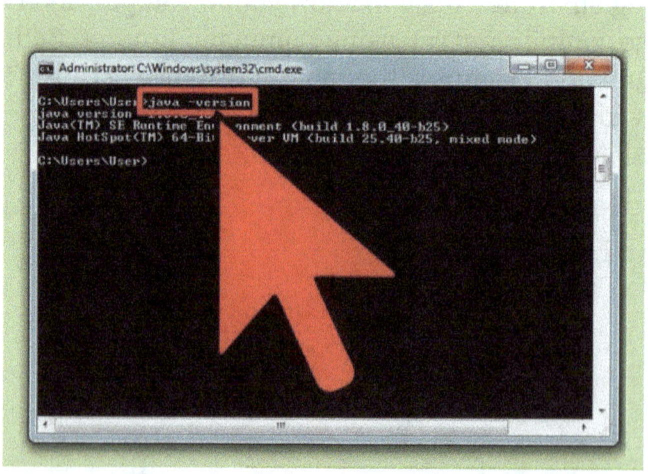

3. Check that Java is installed. Type `java -version` into your command line. If java is installed, you will see a message stating what version of Java is currently installed.

- If not, you may need to install the Java Development Kit from their website.

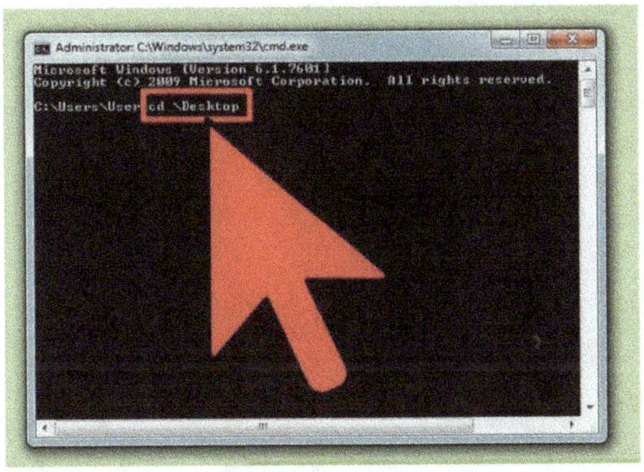

4. Navigate to the correct folder. Use the command cd followed by the directory name to change your working directory.

- For example, if you were operating in `C:\Users\Bob\Project` and wanted to get to C:\Users\Bob\Project\TitanProject , enter in cd TitanProject and press ↵ Enter.
- You can see a list of what is in your current directory by typing `dir` and pressing ↵ Enter.

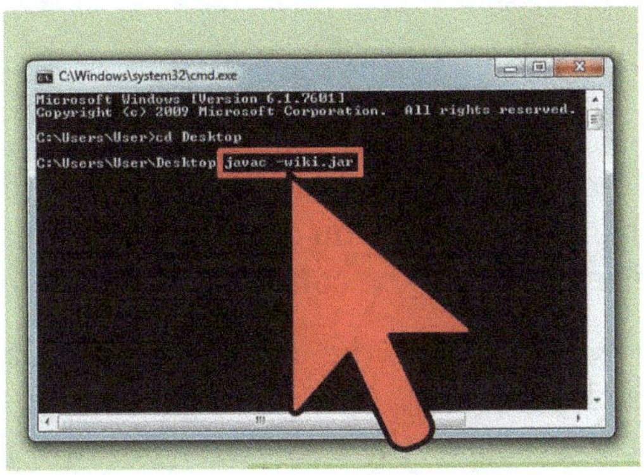

5. Compile the program. Once you are in the correct directory, you can compile the program by typing `javac filename.java` into the command line and pressing enter.

- If you have any errors in your program, or if there is difficultly compiling, the command prompt will notify you.

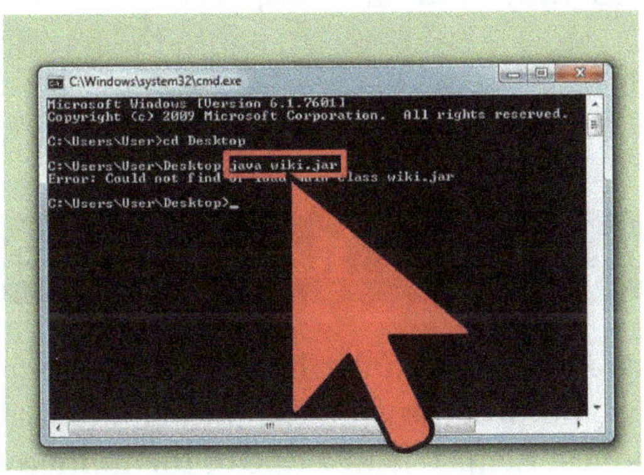

6. Run the program. Enter in java filename and press ↵ Enter. Of course, replace "filename" with whatever the name of your file actually is.

- After pressing ↵ Enter, your program should run. If you receive an error, or if your program fails to run in any way, refer to the troubleshooting method.

Method 2

Troubleshooting

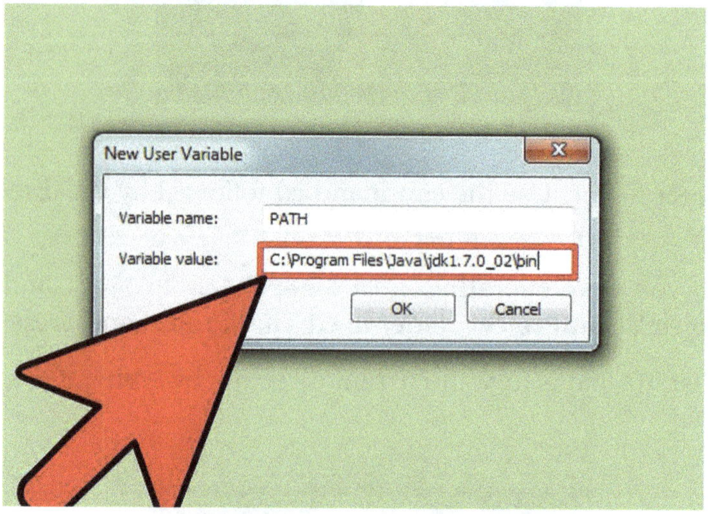

1. Set your path. If you are running a simple program with all of the files in the same directory, you will probably not need to do this. However, if you are running a more complex program with files in multiple directories, you will need to tell the computer where to look for these files.

- Windows: Type `java -version` into the command prompt and press ↵ Enter. Based off the version of Java displayed on the first line, type in `set path=%path%;C:\Program Files\Java\jdk1.5.0_09\bin` to the command prompt and press ↵ Enter. Substitute jdk1.5.0_09 with whatever version of Java you have installed.
- Be sure you are entering in this command while in the directory containing your Java project.
- Mac: Type `/usr/libexec/java_home -v 1.7` into the terminal and press ↵ Enter to ensure Java is installed on your system. Then, type `echo export "JAVA_HOME=\$(/usr/libexec/java_home)" >> ~/.bash_profile` into the terminal and press ↵ Enter. Restart the terminal afterwards.

How to Download, Install, Run JDK and Eclipse

Computer programming using Java is arguably the most important aspect of computing. Many of today's popular applications and programs utilize java as the main source code, ranging from computer games to mobile phones. Eclipse is just one of the numerous script editing applications for developing java programs and allows students to write and compile java code and execute programs.

Steps

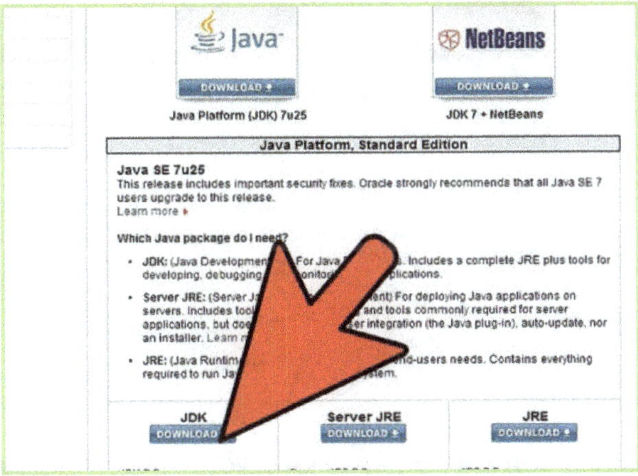

1. Visit the Java downloads page on Oracle's website to find the JDK environment download. Scroll down until you find Java SE 6 Update 43, and download JDK.

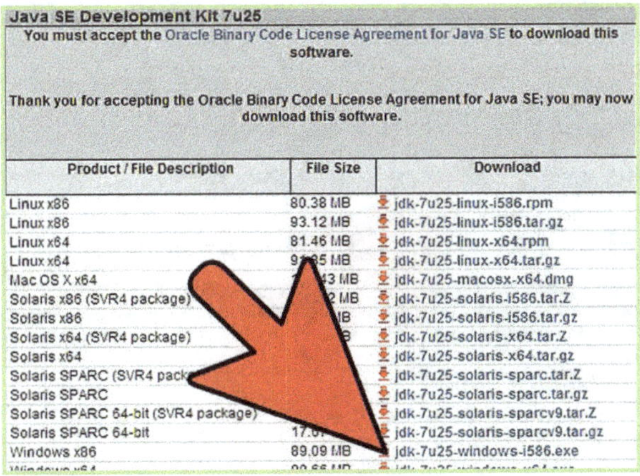

2. Once you have selected download, accept the terms of service and choose the correct OS corresponding for the specific JDK. (Windows, Mac, Linux, etc.)

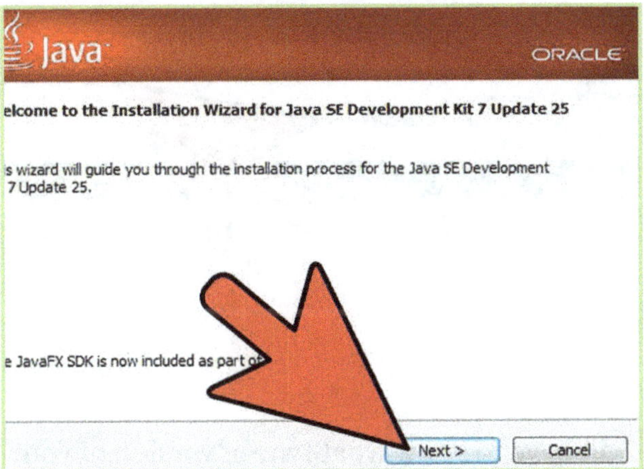

3. Once the download is complete, double click the file to begin the installation of JDK.

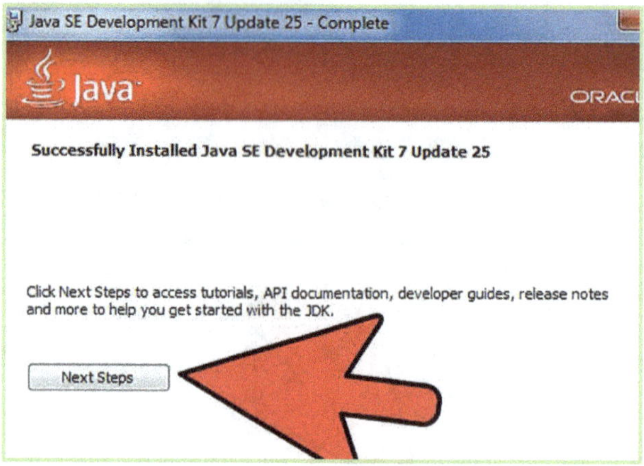

4. After the initial installation is done, a pop up asking you where your source java files will be. You can choose to change where you want to keep your folder but it's best to stick with what you were given first.

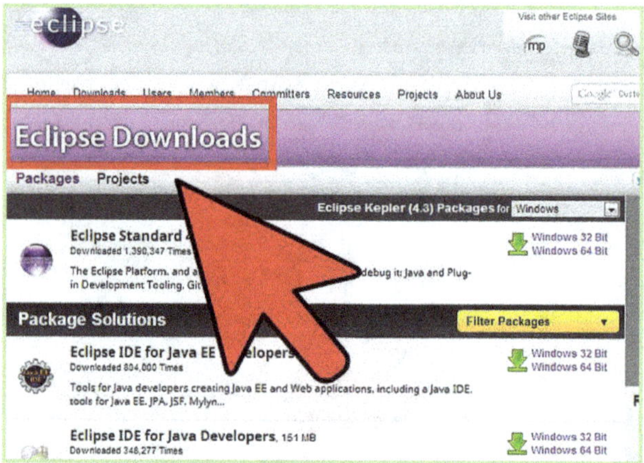

5. When the installation is finished, we will begin to the installation of Eclipse.

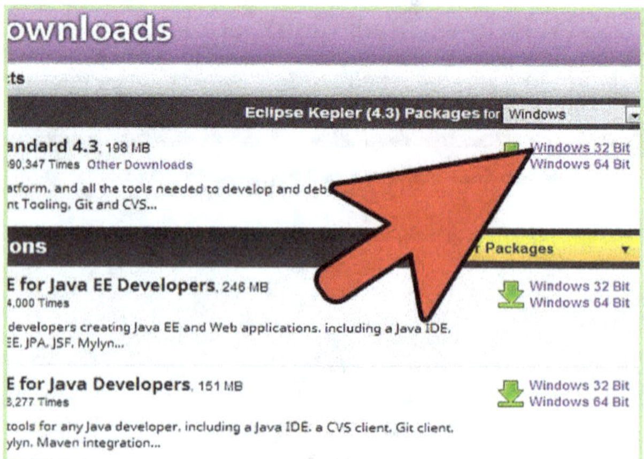

6. For Windows users, you will have to know what type of version of your OS you have. If your computer is a 64 bit Windows, select Windows 64 and if you have a 32 bit Windows, select Windows 32 bit.

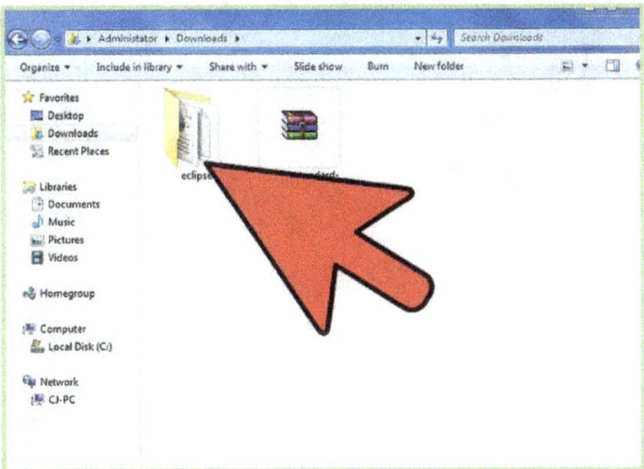

7. Once you have downloaded the Eclipse archive you will need to decompress the zip file, which will create the unzipped Eclipse folder. You may want to extract the archive to the root of C:\ drive, thus creating the folder "C:\eclipse", or just moved the extracted eclipse folder to the root of C:\ drive if you extracted it already. Since Eclipse does not have any installer, there will be a file inside the Eclipse folder named eclipse.exe ( ). You can double click on the file to run Eclipse.

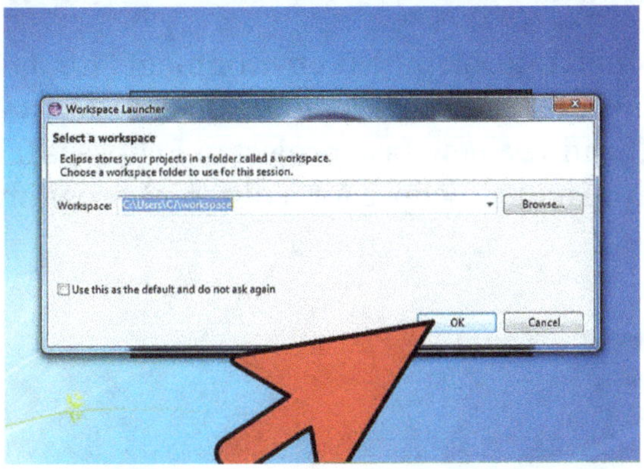

8. After eclipse has been fully installed and extracted, create a workspace folder where you will contain all the program files you create.

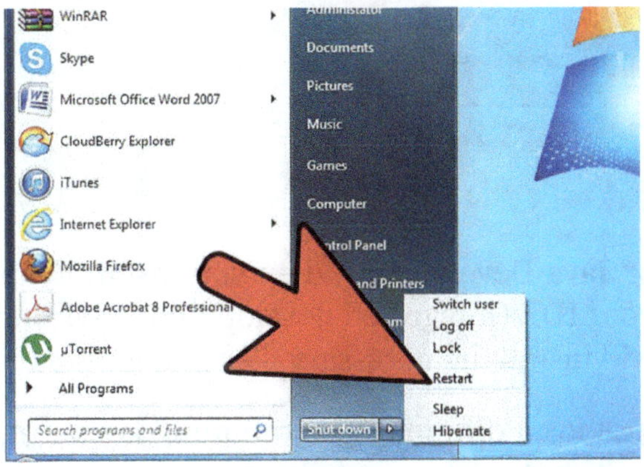

9. Now that you have finished installing Eclipse, restart your computer. Restarting your computer refreshes system memory and allows registration or configuration changes made by installers and uninstallers to take effect.

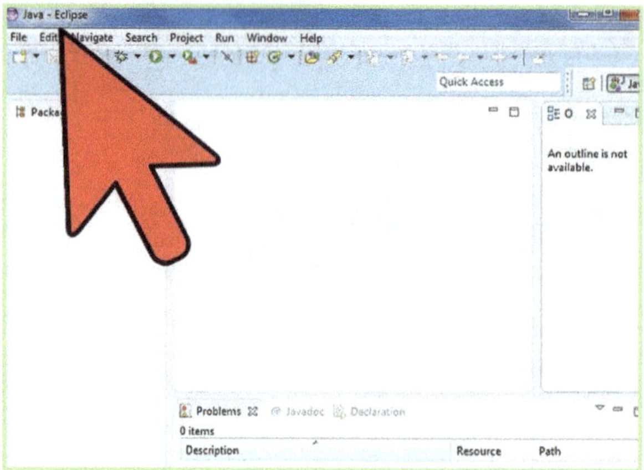

10. From there, create a test program to test the functionality of Eclipse.

How to create a new Java Project in Eclipse

Eclipse is one of the most popular development environments for Java, as it contains everything you need to build a Java project from scratch. Before you can start working on your new project, you'll need to create it first. Creating a new Java project in Eclipse is fairly straightforward, but can be confusing if you've already installed Eclipse for a different programming language.

Steps

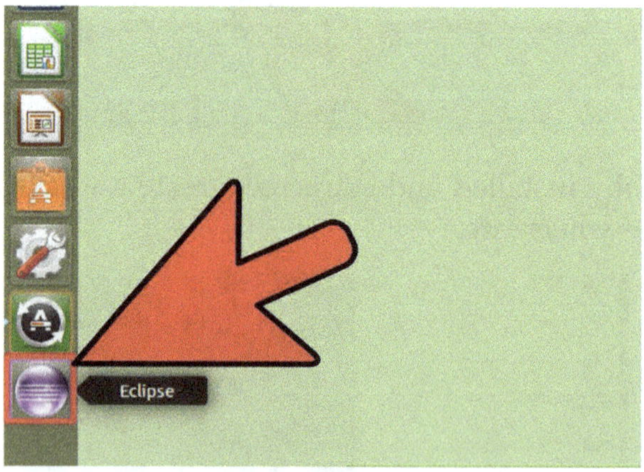

1. Install the Eclipse IDE for Java Developers. When you install Eclipse for the first time, you're given the option to choose your IDE (integrated development environment). Choose "Eclipse IDE for Java Developers". This will install the necessary files and tools to create Java projects.

- If you installed Eclipse for a different programming language, you can add Java support from within Eclipse. Click the "Help" menu and select "Install New Software". Select "All Available Sites" from the top drop-down menu, and then type "java" into the Filter field. Check the "Eclipse Java Development Tools" box and click "Next". Follow the prompts to download and install the Java tools. Eclipse will restart once the installation is complete.

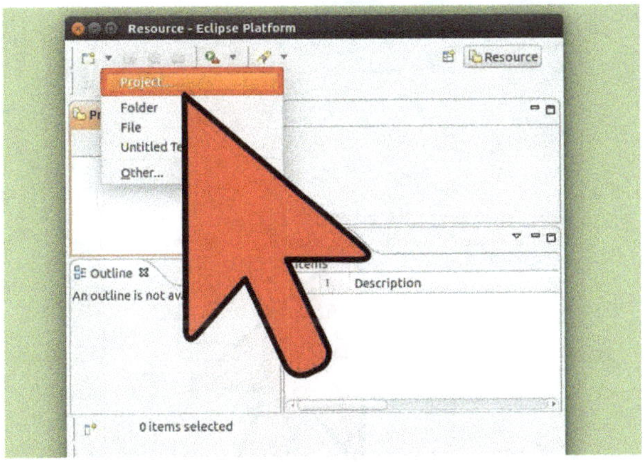

2. Click "File" → "New" → "Java Project". This will open the "New Java Project" window.

- If you don't see the "Java Project" option but have the Java Development Tools installed, select "Project..." from the "New" menu. Expand the "Java" folder and select "Java Project".

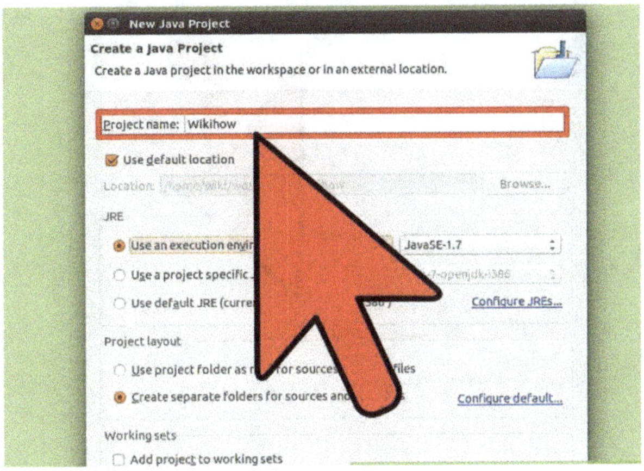

3. Give the project a name. This doesn't have to be the final name for your program, but should help you and others identify the project.

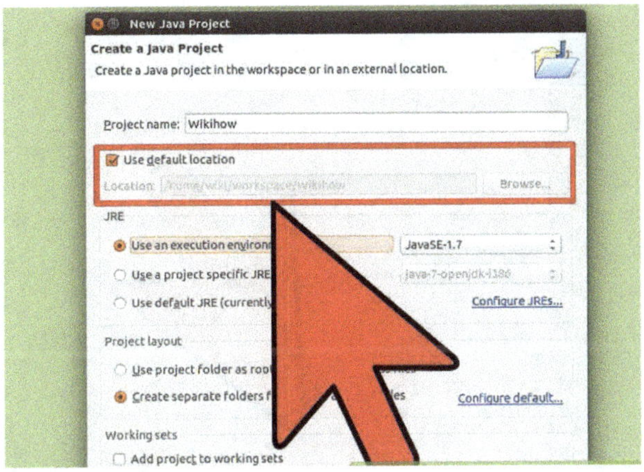

4. Select the location for the project files. The files are saved to the Eclipse directory by default. You can set a custom location if you prefer.

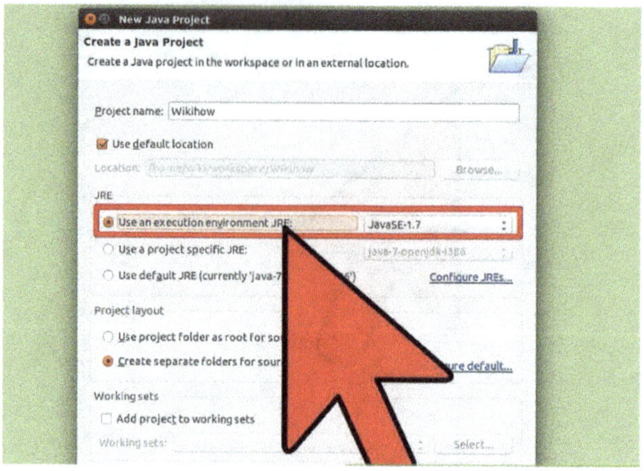

5. Select Java Runtime Environment (JRE) you want to use. If you are creating a program for a specific JRE, select it from the drop-down menu. By default, the newest JRE will be selected.

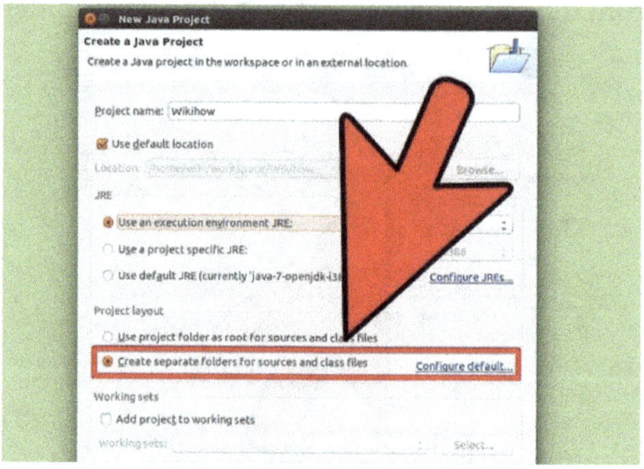

6. Select your project layout. You can choose to either use the project folder, or create separate folders for sources and class files. The default option is "Create separate folders...", though you may need to change depending on the needs of your project.

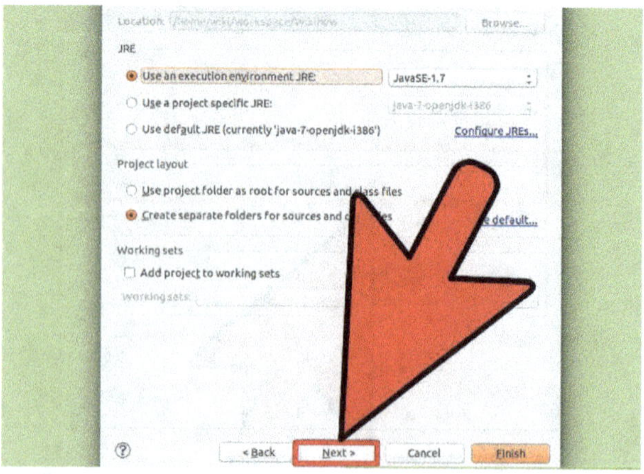

7. Click "Next" to open the "Java Settings" window. This is where you'll define additional sources as well as add libraries to your project.

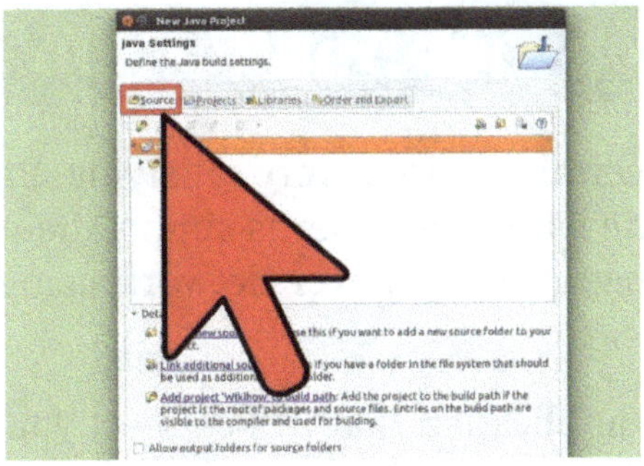

8. Use the Source tab to define your build path. The build path is what the compiler uses to build the program. You can create additional source folders, link external sources, and add or remove folders from the build path. The compiler uses the build path to determine which sources to compile.

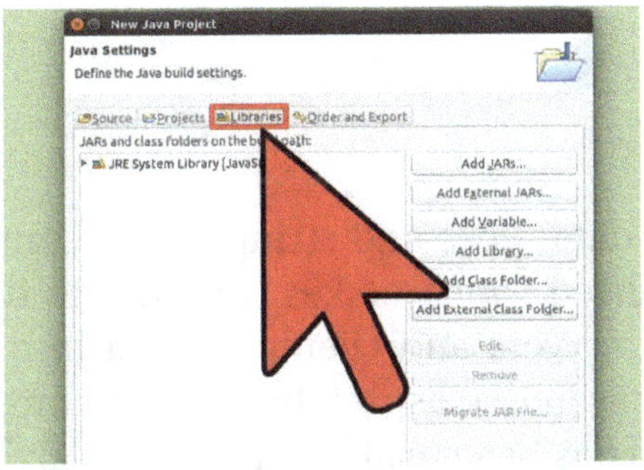

9. Use the Libraries tab to add libraries to the project. This tab will allow you to add JAR files to include in your project, as well as select built-in libraries to use. Importing JAR files allows you to use libraries from other projects.

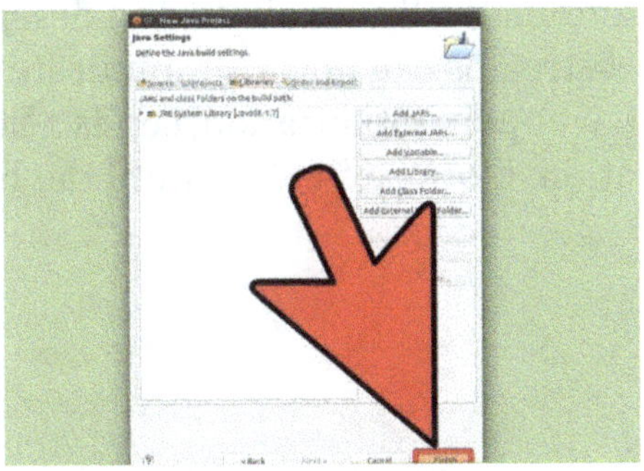

10. Click "Finish" to start working on your new project. You'll be taken to your Java workspace. If you were working in a different programming language before starting the project, you'll be prompted to switch to the Java perspective. This is recommended to get the most out of the IDE.

- Your project will be displayed in the "Package Explorer" frame on the left side of the window. If you just see the Eclipse Welcome tab, click the small Java button on the left side of the window.
- See How to Write Your First Program in Java for a detailed guide on creating your first Java program.

How to create a Network Application in Java

Writing code that executes on a certain device is very satisfying. But, writing code that executes on several devices that communicate with each other is simply life-affirming. This article will teach you how to connect and exchange messages over network using transmission control protocol (TCP).

In this article, you will setup an application that will connect your computer to itself and, essentially, make it *crazy* - talk to itself. You will also learn the difference between the two most widely used streams for networking in Java and how they function.

Data and Object Streams

Before diving into code, the difference between the two streams used in the article needs to be distinguished.

Data Streams

Data streams process primitive data types and strings. Data sent over data streams needs to be manually serialized and deserialized which makes it harder to transfer complex data. But, data streams can communicate with servers and clients written in other languages than Java. Raw streams are similar to data streams in that aspect, but data streams ensure the data is formatted in a platform independent way which is beneficial because both parties will be able to read sent data.

Object Streams

Object streams process primitive data types and objects that implement `Serializable` interface. Data sent over object streams is automatically serialized and deserialized which makes it easier to transfer complex data. But, object streams can only communicate with servers and clients written in Java. Also, `ObjectOutputStream`, upon initialization, sends a header to the `InputStream` of the other party which, upon initialization, blocks execution until the header is received.

Steps

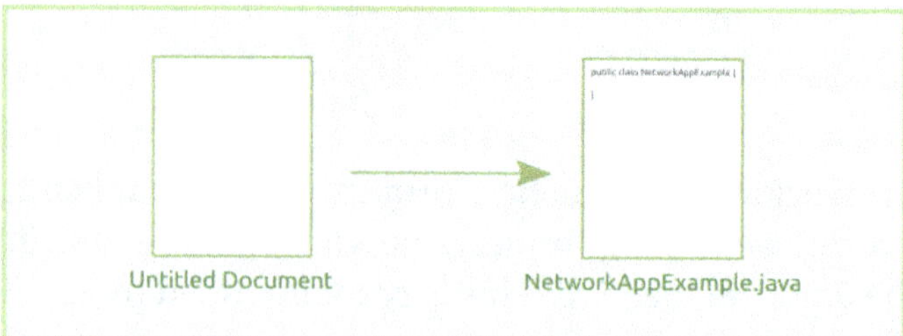

1. Create a class. Create a class and name it however you want. In this article, it will be named `NetworkAppExample`.

```
public class NetworkAppExample {

}
```

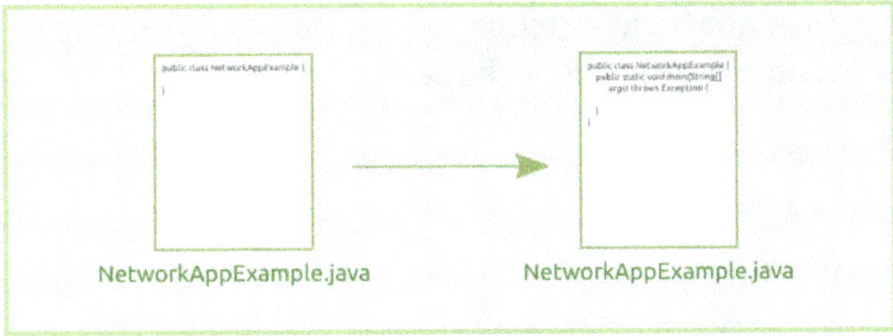

2. Create a main method. Create a main method and declare it might throw exceptions of `Exception` type and any subclass of it - all exceptions. This is considered a bad practice, but is acceptable for barebone examples.

```
public class NetworkAppExample {

    public static void main(String[] args) throws Exception {

    }

}
```

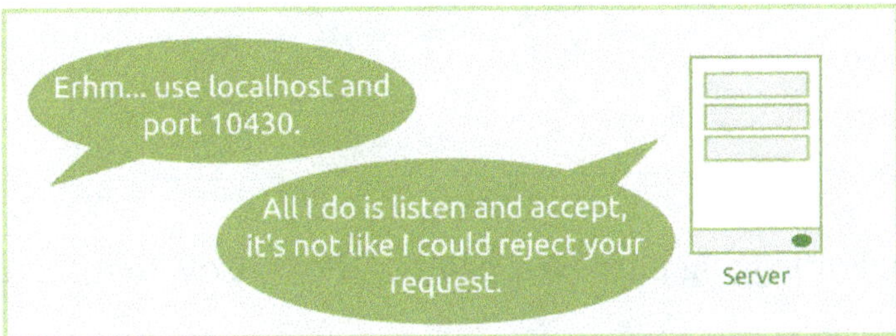

3. Declare server address. This example will use local host address and an arbitrary port number. Port number needs to be in a range from 0 to 65535 (inclusive). However, port numbers to avoid range from 0 to 1023 (inclusive) because they are reserved system ports.

```
public class NetworkAppExample {

    public static void main(String[] args) throws Exception {

        String host = "localhost";

        int port = 10430;

    }

}
```

4. Create a server. Server is bound to the address and port and listens for incoming connections. In Java, `ServerSocket` represents server-side endpoint and its function is accepting new con-

nections. `ServerSocket` does not have streams for reading and sending data because it does not represent connection between a server and a client.

```
import java.net.InetAddress;
import java.net.ServerSocket;
public class NetworkAppExample {
    public static void main(String[] args) throws Exception {
        String host = "localhost";
        int port = 10430;
        ServerSocket server = new ServerSocket(port, 50, InetAddress.getByName(host));
    }
}
```

5. Log server inception. For logging purposes, print to the console that server has been started.

```
import java.net.InetAddress;
import java.net.ServerSocket;
public class NetworkAppExample {
    public static void main(String[] args) throws Exception {
        String host = "localhost";
        int port = 10430;
        ServerSocket server = new ServerSocket(port, 50, InetAddress.getByName(host));
        System.out.println("Server started.");
    }
}
```

6. Create a client. Client is bound to the address and port of a server and listens for packets (messages) after connection is established. In Java, `Socket` represents either a client-side endpoint

connected to the server or a connection (from server) to client and is used to communicate with the party on the other end.

```
import java.net.InetAddress;
import java.net.ServerSocket;
import java.net.Socket;
 public class NetworkAppExample {
    public static void main(String[] args) throws Exception {
        String host = "localhost";
        int port = 10430;
         ServerSocket server = new ServerSocket(port, 50, InetAddress.getByName(host));
        System.out.println("Server started.");
        Socket client = new Socket(host, port);
    }
}
```

7. Log connection attempt. For logging purposes, print to the console that connection has been attempted.

```
import java.net.InetAddress;
import java.net.ServerSocket;
import java.net.Socket;
public class NetworkAppExample {
    public static void main(String[] args) throws Exception {
        String host = "localhost";
        int port = 10430;
        ServerSocket server = new ServerSocket(port, 50, InetAddress.getByName(host));
        System.out.println("Server started.");
        Socket client = new Socket(host, port);
        System.out.println("Connecting to server...");
    }
}
```

8. Establish connection. Clients will never connect unless server listens for and accepts, in other words establishes, connections. In Java, connections are established using `accept()` method of `ServerSocket` class. The method will block execution until a client connects.

```
import java.net.InetAddress;
import java.net.ServerSocket;
import java.net.Socket;
 public class NetworkAppExample {
    public static void main(String[] args) throws Exception {
        String host = "localhost";
        int port = 10430;
         ServerSocket server = new ServerSocket(port, 50, InetAddress.getByName(host));
        System.out.println("Server started.");
        Socket client = new Socket(host, port);
        System.out.println("Connecting to server...");
        Socket connection = server.accept();
    }
}
```

9. Log established connection. For logging purposes, print to the console that connection between server and client has been established.

```
import java.net.InetAddress;
import java.net.ServerSocket;
import java.net.Socket;
public class NetworkAppExample {
```

```
    public static void main(String[] args) throws Exception {
        String host = "localhost";
        int port = 10430;
        ServerSocket server = new ServerSocket(port, 50, InetAddress.getByName(host));
        System.out.println("Server started.");
        Socket client = new Socket(host, port);
        System.out.println("Connecting to server...");
        Socket connection = server.accept();
        System.out.println("Connection established.");
    }
}
```

10. Prepare communication streams. Communication is done over streams and, in this application, raw streams of (connection from) server (to client) and client need to be chained to either data or object streams. Remember, both parties need to use the same stream type.

Data streams

```
import java.io.DataInputStream;
import java.io.DataOutputStream;
import java.net.InetAddress;
import java.net.ServerSocket;
import java.net.Socket;

public class NetworkAppExample {
    public static void main(String[] args) throws Exception {
        String host = "localhost";
        int port = 10430;

        ServerSocket server = new ServerSocket(port, 50, InetAddress.getByName(host));
        System.out.println("Server started.");
```

```
        Socket client = new Socket(host, port);
        System.out.println("Connecting to server...");
        Socket connection = server.accept();
        System.out.println("Connection established.");

        DataOutputStream clientOut = new DataOutputStream(client.getOutputStream());
        DataInputStream clientIn = new DataInputStream(client.getInputStream());
        DataOutputStream serverOut = new DataOutputStream(connection.getOutputStream());
        DataInputStream serverIn = new DataInputStream(connection.getInputStream());
    }
}
```

Object streams

When multiple object streams are used, input streams have to be initialized in the same order as output streams because `ObjectOutputStream` sends a header to the other party and `ObjectInputStream` blocks execution until it reads the header.

```
import java.io.ObjectInputStream;
import java.io.ObjectOutputStream;
import java.net.InetAddress;
import java.net.ServerSocket;
import java.net.Socket;

public class NetworkAppExample {
    public static void main(String[] args) throws Exception {
        String host = "localhost";
        int port = 10430;

        ServerSocket server = new ServerSocket(port, 50, InetAddress.getByName(host));
        System.out.println("Server started.");
        Socket client = new Socket(host, port);
        System.out.println("Connecting to server...");
        Socket connection = server.accept();
        System.out.println("Connection established.");
```

```
        ObjectOutputStream clientOut = new ObjectOutputStream(client.getOutputStream());
            ObjectOutputStream serverOut = new ObjectOutputStream(connection.getOutput-
Stream());
        ObjectInputStream clientIn = new ObjectInputStream(client.getInputStream());
        ObjectInputStream serverIn = new ObjectInputStream(connection.getInputStream());
    }
}
```

Order as specified in the code above might be easier to remember - first initialize output streams then input streams in the same order. However, another order for initialization of object streams is the following:

```
ObjectOutputStream clientOut = new ObjectOutputStream(client.getOutputStream());
ObjectInputStream serverIn = new ObjectInputStream(connection.getInputStream());
ObjectOutputStream serverOut = new ObjectOutputStream(connection.getOutputStream());
ObjectInputStream clientIn = new ObjectInputStream(client.getInputStream());
```

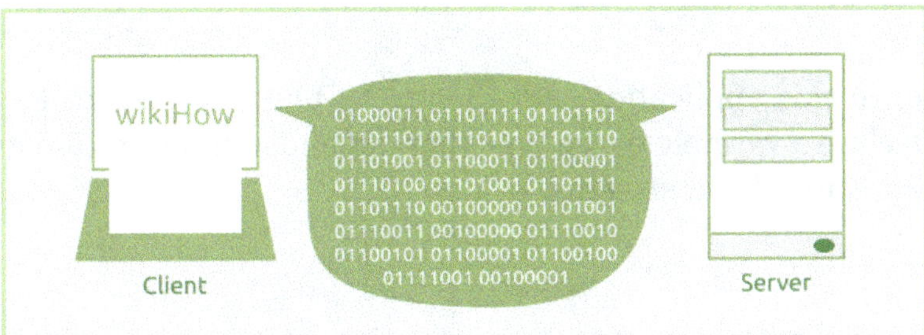

11. Log that communication is ready. For logging purposes, print to the console that communication is ready.

```
// code omitted
import java.net.InetAddress;
import java.net.ServerSocket;
import java.net.Socket;
public class NetworkAppExample {
    public static void main(String[] args) throws Exception {
        String host = "localhost";
        int port = 10430;
        ServerSocket server = new ServerSocket(port, 50, InetAddress.getByName(host));
        System.out.println("Server started.");
```

```
        Socket client = new Socket(host, port);
        System.out.println("Connecting to server...");
        Socket connection = server.accept();
        System.out.println("Connection established.");
        // code omitted
        System.out.println("Communication is ready.");
    }
}
```

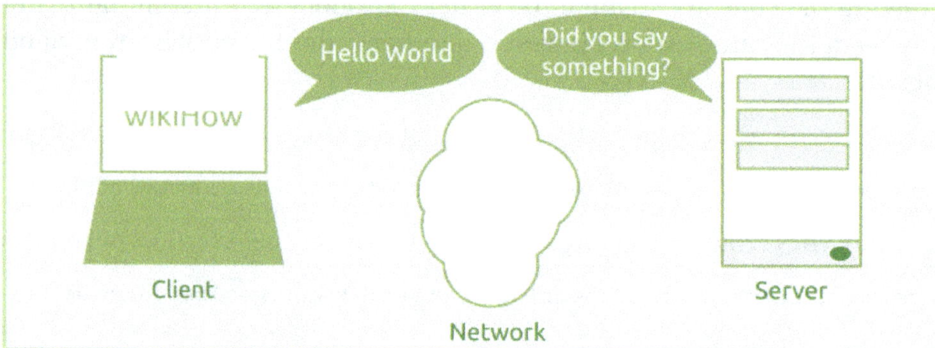

12. Create a message. In this application, `Hello World` text will be sent to the server either as `byte[]` or `String`. Declare a variable of the type that depends on the stream used. Use `byte[]` for data streams and `String` for object streams.

Data streams

Using data streams, serialization is done by converting objects into primitive data types or a `String`. In this case, `String` is converted to `byte[]` instead of written using `writeBytes()` method to show how it would be done with other objects, such as images or other files.

```
import java.io.DataInputStream;
import java.io.DataOutputStream;
import java.net.InetAddress;
import java.net.ServerSocket;
import java.net.Socket;

public class NetworkAppExample {
    public static void main(String[] args) throws Exception {
        String host = "localhost";
        int port = 10430;
```

```
        ServerSocket server = new ServerSocket(port, 50, InetAddress.getByName(host));
        System.out.println("Server started.");
        Socket client = new Socket(host, port);
        System.out.println("Connecting to server...");
        Socket connection = server.accept();
        System.out.println("Connection established.");

        DataOutputStream clientOut = new DataOutputStream(client.getOutputStream());
        DataInputStream clientIn = new DataInputStream(client.getInputStream());
        DataOutputStream serverOut = new DataOutputStream(connection.getOutputStream());
        DataInputStream serverIn = new DataInputStream(connection.getInputStream());
        System.out.println("Communication is ready.");

        byte[] messageOut = "Hello World".getBytes();
    }
}
```

Object streams

```
import java.io.ObjectInputStream;
import java.io.ObjectOutputStream;
import java.net.InetAddress;
import java.net.ServerSocket;
import java.net.Socket;

public class NetworkAppExample {
    public static void main(String[] args) throws Exception {
        String host = "localhost";
        int port = 10430;

        ServerSocket server = new ServerSocket(port, 50, InetAddress.getByName(host));
        System.out.println("Server started.");
        Socket client = new Socket(host, port);
        System.out.println("Connecting to server...");
```

```
        Socket connection = server.accept();
        System.out.println("Connection established.");

        ObjectOutputStream clientOut = new ObjectOutputStream(client.getOutputStream());
            ObjectOutputStream serverOut = new ObjectOutputStream(connection.getOutput-
Stream());
        ObjectInputStream clientIn = new ObjectInputStream(client.getInputStream());
        ObjectInputStream serverIn = new ObjectInputStream(connection.getInputStream());
        System.out.println("Communication is ready.");

        String messageOut = "Hello World";
    }
}
```

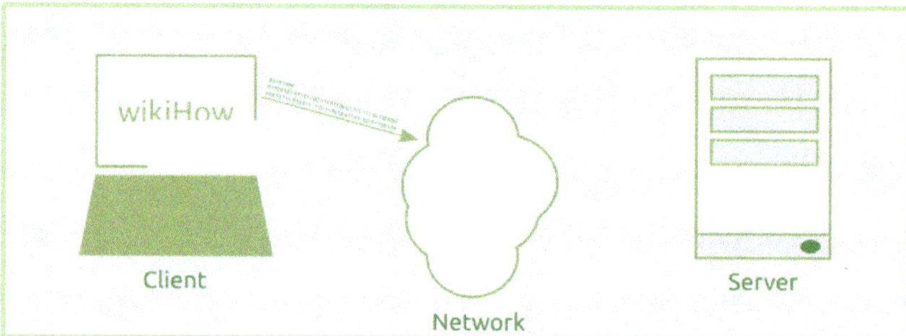

13. Send the message. Write data to the output stream and flush the stream to ensure the data has been written entirely.

Data streams

Length of a message needs to be sent first so the other party knows how many bytes it needs to read. After the length is sent as a primitive integer type, bytes can be sent.

```
import java.io.DataInputStream;
import java.io.DataOutputStream;
import java.net.InetAddress;
import java.net.ServerSocket;
import java.net.Socket;

public class NetworkAppExample {
    public static void main(String[] args) throws Exception {
        String host = "localhost";
```

```
        int port = 10430;

        ServerSocket server = new ServerSocket(port, 50, InetAddress.getByName(host));
        System.out.println("Server started.");
        Socket client = new Socket(host, port);
        System.out.println("Connecting to server...");
        Socket connection = server.accept();
        System.out.println("Connection established.");

        DataOutputStream clientOut = new DataOutputStream(client.getOutputStream());
        DataInputStream clientIn = new DataInputStream(client.getInputStream());
        DataOutputStream serverOut = new DataOutputStream(connection.getOutputStream());
        DataInputStream serverIn = new DataInputStream(connection.getInputStream());
        System.out.println("Communication is ready.");

        byte[] messageOut = "Hello World".getBytes();
        clientOut.writeInt(messageOut.length);
        clientOut.write(messageOut);
        clientOut.flush();
    }
}
```

Object streams

```
import java.io.ObjectInputStream;
import java.io.ObjectOutputStream;
import java.net.InetAddress;
import java.net.ServerSocket;
import java.net.Socket;

public class NetworkAppExample {
    public static void main(String[] args) throws Exception {
        String host = "localhost";
        int port = 10430;
```

```
        ServerSocket server = new ServerSocket(port, 50, InetAddress.getByName(host));
        System.out.println("Server started.");
        Socket client = new Socket(host, port);
        System.out.println("Connecting to server...");
        Socket connection = server.accept();
        System.out.println("Connection established.");

        ObjectOutputStream clientOut = new ObjectOutputStream(client.getOutputStream());
        ObjectOutputStream serverOut = new ObjectOutputStream(connection.getOutput-
Stream());
        ObjectInputStream clientIn = new ObjectInputStream(client.getInputStream());
        ObjectInputStream serverIn = new ObjectInputStream(connection.getInputStream());
        System.out.println("Communication is ready.");

        String messageOut = "Hello World";
        clientOut.writeObject(messageOut);
        clientOut.flush();
    }
}
```

14. Log sent message. For logging purposes, print to the console that message has been sent.

Data streams

```
import java.io.DataInputStream;
import java.io.DataOutputStream;
import java.net.InetAddress;
import java.net.ServerSocket;
```

```
import java.net.Socket;

public class NetworkAppExample {
    public static void main(String[] args) throws Exception {
        String host = "localhost";
        int port = 10430;

        ServerSocket server = new ServerSocket(port, 50, InetAddress.getByName(host));
        System.out.println("Server started.");
        Socket client = new Socket(host, port);
        System.out.println("Connecting to server...");
        Socket connection = server.accept();
        System.out.println("Connection established.");

        DataOutputStream clientOut = new DataOutputStream(client.getOutputStream());
        DataInputStream clientIn = new DataInputStream(client.getInputStream());
        DataOutputStream serverOut = new DataOutputStream(connection.getOutputStream());
        DataInputStream serverIn = new DataInputStream(connection.getInputStream());
        System.out.println("Communication is ready.");

        byte[] messageOut = "Hello World".getBytes();
        clientOut.writeInt(messageOut.length);
        clientOut.write(messageOut);
        clientOut.flush();
        System.out.println("Message sent to server: " + new String(messageOut));
    }
}
```

Object streams

```
import java.io.ObjectInputStream;
import java.io.ObjectOutputStream;
import java.net.InetAddress;
import java.net.ServerSocket;
```

```
import java.net.Socket;

public class NetworkAppExample {
    public static void main(String[] args) throws Exception {
        String host = "localhost";
        int port = 10430;

        ServerSocket server = new ServerSocket(port, 50, InetAddress.getByName(host));
        System.out.println("Server started.");
        Socket client = new Socket(host, port);
        System.out.println("Connecting to server...");
        Socket connection = server.accept();
        System.out.println("Connection established.");

        ObjectOutputStream clientOut = new ObjectOutputStream(client.getOutputStream());
        ObjectOutputStream serverOut = new ObjectOutputStream(connection.getOutput-
Stream());
        ObjectInputStream clientIn = new ObjectInputStream(client.getInputStream());
        ObjectInputStream serverIn = new ObjectInputStream(connection.getInputStream());
        System.out.println("Communication is ready.");

        String messageOut = "Hello World";
        clientOut.writeObject(messageOut);
        clientOut.flush();
        System.out.println("Message sent to server: " + messageOut);
    }
}
```

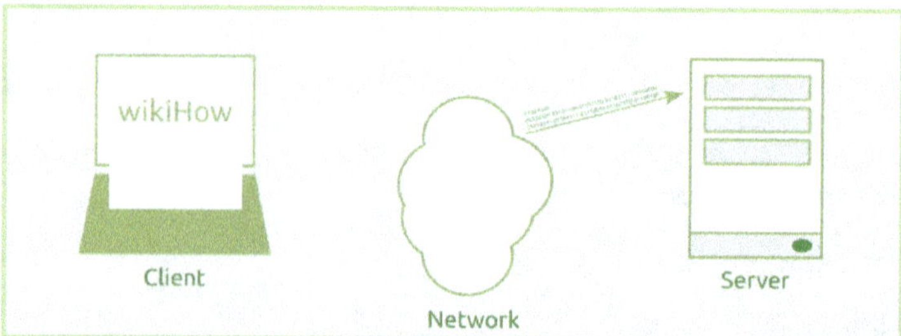

15. Read the message. Read data from the input stream and convert it. Since we know exactly the

type of sent data, we will either create a `String` from `byte[]` or cast `Object` to `String` without checking, depending on the stream used.

Data streams

> As length was sent first and bytes afterward, reading has to be done in the same order. In case length is zero, there is nothing to read. Object is deserialized when bytes are converted back into an instance, in this case, of String.

```
import java.io.DataInputStream;

import java.io.DataOutputStream;

import java.net.InetAddress;

import java.net.ServerSocket;

import java.net.Socket;


public class NetworkAppExample {

    public static void main(String[] args) throws Exception {

        String host = "localhost";

        int port = 10430;


   ServerSocket server = new ServerSocket(port, 50, InetAddress.getByName(host));

        System.out.println("Server started.");

        Socket client = new Socket(host, port);

        System.out.println("Connecting to server...");

        Socket connection = server.accept();

        System.out.println("Connection established.");


        DataOutputStream clientOut = new DataOutputStream(client.getOutputStream());

        DataInputStream clientIn = new DataInputStream(client.getInputStream());

        DataOutputStream serverOut = new DataOutputStream(connection.getOutputStream());

        DataInputStream serverIn = new DataInputStream(connection.getInputStream());

        System.out.println("Communication is ready.");


        byte[] messageOut = "Hello World".getBytes();

        clientOut.writeInt(messageOut.length);
```

```
        clientOut.write(messageOut);
        clientOut.flush();
        System.out.println("Message sent to server: " + new String(messageOut));

        int length = serverIn.readInt();
        if (length > 0) {
            byte[] messageIn = new byte[length];
            serverIn.readFully(messageIn, 0, messageIn.length);
        }
    }
}
```

Object streams

```
import java.io.ObjectInputStream;
import java.io.ObjectOutputStream;
import java.net.InetAddress;
import java.net.ServerSocket;
import java.net.Socket;

public class NetworkAppExample {
    public static void main(String[] args) throws Exception {
        String host = "localhost";
        int port = 10430;

        ServerSocket server = new ServerSocket(port, 50, InetAddress.getByName(host));
        System.out.println("Server started.");
        Socket client = new Socket(host, port);
        System.out.println("Connecting to server...");
        Socket connection = server.accept();
        System.out.println("Connection established.");

        ObjectOutputStream clientOut = new ObjectOutputStream(client.getOutputStream());
            ObjectOutputStream serverOut = new ObjectOutputStream(connection.getOutput-
Stream());
        ObjectInputStream clientIn = new ObjectInputStream(client.getInputStream());
```

```
        ObjectInputStream serverIn = new ObjectInputStream(connection.getInputStream());
        System.out.println("Communication is ready.");

        String messageOut = "Hello World";
        clientOut.writeObject(messageOut);
        clientOut.flush();
        System.out.println("Message sent to server: " + messageOut);

        String messageIn = (String) serverIn.readObject();
    }
}
```

16. Log read message. For logging purposes, print to the console that message has been received and print its content.

Data streams

```
import java.io.DataInputStream;
import java.io.DataOutputStream;
import java.net.InetAddress;
import java.net.ServerSocket;
import java.net.Socket;

public class NetworkAppExample {
    public static void main(String[] args) throws Exception {
        String host = "localhost";
        int port = 10430;

        ServerSocket server = new ServerSocket(port, 50, InetAddress.getByName(host));
        System.out.println("Server started.");
```

```
        Socket client = new Socket(host, port);
        System.out.println("Connecting to server...");
        Socket connection = server.accept();
        System.out.println("Connection established.");

        DataOutputStream clientOut = new DataOutputStream(client.getOutputStream());
        DataInputStream clientIn = new DataInputStream(client.getInputStream());
        DataOutputStream serverOut = new DataOutputStream(connection.getOutputStream());
        DataInputStream serverIn = new DataInputStream(connection.getInputStream());
        System.out.println("Communication is ready.");

        byte[] messageOut = "Hello World".getBytes();
        clientOut.writeInt(messageOut.length);
        clientOut.write(messageOut);
        clientOut.flush();
        System.out.println("Message sent to server: " + new String(messageOut));

        int length = serverIn.readInt();
        if (length > 0) {
            byte[] messageIn = new byte[length];
            serverIn.readFully(messageIn, 0, messageIn.length);
            System.out.println("Message received from client: " + new String(messageIn));
        }
    }
}
```

Object streams

```
import java.io.ObjectInputStream;
import java.io.ObjectOutputStream;
import java.net.InetAddress;
import java.net.ServerSocket;
import java.net.Socket;

public class NetworkAppExample {
    public static void main(String[] args) throws Exception {
```

```
        String host = "localhost";
        int port = 10430;

        ServerSocket server = new ServerSocket(port, 50, InetAddress.getByName(host));
        System.out.println("Server started.");
        Socket client = new Socket(host, port);
        System.out.println("Connecting to server...");
        Socket connection = server.accept();
        System.out.println("Connection established.");

        ObjectOutputStream clientOut = new ObjectOutputStream(client.getOutputStream());
          ObjectOutputStream serverOut = new ObjectOutputStream(connection.getOutput-
Stream());
        ObjectInputStream clientIn = new ObjectInputStream(client.getInputStream());
        ObjectInputStream serverIn = new ObjectInputStream(connection.getInputStream());
        System.out.println("Communication is ready.");

        String messageOut = "Hello World";
        clientOut.writeObject(messageOut);
        clientOut.flush();
        System.out.println("Message sent to server: " + messageOut);

        String messageIn = (String) serverIn.readObject();
        System.out.println("Message received from client: " + messageIn);
    }
}
```

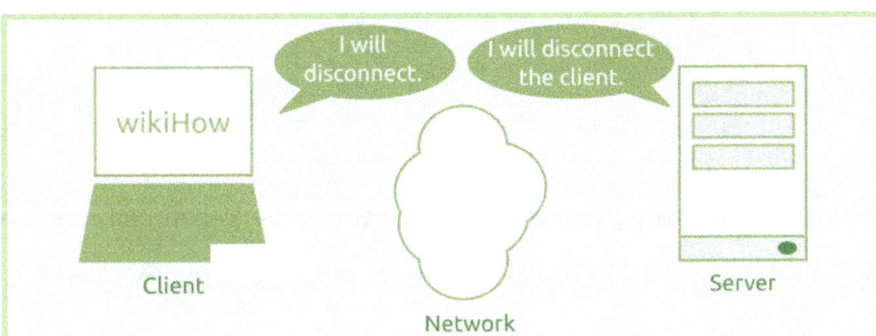

17. Disconnect connections. Connection is disconnected when one party closes its streams. In

Java, by closing the output stream, associated socket and input stream are closed, as well. Once a party on the other end finds out connection is dead, it needs to close its output stream, as well, to prevent memory leaks.

```
// code omitted
import java.net.InetAddress;
import java.net.ServerSocket;
import java.net.Socket;
public class NetworkAppExample {
    public static void main(String[] args) throws Exception {
        String host = "localhost";
        int port = 10430;
        ServerSocket server = new ServerSocket(port, 50, InetAddress.getByName(host));
        System.out.println("Server started.");
        Socket client = new Socket(host, port);
        System.out.println("Connecting to server...");
        Socket connection = server.accept();
        System.out.println("Connection established.");
        // code omitted
        System.out.println("Communication is ready.");
        // code omitted
        clientOut.close();
        serverOut.close();
    }
}
```

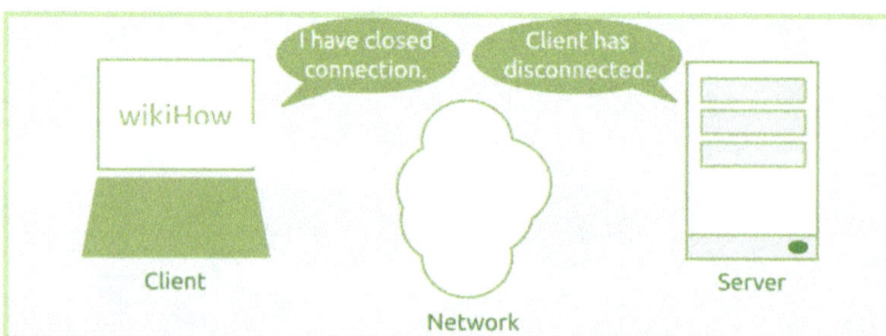

18. Log disconnection. For logging purposes, print to the console connections have been disconnected.

```
// code omitted
import java.net.InetAddress;
import java.net.ServerSocket;
```

```
import java.net.Socket;
public class NetworkAppExample {
    public static void main(String[] args) throws Exception {
        String host = "localhost";
        int port = 10430;
        ServerSocket server = new ServerSocket(port, 50, InetAddress.getByName(host));
        System.out.println("Server started.");
        Socket client = new Socket(host, port);
        System.out.println("Connecting to server...");
        Socket connection = server.accept();
        System.out.println("Connection established.");
         // code omitted
        System.out.println("Communication is ready.");
        // code omitted
        clientOut.close();
        serverOut.close();
        System.out.println("Connections closed.");
    }
}
```

19. **Terminate server. Connections are disconnected, but server is still up and running. As `ServerSocket` is not associated with any stream, it needs to be explicitly closed by calling `close()` method.**

```
// code omitted
import java.net.InetAddress;
import java.net.ServerSocket;
import java.net.Socket;
public class NetworkAppExample {
    public static void main(String[] args) throws Exception {
        String host = "localhost";
        int port = 10430;
         ServerSocket server = new ServerSocket(port, 50, InetAddress.getByName(host));
```

```
        System.out.println("Server started.");
        Socket client = new Socket(host, port);
        System.out.println("Connecting to server...");
        Socket connection = server.accept();
        System.out.println("Connection established.");
         // code omitted
        System.out.println("Communication is ready.");
         // code omitted
        clientOut.close();
        serverOut.close();
        System.out.println("Connections closed.");
        server.close();
    }
}
```

20. Log server termination. For logging purposes, print to the console server has been terminated.

```
// code omitted
import java.net.InetAddress;
import java.net.ServerSocket;
import java.net.Socket;
public class NetworkAppExample {
    public static void main(String[] args) throws Exception {
        String host = "localhost";
        int port = 10430;
         ServerSocket server = new ServerSocket(port, 50, InetAddress.getByName(host));
        System.out.println("Server started.");
        Socket client = new Socket(host, port);
        System.out.println("Connecting to server...");
        Socket connection = server.accept();
```

```
        System.out.println("Connection established.");
        // code omitted
        System.out.println("Communication is ready.");
         // code omitted
         clientOut.close();
        serverOut.close();
        System.out.println("Connections closed.");
        server.close();
        System.out.println("Server terminated.");
    }
}
```

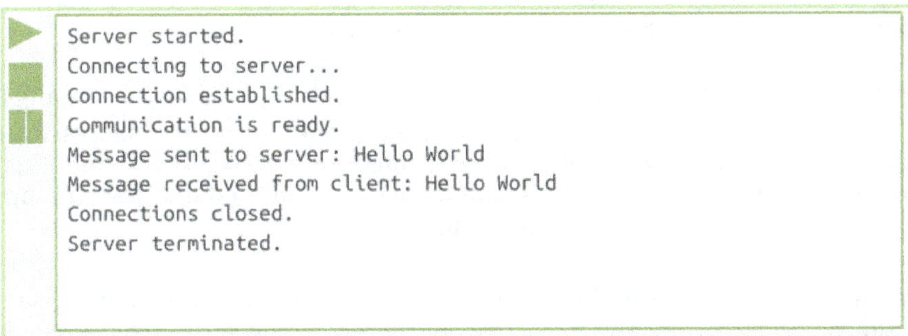

21. Compile and run. Logging enabled us to know if the application was successful or not. Expected output:

```
Server started.
Connecting to server...
Connection established.
Communication is ready.
Message sent to server: Hello World
Message received from client: Hello World
Connections closed.
Server terminated.
```

In case your output is not like the one above, which is unlikely to happen, there are a few solutions:

- If the output stops at the line `Connection established.` and object streams are used, flush each `ObjectOutputStream` immediately after initialization because headers, for some reason, were not sent.
- If the output prints `java.net.BindException: Address already in use`, choose a different port number because the one specified is already used.

Permissions

All chapters in this book are published with permission under the Creative Commons Attribution Share Alike License or equivalent. Every chapter published in this book has been scrutinized by our experts. Their significance has been extensively debated. The topics covered herein carry significant information for a comprehensive understanding. They may even be implemented as practical applications or may be referred to as a beginning point for further studies.

We would like to thank the editorial team for lending their expertise to make the book truly unique. They have played a crucial role in the development of this book. Without their invaluable contributions this book wouldn't have been possible. They have made vital efforts to compile up to date information on the varied aspects of this subject to make this book a valuable addition to the collection of many professionals and students.

This book was conceptualized with the vision of imparting up-to-date and integrated information in this field. To ensure the same, a matchless editorial board was set up. Every individual on the board went through rigorous rounds of assessment to prove their worth. After which they invested a large part of their time researching and compiling the most relevant data for our readers.

The editorial board has been involved in producing this book since its inception. They have spent rigorous hours researching and exploring the diverse topics which have resulted in the successful publishing of this book. They have passed on their knowledge of decades through this book. To expedite this challenging task, the publisher supported the team at every step. A small team of assistant editors was also appointed to further simplify the editing procedure and attain best results for the readers.

Apart from the editorial board, the designing team has also invested a significant amount of their time in understanding the subject and creating the most relevant covers. They scrutinized every image to scout for the most suitable representation of the subject and create an appropriate cover for the book.

The publishing team has been an ardent support to the editorial, designing and production team. Their endless efforts to recruit the best for this project, has resulted in the accomplishment of this book. They are a veteran in the field of academics and their pool of knowledge is as vast as their experience in printing. Their expertise and guidance has proved useful at every step. Their uncompromising quality standards have made this book an exceptional effort. Their encouragement from time to time has been an inspiration for everyone.

The publisher and the editorial board hope that this book will prove to be a valuable piece of knowledge for students, practitioners and scholars across the globe.

Index

www.ingramcontent.com/pod-product-compliance
Lightning Source LLC
LaVergne TN
LVHW080905210926
848485LV00004B/593